D1476856

Studies in War, Society, and the Military

I Die with My Country

# I Die with My Country

Perspectives on the Paraguayan War, 1864–1870

Edited by Hendrik Kraay and Thomas L. Whigham

University of Nebraska Press
Lincoln and London

Library of Congress Cataloging-in-
Publication Data
I die with my country : perspectives
on the Paraguayan War, 1864–1870 /
edited by Hendrik Kraay and
Thomas L. Whigham.
p. cm.—(Studies in war, society,
and the military)
Includes bibliographical references
and index.
ISBN 0-8032-2762-0 (hardcover : alk.
paper)
1. Paraguayan War, 1865–1870.
2. Paraguay—History—19th century.
3. Brazil—History—19th century.
4. Uruguay—History—19th century.
5. Argentina—History—19th century.
I. Kraay, Hendrik, 1964– .
II. Whigham, Thomas, 1955– .
III. Series.
F2687.I62 2004
989.2'05—dc22
2004007730

*In Memoriam*
*Miguel Angel Cuarterolo*
*1950–2002*

# Contents

# Maps and Illustrations

## Maps

## Illustrations

# Preface

This book originated as a panel on the Paraguayan War organized by Hendrik Kraay for the Society for Military History (SMH) annual conference at the University of Calgary in May 2001. The timing for this panel seemed perfect, reflecting a renewed interest in that war among historians in Argentina, Brazil, and the United States. The rapt attention that the audience gave the panel was another positive indicator. Jerry Cooney, Roger Kittleson, Juan Manuel Casal, and Kraay presented papers, and Thomas L. Whigham provided commentary. Over dinner Whigham also suggested collecting the essays together into a book. We subsequently laid the groundwork for this volume during a hike in the beautiful Canadian Rockies just outside Banff. Cooney and Kittleson revised their SMH papers, while Casal, Kraay, and Whigham wrote new ones. In the months that followed, four other contributors joined the project.

Assembling a coherent compilation from the work of nine historians based in six countries and speaking four languages presented more than a few editorial headaches. For the sake of consistency we have adopted a number of conventions. Argentine, Brazilian, Paraguayan, and Uruguayan place names are spelled according to the modern orthography in their respective countries. Thus the Brazilian town of Uruguaiana always appears with its modern Portuguese spelling, though its Spanish-speaking neighbors know it as "Uruguayana." Similarly, for battles we use the Spanish name, given that the major ones took place in Spanish-speaking countries. In a few cases, however, where the Brazilians know the battle by a completely different name, we include the alternative in brackets. Following contemporary (and modern) Brazilian usage, people mentioned in chapters 4, 5, and 6 are referred to by the name by which they were most commonly known, frequently the most distinctive part of their first or last names. For example, Benjamin Constant Botelho de Magalhães, the subject of Renato Lemos's chapter, is known as Benjamin Constant, his two first names and not his last name. No disrespect is implied in this usage.

As editors we have accumulated some considerable debts in putting together this compilation. At various points in the project we benefited from the counsel of Loren "Pat" Patterson, Barbara Ganson, Peter Beattie, and Daniel Hayworth. Wendy Giminski and the staff at the University of Georgia's Graphic Arts Department did an excellent job in designing maps for the volume. As readers for the University of Nebraska Press, Peter Beattie and Vitor Izecksohn provided helpful comments and suggestions for revision. Our thanks to all.

While the manuscript of this book was under review, we were saddened to learn of Miguel Angel Cuarterolo's sudden death in Buenos Aires. South America lost a pioneer historian of photography and we a supportive colleague. His widow, Mirta, assisted in seeing Miguel Angel's chapter through the publication process. We thank her for this help and dedicate this book to Miguel Angel's memory.

# I Die with My Country

*Thomas L. Whigham*
*Hendrik Kraay*

# 1. Introduction

## War, Politics, and Society in South America, 1820s–60s

"*Muero con mi patria* [I die with my country]!" These words, shouted defiantly at his Brazilian pursuers by Paraguayan president Francisco Solano López, brought to an end the most costly interstate war in South American history. As he slid mortally wounded into the red muck of the Aquidabán River on 1 March 1870, his last view was of a country devastated. Paraguay had doggedly held off Brazil and its Uruguayan and Argentine allies for nearly six years, wrecking a good portion of South America in the process. And now Brazilian forces had finally caught up with the remnants of López's army and destroyed it.

The Paraguayan War (or the War of the Triple Alliance) profoundly shaped the histories of the four countries involved, yet it remains little known outside South America. It readily lends itself to superlatives: Leslie Bethell notes that, after the Crimean War, it was the bloodiest interstate conflict between 1815 and 1914, and according to Miguel Angel Centeno's calculations, it accounts for more than half of the casualties in all of Latin America's interstate wars combined.[1] Others have called it one of the first total wars.[2] With more than 60 percent of its population dead by 1870, Paraguay enjoys the dubious distinction of suffering the highest rate of civilian and military casualties recorded in any modern war.[3] In its long periods of grinding, static trench warfare, the conflict between Paraguay and its three allied opponents foreshadowed the First World War on the western front.

For the people of South America these years marked a watershed as profound as that of the Civil War for those of the United States or the First World War for those of Europe. As the great Brazilian writer Machado de Assis put it in 1894, "there is no doubt that, after López's death, clocks have run faster."[4] Those generations of Argentine, Uruguayan, and Brazilian soldiers molded by the war returned to countries undergoing rapid social and economic changes. Urbanization, incipient industrialization, immigration, the final decline and abolition of slavery in Brazil, and the expansion of agricultural frontiers in Argentina and Uruguay were all hastened by the definitive consolidation of three nation-states. Although many of these changes had only indirect links to the war, those who experienced the conflict tended to see their societies through the prism of their wartime experience. To them everything bore its stain. This was also the case for the prostrate Paraguay, where the war's effects hung over the population for more than a generation.

The nine chapters that follow, all original works, provide perspectives on the Paraguayan War as it was lived by men and women in Brazil, Paraguay, Uruguay, and Argentina. The authors share a concern with social history and the experience of societies at war. Wars yield to analysis at many levels— the national, the local, and the individual. Nation-states may go to war, but individuals approach war in distinct ways, often as part of the social groups or local communities that define them and through which they are mobilized.[5] The contributors to this book look beneath the political, military, and diplomatic questions that have dominated scholarship to understand how men and women saw this conflict and how it shaped them and their societies.

## The Luso-Spanish Conflict in the Plata, 1600s–1800s

War had always shaped the relations between Spanish and Portuguese South America. Indeed the Paraguayan War was just the last chapter in a two-century conflict between the Spanish and Portuguese over the region defined by the Platine river system. The Portuguese advance beyond the nominal bounds of their colonial domain brought them into contact and conflict with Spanish settlers along the frontier as early as the seventeenth century. Both craved the land as well as the Indians who lived upon it. In 1680 the Portuguese establishment of Colônia do Sacramento along the Río de la Plata opposite Buenos Aires marked a new stage in the struggle for hegemony in this region. The Portuguese aimed to tap directly into the contraband trade through the future Argentine capital to the rich silver mines of Peru. Spanish authorities had no intention of tolerating this challenge to their imperial commercial monopoly. They promptly destroyed the outpost, but the Portuguese rebuilt it three years later. For more than a century afterward the two colonial powers fought over the mouth of the Plata. None of the treaties negotiated during these years endured, and the empires' boundaries shifted back and forth in response to changing political fortunes.[6]

The outbreak of the independence struggles in the Americas added new dimensions to these conflicts. Napoleon's occupation of the respective mother countries (and the capture of the Spanish king) produced far-reaching challenges. The Platine viceroyalty fractured into its pieces, with Bolivia, Paraguay, and ultimately Uruguay breaking free from Buenos Aires's administrative control. Argentina itself turned into a loose confederation of

South America, circa 1864

more or less autonomous provinces, none save Buenos Aires really viable, given its exclusive control of the customs house and its revenues. Under the dictatorship of Dr. José Gaspar de Francia (1814–40), Paraguay adopted a policy of isolation from the outside world, which insulated it from the political anarchy to the south and had the effect—probably unintended—of reinforcing the population's Hispano-Guaraní identity.[7]

In contrast to Paraguay, Buenos Aires emerged as a center of patriot sympathies, sending armies as far afield as Peru to defeat royalist forces in the second decade of the nineteenth century. Despite their success in liberating South America, *porteños* (residents of Buenos Aires) failed to impose their will on the provinces. The relatively centralized and businesslike government of the United Provinces of the Plata, established in 1816–19, collapsed in the face of caudillo opposition in 1820. Bernardino Rivadavia's liberal, modernizing efforts in the 1820s enjoyed some limited success in the port. But when he attempted to build a unitary government for the United Provinces, he lost the support of ranchers in Buenos Aires Province, who feared losing control of the capital's all-important customs house. Intractable ideological differences and competing visions of the relationship between the provinces and Buenos Aires rendered Argentina virtually ungovernable.

Portuguese America went through a significantly different trajectory. Prince-Regent (after 1816, King) João VI avoided the fate of his Spanish counterpart and escaped the French invaders, reaching Rio de Janeiro in 1808. There he established his capital, governing the entire Portuguese empire from this tropical court until 1821. The ambitions of his Spanish-born wife, Carlota Joaquina, to dominate Platine affairs coincided with the interests of southern Brazilian ranchers. This led to a full-scale Portuguese invasion of the Banda Oriental (modern-day Uruguay) in 1816 that displaced the nascent Federal League of José Gervasio Artigas. Soon Brazil incorporated the region as the Cisplatine Province. The 1820 revolution in Porto, Portugal, prompted a reluctant João to return to Lisbon; by 1822 his son had turned himself into Emperor Pedro I of Brazil. Relatively little fighting was required to expel troops loyal to Portugal (except in Bahia) or to ensure the loyalty of the far-flung provinces to the new government in Rio de Janeiro. Even the Cisplatine Province—loyal longer to Lisbon thanks to its large Portuguese garrison—eventually fell into line. By 1824 the empire was secure, with British and Portuguese recognition coming one year later.

Brazilian rhetoric that heralded the Río de la Plata as the country's natural southern frontier could not be sustained. In 1825 exiles led by Juan

Lavalleja crossed onto the east bank of the Uruguay River, the Banda Oriental, and raised the standard of revolt against Brazil. Receiving strong backing from *porteños,* the rebellion soon attracted support from rural caudillos. Within six months the Brazilians controlled only Colônia do Sacramento and Montevideo. Brazil declared war against Buenos Aires, but the ensuing conflict, known as the Cisplatine War, ended in a stalemate. A British-mediated peace in 1828 led to the creation of the independent República Oriental del Uruguay the following year. Political instability in Brazil during the nine-year regency that followed Pedro I's abdication in 1831 and the early years of Pedro II's personal reign prompted a temporary Brazilian withdrawal from Platine affairs.

This retreat coincided with the rise in Buenos Aires of Juan Manuel de Rosas, the Federalist caudillo. Rejecting all that smacked of Rivadavia's liberal and centralizing (Unitarian) reforms, this rancher proclaimed his unbending opposition against "savage Unitarians." Nominally the governor of Buenos Aires Province, Rosas in fact exercised control over the thirteen other provinces through a complex web of patronage and alliances backed by force. Unitarians sought refuge in Montevideo (and further abroad), vilifying Rosas as a barbarian. Rosas's ally in Uruguay, Manuel Oribe, and his Blanco Party controlled the countryside, while Colorados and Unitarian exiles hung on in the capital, surviving a nearly nine-year siege (1843–51). Immigrant volunteers—including Giuseppe Garibaldi—and the timely interventions of Britain and France ensured Montevideo's survival.

Southern Brazil had its share of civil war as well. The ranchers of Rio Grande do Sul retained extensive interests in Uruguay after its independence, and they had numerous grievances against the imperial government, notably the lack of protection for their *charque* (dried beef) in the domestic market (it was a major part of the slaves' diet). In 1836 leaders of the so-called Farroupilha Rebellion proclaimed a republic in Rio Grande do Sul. Some sought ties with Uruguay and Argentine provinces, but little came of these initiatives. Concessions by the imperial government combined with war weariness finally produced a settlement in 1844–45. The Farrapo defeat proved easier to stomach given the generous bribes distributed by the imperial commander, Luis Alves de Lima e Silva, the Baron (later Marquis and Duke) of Caxias.

Having "pacified" Rio Grande do Sul and defeated the other internal revolts by midcentury, a politically unified Brazil under Emperor Pedro II stood poised to resume its historic imperial role in the Plata. This included its strategic interest in ensuring free navigation along the regional river system, the only easy access to the interior province of Mato Grosso. By then Rosas's position in Buenos Aires had weakened. Opposition crystallized around the Federalist caudillo of Entre Ríos, Justo José de Urquiza, a wealthy rancher and old ally of the Bonaerense strongman. A mixed alliance of *porteño* Unitarians, Montevideo Colorados, and interior Federalists, backed by Brazilian money and troops (and verbal support from Paraguay), defeated Rosas at Caseros (2 February 1852), sending him into a long English exile. Uruguay became virtually a Brazilian protectorate, its government financed by Rio de Janeiro (previous regimes had mortgaged the Montevideo customs revenue); Brazilian troops remained in the country until 1855. Even then Uruguayans lacked a principle around which they could unite. Attempts to meld the rival Colorado and Blanco factions into a Fusionist government of national unity in the late 1850s came to naught when dogmatic Colorados vetoed the policy.

With Rosas out of the way, Urquiza presided over a constituent assembly that created a federal constitution for the Argentine Confederation. Buenos Aires, however, felt most uncomfortable with any system that curtailed provincial privileges. On several occasions, the province rebelled. In 1861 the Unitarian governor of Buenos Aires, Bartolomé Mitre (aided by Uruguayan Colorados under Venancio Flores), destroyed the confederation at the battle of Pavón. Mitre, elected president of a new Argentina that included Buenos Aires in 1862, proceeded to build a central state and waged war against the remaining Federalist caudillos.

Mitre's interests extended beyond the bounds of Argentina. As Juan Manuel Casal notes in chapter 7, Mitre lent support to Flores in his 1863 war against the regime of Bernardo Berro. This government also came under considerable pressure from Brazil, whose nationals accounted for more than one-tenth of Uruguay's population and controlled much of the best ranching land bordering Rio Grande do Sul. Berro's attempts to impose Montevideo's control over this district lay behind the numerous appeals for intervention heard in Rio de Janeiro over the next year. In September 1864, after issuing an ultimatum that Berro could never accept, Brazil invaded Uruguay to support Flores's rebellion. Anticipating an amenable Flores administration, Mitre acquiesced in the Brazilian intervention, marking a significant shift in the historic pattern of regional rivalries. Instead of enemies the governments in Buenos Aires and Rio de Janeiro now acted as allies, and in February 1865 they placed the presidential sash over their client, Flores.

Meanwhile the Paraguayan president, Francisco Solano López, regarded these developments with increasing dismay. After Francia's death in 1840, his successor, Carlos Antonio López, had initiated modest political reforms, writing a limited constitution in 1844 and, more importantly, beginning an extensive construction program. His government built roads, a shipyard, an iron foundry, a railroad to link Asunción and Cerro León, and other military facilities. Foreign, especially British, technicians provided the expertise necessary to complete these projects. The more-activist post-Francia state relied heavily on conscript labor and financed its public works with revenue derived from monopolies in yerba mate (Paraguayan tea) and timber in addition to profits from the state-owned ranches.

In a relatively quiet way the elder López had attempted to open Paraguay and expand his country's role in the Plata region. A military expedition to Corrientes in 1845–46, commanded by nineteen-year-old general Francisco Solano López, sought to dislodge Rosas's allies from the Argentine northeast as part of a rapprochement with Brazil and the Unitarians. In the 1850s López obtained free navigation on the river system for Paraguay and signed treaties with a number of foreign powers, though border issues with Argentina and Brazil remained unresolved. The construction of Humaitá, a massive fortress that controlled the river access to Asunción, reflected the president's continuing worries about relations with his neighbors.

Shortly before his death in 1862, Carlos Antonio López handed the mantle of presidential authority to his son, Francisco Solano López, who dreamed of making Paraguay into the regional arbiter. He accelerated the military build-up that his father had initiated, raising the regular army's strength to some twenty-eight thousand men. Mitre's success in creating a liberal and centralized Argentina worried the younger López, for even in the 1860s, many Argentines continued to regard Paraguay as little more than a renegade province. Moreover the remaining Federalists and interior caudillos heralded Paraguay as the last defender of their political model. To the new dictator Argentine and Brazilian intervention in Uruguay presaged Paraguay's own fate. López thus issued an ultimatum demanding that the empire not invade Uruguay. When Brazil did so anyway, the Paraguayan navy seized the Brazilian steamer *Marquês de Olinda,* carrying the new provincial president (governor) of Mato Grosso. The republic then launched a quick and successful (though strategically unwise) invasion of Mato Grosso.

Historians have made much of López's miscalculations. He expected to receive support from Argentine Federalist caudillos, like Urquiza of Entre Ríos, who had yet to fully reconcile themselves to Mitre's regime. López

The Plata, 1864

also doubted that a Brazil–Argentina alliance was viable, given the two states' historic rivalries. The Mato Grosso invasion, while yielding booty and stocks of arms, delayed action directly on behalf of the Uruguayan Blancos for several months. While Paraguay enjoyed some initial military advantages, the country was hardly the South American juggernaut that its enemies feared. In terms of population, resources, and access to outside supplies of materiel, it proved no match for Brazil, let alone the empire and its future allies. Paraguay's population of less than 450,000 was dwarfed by Brazil's roughly

10 million (though the latter figure included about 1.5 million slaves). When Argentina and Uruguay joined in the alliance against Paraguay, they added 1.7 million and 250,000 respectively to the total allied population.[8] López's only hope for winning the war lay in a quick and decisive military victory, coupled with skilled diplomacy to make the most of the divisions among his enemies. The former eluded him, and he lacked the capacity for the latter. As a result Paraguay ended up fighting a bitter defensive war, resisting far longer than anyone expected.

## The Course of the War, 1865–70

The aggressive Paraguayan response to the Brazilian intervention in Uruguay caught the empire by surprise.[9] A wave of patriotic indignation at the Paraguayan attacks swept Brazil. Units from the small standing army stationed throughout the country hastily embarked for the capital and then on to Rio Grande do Sul and Montevideo. During the first week of January the Brazilian government created a new corps, the Voluntários da Pátria (Volunteers of the Fatherland), whose soldiers received higher pay and benefits than men in the mostly conscript regular army. As war fever gripped the country in the first months of 1865, dozens of such battalions were raised (see chapter 4). Naive dreams of glory took hold of these men who, like their counterparts in all wars, expected to be home before Christmas.

Having completed the occupation of southern Mato Grosso, López finally turned southward to aid his now-defeated Blanco allies in Uruguay. Mitre's government in Buenos Aires refused him permission to cross Corrientes into Rio Grande do Sul, upon which the Paraguayan Congress promptly declared war against Argentina. Paraguayan forces captured the town of Corrientes in mid-April and advanced down the Paraná River. On 1 May Brazilian, Argentine, and Uruguayan representatives signed the Triple Alliance Treaty, which committed their countries to the removal of López and, in a secret protocol, to the satisfaction of their respective territorial claims on Paraguay.

The alliance between Rio de Janeiro and Buenos Aires marked a major shift in the historic pattern of regional politics as the two states put aside their traditional rivalries in order to destroy Paraguay. Soon after the treaty's signing, a second Paraguayan force crossed Misiones toward Brazil, sacking ranches before splitting into two columns that moved down both banks of the Uruguay River. Meanwhile the Brazilian navy overwhelmed the Paraguayan fleet at the Riachuelo, just south of Corrientes, on 11 June 1865. This effectively isolated Paraguay and put an end to the advance along the Paraná River. Allied forces under Flores destroyed part of the other invading force at Yataí near the right bank of the Uruguay River (17 August). The Paraguayan forces in Rio Grande do Sul entered Uruguaiana at about the same time but soon found themselves surrounded by allied troops. Facing starvation, the surviving invaders surrendered on 18 September. Emperor Pedro II, who had hastened to the front, witnessed the capitulation.

With the fall of Uruguaiana, strategic initiative passed to the allies, who spent the next seven months organizing their forces for the attack on Paraguay. This proved no easy task. Allied armies had never fought together, and supply, especially for the Brazilians, proved a perennial problem. In mid-April 1866 allied troops finally crossed the Paraná River into southern Paraguay. Their target was Humaitá, the fortress that commanded a sharp bend in the Paraguay River and controlled the most direct route to Asunción. Hampered by swampy terrain, poor weather, and long supply lines, the allies also met stiff resistance. In a strategic gamble López attacked the main allied forces at Tuyutí on 24 May. Thousands of men died before the allies emerged victorious. But the war was far from over. On 3 September the allies successfully stormed Humaitá's defensive perimeter at Curuzú. A meeting between Bartolomé Mitre (then the allied commander in chief) and Solano López nine days later failed to bring an end to hostilities, and on 22 September the allies suffered a massive reverse in their attempt to take Paraguayan earthworks at Curupayty.

This engagement effectively stalled the allied advance for the next two years, with the war now taking the form of a slow siege of the Humaitá fortifications. By this time the Uruguayan contribution to the war effort was token at best, while the Argentine troops, who had borne the brunt of the fighting at Curupayty, diminished noticeably as a proportion of the allied forces. In 1867 still more were withdrawn from the front to suppress domestic rebellions, which are analyzed by Ariel de la Fuente in his contribution to this book. Expectations of a quick victory faded among the allied troops, and disillusioned officers like Benjamin Constant spoke with contempt of the hollow assurances of victory trumpeted in the Rio de Janeiro newspapers (see chapter 5). Curupayty forced Brazil into increasingly desperate measures to maintain its army in Paraguay. Orders for new levies of national guardsmen brought increasingly brutal impressment throughout the country; six weeks after the defeat, the government resolved to recruit slaves systematically for the ranks. The Marquis of Caxias, the country's most experienced general,

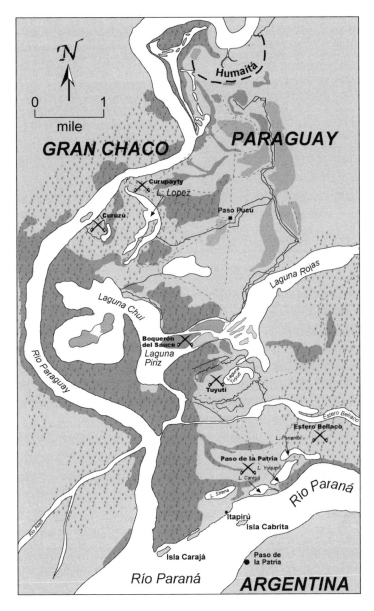

Humaitá and Its Defenses, 1866–68

received command over the Brazilian forces, and in January 1868 he became allied commander in chief as Mitre left for Buenos Aires.

Soon thereafter the Brazilian squadron succeeded in forcing its way past Humaitá, a feat of limited military significance but nevertheless much celebrated in Brazil. In July López ordered the evacuation of Humaitá's remaining troops, all of them starved and in rags. Their resistance had kept the allies at bay for two years, but there was a limit to what men can do; as Jerry Cooney makes clear in chapter 2, Paraguay had exhausted its resources. Allied forces finally advanced toward Asunción, overcoming a series of improvised defenses. In November a Brazilian contingent prepared a road through the Chaco on the west bank of the Paraguay River. This allowed the allies to take up positions between Asunción and the main Paraguayan forces. In a series of desperate battles, culminating at Lomas Valentinas (Pykysyry, 21–27 December), Caxias's troops crushed the Paraguayan army, but Marshal López managed to escape eastward to Piribebuí, where he reestablished his capital. On 1 January 1869 the allies finally entered a largely deserted Asunción. López had ordered repeated evacuations of the mostly female civilian population as the allies pushed forward (see chapter 3).

Despite having failed to capture the Paraguayan president, the ailing Caxias declared the war over. He returned to Brazil to restore his health and reenter politics. For several months allied forces left López alone in the hills east of Asunción. He managed somehow to put together an army of ten thousand boys and old men, still loyal, still stubborn defenders of Paraguay. They began some modest raids against the allied troops.

In April 1869 Pedro II assigned his son-in-law, the Count of Eu, to command the allied forces. Some months later he went on the offensive, overrunning Piribebuí and defeating Paraguay's child soldiers at Acosta Ñu (Campo Grande) on 16 August. Once again López eluded capture, retreating north with a shrinking band of followers. Brazilian forces took another six months before finally catching up with him at the Aquidabán.

Meanwhile new governments in Buenos Aires and Rio de Janeiro both returned to more traditional foreign-policy stances. The two principal allies, Brazil and Argentina, fell out over postwar policy toward Paraguay. In 1869, Brazilian occupiers helped put together a provisional government consisting of anti-López Paraguayans; the new regime signed a peace treaty the following year. The allied powers, however, continued to meddle in the country's governance. They imposed separate territorial settlements but referred the Argentine claim over the Chaco Boreal to U.S. arbitration. President

Rutherford B. Hayes ruled in Paraguay's favor, and the last Brazilian troops left Paraguay in 1876, with the Argentines following three years later. Even after the troops' departure the Brazilian and Argentine embassies remained important players in Paraguayan politics. [10]

## The Experience of War, 1864–70

Little has been written on the wartime experience of the tens of thousands of men who fought on the muddy battlefields of southern Paraguay. In comparison with the U.S. Civil War few soldiers kept diaries or maintained extensive correspondence with family and friends (Benjamin Constant's letters, analyzed in this book by Renato Lemos, are thus a rare exception). Surviving letters, memoirs, and diaries suggest a number of common experiences. In the great mobilization of 1865–66 the majority of soldiers from all four countries headed to the front together with men from their hometowns. Despite repeated military reorganizations such small groups tended to remain together (at least judging by letters home, in which the soldiers relayed news of their comrades). [11] Middle- and upper-class officers met up with acquaintances and colleagues from other parts of their countries, forming invaluable networks that advanced careers and endured after the war. [12] All suffered from the inclement weather, and no memoir omits mention of the unfamiliar cold. Death and disease were likewise constant companions; in the second half of 1867, for instance, the roughly forty-thousand-strong Brazilian contingent never had fewer than ten thousand soldiers listed as sick. [13]

The first engagements left a profound impression on men with no prior combat experience. An elderly volunteer from Santa Catarina recalled in 1920 the shock that he had felt at seeing the allied camp surrounded by Paraguayan cadavers on the day after the battle of Tuyutí. Letters written at that time suggest an enthusiasm for the fight on the part of many volunteers. A Brazilian sergeant wrote to his brother that the bearer of his letter would describe "the crazy things that I did in combat," which according to his captain would surely earn him a decoration. Disillusionment set in as the sergeant's hopes for promotion were repeatedly dashed; in mid-1868 he advised his brother to pay no attention to the tales of imminent victory, for the war will certainly "see out the year '68 and, who knows, '69, for hopes for its end have vanished."[14] Sympathy for the enemy on the part of Brazilian soldiers is suggested by Dionísio Cerqueira's recollection after the battle of

Acosta Ñu that "it was no fun fighting against so many children." Others, such as Benjamin Constant, admired (if sometimes grudgingly) the tenacity with which the Paraguayans fought, but evidence suggests that allied troops systematically killed prisoners of war in the last stages of the conflict.[15] For their part the Paraguayans invariably portrayed the slow-moving Brazilians as monkeys, turtles, or toads.[16]

Over the course of the war the social composition of the armies changed significantly. As Paraguay plumbed the bottom of her demographic well, boys and old men came to dominate her ranks. The generally enthusiastic Brazilian volunteers of the first half of 1865 gave way to levies of ever-less-willing conscripts, and officers felt deeply frustrated about the quality of their manpower, especially after slave recruitment began systematically in late 1866.[17] Already in 1865 Argentine and Uruguayan commanders resorted to enlisting Paraguayan prisoners of war.[18] Impressment in Uruguay and Argentina prompted as much complaint as it did in Brazil and on some occasions contributed to outright rebellion (see chapters 7 and 8). Not surprisingly discipline remained a constant headache for allied commanders. Flogging and beatings maintained a semblance of order in the ranks but belied the rhetoric of citizenship and service to the nation that motivated the early mobilizations.[19] Of course such soldiers had little interest in dangerous offensive operations. Caxias complained bitterly about his men's reluctance to enter the fray during the December 1868 battles that brought about the Paraguayan army's defeat.[20] By contrast the Paraguayan defenders' determination to resist never flagged, even as their cause became ever more hopeless.

Victory came as a relief to the allies. Since 1868, patriotic committees in Brazil and Argentina had been preparing to celebrate the allied triumph. Judging by newspaper accounts, Brazil's cities now erupted into a frenzy of celebration. Reactions in Buenos Aires and Montevideo were more subdued, for the fight against Paraguay had mostly been a Brazilian matter for some time. Brazilian authorities worried that the return of the surviving Voluntários units in 1870 would occasion disorder and quickly disbanded them, often sending the men home without meeting their arrears of pay. The state made few provisions for the numerous disabled veterans who had returned since the beginning of the war, and thousands later showered the imperial and provincial governments with petitions for aid. As Roger Kittleson and Hendrik Kraay show in their chapters, Brazil offered little to its veterans. Those who had imbibed the wartime rhetoric of citizenship and patriotic service to the nation suffered painful disappointment.

## Interpreting the War

While most veterans struggled to survive, some individuals who lived through the war generated the first interpretations of it. Much of this was hagiography —artists like Brazilian Vitor Meireles produced panoramic paintings to extol their countrymen's feats of arms. But some, such as Cándido López, José Ignacio Garmendia, and the other Argentine and Uruguayan painters discussed by Miguel Angel Cuarterolo, set "objective" standards of truth for themselves and painted scenes of camp life and battlefields based on photographs and survivors' recollections that did not always sanitize warfare or extol their compatriots' heroism. Alfredo d'Escragnolle Taunay, who served in the disastrous Brazilian expedition that sought to open a second front in Mato Grosso, immortalized the retreat from Laguna in a literary classic that celebrated the heroic achievements of ordinary backlanders in the column's rank and file. Characteristically, however, he published the book's first edition in French (1871), leaving a Portuguese-language edition to appear three years later.[21] As the young officers of the war years aged, they produced the memoirs that are often cited in this compilation. Invariably they dedicated these works to the memory and glory of their countries' fallen soldiers.[22]

Polemics about the war erupted even before the guns fell silent. The Argentine essayist Carlos Guido y Spano denounced Mitre's alliance with Brazil as early as 1865 and was later willing to enter into protracted debate with him.[23] But perhaps the loudest Argentine opponent of Mitre's pro-Brazilian policy was also the country's greatest polemicist, Juan Bautista Alberdi, the author of the 1853 Constitution, who effectively castigated the Argentine president as a Brazilian dupe.[24]

The quick translation into either Spanish or Portuguese of foreigners' accounts added grist to the mill of increasingly acrimonious relations between Brazil and Argentina. George Thompson, the British civil engineer who served in López's army as a colonel, published his memoirs, *The War in Paraguay*, in London in 1869, several months before the marshal's death. Portuguese and Spanish translations appeared in the same year, and he found his generally trustworthy account picked apart at every detail.[25] Decades later, in the aftermath of a dispute over the Misiones territory, journalists in Brazil and Argentina saw fit to reopen the question of who had been the more effective commander, Mitre or Caxias. In retrospect the whole business seems sterile and anachronistic, but commentators at the time argued the question with much rancor, and an elderly but still combative Mitre weighed in to defend his reputation.[26]

Twentieth-century historiography on the war went through several major phases. By midcentury a substantial corpus of diplomatic and military history had appeared. The best of these studies are still useful to historians, though their tendency to blame the war on the overweening ambitions of the tyrannical López amounts to a repetition of allied wartime propaganda.[27] At the same time, the Paraguayan dictator fared relatively well at the hands of certain nationalist historians who portrayed him as the maximum hero in a nation of heroes. Such interpretations, which some modern scholars have repeated, helped fire Paraguayan patriotism during the Chaco War of the 1930s. Afterward the same sympathies provided a historical buttress for the Alfredo Stroessner dictatorship (1954–89), linking two dissimilar periods with the sheen of the same "martial spirit."[28]

During the 1960s, revisionists influenced by both left-wing dependency theory and, paradoxically, an older, right-wing nationalism (especially in Argentina) focused on Britain's role in the region. They saw the war as a plot hatched in London to open up a supposedly wealthy Paraguay to the international economy. With more enthusiasm than evidence revisionists presented the loans contracted in London by Argentina, Uruguay, and Brazil as proof of the insidious role of foreign capital. Much of their argument rested on a spurious reading of Paraguayan history that portrayed the country's efforts at economic development as profound and unacceptable challenges to the British free-trade model. Instead of an arch-villain, they presented López as an anti-imperialist crusader. Widely popularized by Eduardo H. Galeano and others in the 1970s, this view of the war retains much popular currency in the region.[29]

Little evidence for these allegations about Britain's role has emerged, and the one serious study to analyze this question has found nothing in the documentary base to confirm the revisionist claim.[30] If anything, as several Brazilian historians have noted, *their* country was the imperial power that repeatedly intervened in the Plata during the half century before the war, and it hardly acted as a tool of British interests.[31] At the time, allied propaganda presented the war as a campaign to bring civilization to a benighted Paraguay by destroying its despotic government and freeing its people from slavery. The Brazilian plenipotentiary, in fine imperialist fashion, once predicted that the wartime demonstration of Brazil's "unity, patriotism, and resources" would bring into line the fractious peoples of the region, who had already cost his country so much blood and money.[32] Yet all this talk of "civilizing" would have sounded more convincing had it not been mouthed by slavocrats—a fact that was broadly recognized at the time.

More-recent historiography has sought to understand the war as a product of the difficult process of state formation in the region.[33] Given the complex alliances that cut across state boundaries, we must not limit our analysis to interstate confrontation. The conflicts of the 1860s make more sense if seen as an extension of a regional civil war. Argentina, after all, suffered more casualties in the rebellions against Mitre's government than in the fight against Paraguay.[34] As Casal notes in chapter 7, most Uruguayans saw the conflict as another episode in the long partisan struggle between Blancos and Colorados. In Corrientes in early 1867 Benjamin Constant perceived more hostility against Brazilians than against Paraguayans (see chapter 5), and it was no different in Entre Ríos. As Thomas Whigham argues in the concluding chapter to this book, Paraguay's defeat accelerated the process of state formation by foreclosing alternatives and helping crystallize the nationalism of these four states.

Brazilian scholarship on the war has focused on the conflict's influence on the two great social and political changes of the late nineteenth century—the May 1888 abolition of slavery and the overthrow of the empire by military coup a year and a half later. In 1898 Joaquim Nabuco argued that the war not only constituted a "watershed in contemporary history" that marked "the empire's apogee" but also sowed the seeds of its destruction. It enhanced the aspirations of military men to play a greater role in politics, while contact with republicans in the Plata region influenced the disillusion that officers felt with the monarchy. According to Nabuco the war also contributed powerfully to the quest for abolition as Brazilian officers experienced life in societies without slavery, bore the Paraguayan recriminations about the continuation of the institution in the empire, and saw how slavery undermined Brazil's military effectiveness. In an earlier polemical work he added that the shared experience of officers and recently freed enlisted men turned the army into an abolitionist institution.[35]

Numerous historians have returned to Nabuco's assessments of the war's political effect, and his interpretation has largely stood the test of time. Some of its exponents, however, adopt an overly teleological approach in focusing on the structural incompatibility between a professional army and the slavocratic imperial regime.[36] As Lemos points out in chapter 5, Benjamin Constant, a central figure in the 1889 coup, showed little enthusiasm for the war and much less for Brazil's republican allies.

Nabuco's relatively favorable view of the war as an event that accelerated abolition was challenged by a popular revisionist of the 1980s, Júlio José Chiavenato, who portrayed the conflict as a genocide deliberately perpetrated against the Paraguayan people and Brazil's slave and Afro-Brazilian populations. This improbable assertion many in Brazil and Paraguay accept as gospel truth.[37] Among other things, Chiavenato also alleged, citing a document that has never come to light, that Caxias (with Mitre's connivance) deliberately spread cholera in Corrientes and other provinces hostile to the war effort by having infected corpses thrown into the rivers. These allegations resurfaced in October and November 2001 and occasioned spirited debate in the Brazilian press as army spokesmen denied that Caxias, today the corporation's greatest hero, could have perpetrated such a crime.[38]

This was not the first public conflict over Caxias's reputation. In 1988, during the celebrations of the centenary of abolition, police and the army prevented representatives of the black movement from parading past the duke's pantheon, fearing that the marchers might use the occasion to sully his reputation by accusing him of the genocide of Afro-Brazilian soldiers.[39] While no evidence that Brazilian commanders deliberately used black men as cannon fodder has come to light, and the number of slaves forced into the army and navy was actually quite small (about seven thousand), there are also no indications of army officer sympathy for the slave-soldiers.[40] The debate over these issues is likely to continue, given the army's investment in Caxias's symbolic role; right-wing historiography still presents the Paraguayan War as the patriotic crusade of an army united with the nation.[41] These arguments provide tempting targets for iconoclasts.

In contrast to the considerable attention paid by historians to Afro-Brazilian involvement in the war—both free and slave[42]—few have looked at indigenous peoples during the conflict. In general, Indian populations managed to stay well clear of the conflict, but some were forcibly drawn into it. Travelers reported extensive impressment efforts along the Amazon River, to which people reacted in the usual way, by abandoning their homes; decades later the Tukuna still recalled the horrors of those days. In 1865 the Brazilian province of Bahia recruited a company of "uniformed Indians" from its surviving villages; a remnant group of Payaguá mustered fully five hundred men for Paraguay's army; and the Argentine province of Santa Fe included Guaycurúan auxiliaries in its contingents.[43] Indigenous groups in Mato Grosso adopted different strategies when Paraguayans occupied their lands in 1864–65. Some maintained a precarious neutrality, while others fought against all comers. The Kadiwéu or Caduveo (Mbaya) sided with the empire, obtaining supplies and equipment to launch raids deep into Paraguayan territory. In return they later received formal recognition of their land claim, and well into the twentieth century, elders donned Paraguayan War–era uniforms to greet visitors.[44] To be sure, such indigenous participation had little direct effect on the course of the war, but it certainly affected indigenous peoples' perception of their relationship to the warring states and remains an area for future research.

The question of the war's demographic consequences has surged to the forefront of Paraguayan historiography. In their willingness to die or to go on fighting for a hopeless cause, the Paraguayans seemed to their enemies as something other than human beings. The result was frightening: every traditional account of the postwar years had both Asunción and the country-side utterly denuded of men, with women and children the only inhabitants. Paraguayans touted this circumstance as proof of their patriotism, the allies as proof of their fanaticism. No one seemed to realize that starvation and disease respected neither patriots nor cowards nor people who were in the wrong place at the wrong time. Nor did any scholars initially question the traditional estimates that over 50 percent of the Paraguayan population died in the war. If accurate, the historical ramifications of such statistics are striking, for no modern society has tolerated such loses before forcing an end to hostilities. Nor has any modern society seen women left in so dominant a position.

In 1988–90 Vera Blinn Reber argued that Paraguay's wartime losses had been greatly exaggerated. Her writings stimulated a lively debate between "high-counters" and "low-counters."[45] A previously unknown census from 1870–71 discovered a few years later indicated an even greater loss than previously suspected—somewhat over 60 percent.[46] This census, with its stark numerical depiction of a national tragedy, would seem to put an end to the debate about numbers, though not about their interpretation. New critiques are even now appearing.[47] All that is sure is that the demographic question, with all of its curious historical implications, and the allegations of geno-cide will continue to draw attention to the most grotesque aspects of the Paraguayan War.

The chapters that follow share broad concerns about the human cost of the war, the effects of mobilization, and the political changes in Paraguay and the three allied countries. The first chapters deal with Francisco Solano López's Paraguay. Jerry W. Cooney examines the all-important material aspects of that country's resistance. Skilled improvisation to supply Humaitá with food and domestically manufactured weaponry allowed the army to fend off the much better equipped allies. To be sure, the enlistment of all available manpower and the seemingly endless sacrifices of the civilian population could not win a war of attrition. Yet Paraguayan ingenuity, patriotism, and hard work sustained the resistance for years longer than anyone could have predicted. The conflict's social significance for women—who by the end of war constituted a large majority of Paraguay's population—is the subject of Barbara Potthast's chapter. She examines both the rhetoric and the reality of women's role in the war. Although subsequently hailed as full partners in the "epic national struggle" and in fact responsible for much of the rural labor that sustained the army, women's status in Paraguay changed little as a result of the conflict. Despite the enormous casualty rate (from which men suffered disproportionately), traditional gender roles endured and in fact reconstituted themselves stronger than ever by the end of the century.

The next section focuses on Brazil, the largest allied country and the one that bore the brunt of the fighting after 1866. Hendrik Kraay examines the early mobilization for the war effort in Bahia, focusing on the creation of all-black companies, the so-called Zuavos Baianos. These units exemplified the popular side of Brazil's mobilization, which drew on little-known patriotic traditions and linked broad sectors of the free poor to the imperial state. Despite distinguished service in 1865–66, the Zuavos lost their separate institutional identity during the reorganizations that the Brazilian army accomplished in the field. Few of their officers and soldiers survived the war, but those who did shared the same disillusionment as other veterans. Renato Lemos analyzes the 1866–67 battlefield letters of Benjamin Constant Botelho de Magalhães, a young army captain better known for his central role in the 1889 republican coup that overthrew Pedro II. His correspondence reveals the frustrations of Brazilian military men at their lack of progress against the Paraguayans—a nagging reality that he blamed on incompetent leadership. The tensions within the officer corps divided educated professionals like Benjamin Constant from political lackeys and men who had risen through the ranks. Yet this friction failed to bring an immediate rejection of the imperial regime. If anything, Benjamin Constant developed an even dimmer view of Argentines and Uruguayans and their republican system of government. Roger Kittleson, for his part, examines the consequences of the war in Rio Grande do Sul. He traces the social dislocation that mobilization brought and examines the political ideology of Gaúcho veterans. In Porto Alegre, after the conflict, they demanded but failed to receive recognition as citizens and members of the nation by virtue of their wartime service.

The three chapters on the Spanish-speaking allies underscore the complex political fault lines in the Plata region. Juan Manuel Casal argues that Uruguay's participation in the war is best understood as a Colorado cause:

after regaining control over the country in 1864–65, Flores joined his Brazilian and *porteño* patrons in the struggle against the Blancos' allies. Decimated early in the conflict, the Oriental Division lingered on as a token force until the end of the war, and even then it was composed largely of Paraguayans. Ariel de la Fuente's chapter analyzes the wartime divisions in an Argentina that had purportedly settled its internal differences with the rise of Bartolomé Mitre. The *porteño* project of unification remained unpopular in the interior provinces, which were more attuned to a decentralized "Americanist" model that had more in common with that of Paraguay than with that of Buenos Aires. For his part the late Miguel Angel Cuarterolo discusses the social context of war iconography and how the work of photographers and sketch artists served as the basis for patriotic war art. He focuses on the work of Bate & Co. W., Uruguayan photographers who took a series of battlefield views in 1865 and 1866, hoping to sell them in Montevideo and Buenos Aires. Although the company went bankrupt, their photographs remained essential references for late-nineteenth-century artists and today's historians.

In the concluding chapter Thomas Whigham surveys the war's consequences for nation-building and state-formation projects in the region, arguing that it contributed directly to the emergence of modern states in the region. Modernity, of course, is a highly relative thing. Argentina went on to experience an economic revolution in cereal production and, after the advent of refrigerated cargo holds, in the export of beef. All this was accompanied by an enormous wave of Spanish and Italian immigrants. Something similar happened in Uruguay (though mutton takes the place of beef in the description). Brazil also modernized by abolishing slavery, fostering immigration, and putting a republican political system into place. Where Argentina had its beef, Brazil had its coffee, which assumed a dominant role in the world market. Millionaire exporters in both countries (and in Uruguay) reaped bonanza profits from these modern links to the Atlantic economy. In Paraguay, by contrast, modernization affected only the tiniest sliver of the population (in ranching and in the export of yerba mate and petigraine oil). Most people still had their small portion of tobacco, beef, and manioc root, and they had their memories of the "*gran epopeya*," which, compared to the challenges of day-to-day survival in the late nineteenth century, looked increasingly "glorious" as the years went by. So it was with the veterans of all four armies.

In the chapters that follow, the authors display little interest in glory. They do claim an interest, however, in ferreting out the human dimension of the Paraguayan War, in seeing what motivated people, what made them tick under the worst imaginable circumstances. If the modernity of the late 1800s, with its gas lampposts, imported kippers, and starched collars, was a poor reward for their services in the war, perhaps now we can at least recognize their humanity and understand that as the war changed them, so too did they change history.

# 2. Economy and Manpower

## Paraguay at War, 1864–69

In the early morning of 1 March 1870 in remote northeastern Paraguay, a bullet in the back from a Brazilian army carbine ended the life of President-Marshal Francisco Solano López. After five bloody years of struggle, the most destructive international war ever fought in South America was over. For four years the landlocked Republic of Paraguay, with its population of less than half a million, had fended off the military might of Brazil, Argentina, and Uruguay.[1] The war placed great strains upon Paraguay's internal economy, and yet the republic managed to resist a much more powerful coalition. How it accomplished that feat is a complex tale, involving the internal financing of the war, the countering of the allied economic blockade, a maximum mobilization of manpower, and overcoming the difficulties of the production and transportation of supplies to the fighting forces.[2]

### Administration and Finance

The mobilization of resources for war presented few administrative problems. Since independence in 1813, Paraguay had been a highly centralized state, and its leaders had created a crude but effective command economy. Subordinates in the countryside followed orders from Asunción to direct needed labor and resources for national purposes. The people obeyed with little protest. Communications from the seat of government to rural officials were facilitated by the republic's relative small size, for at least 50 percent its population and many of its resources lay within an eighty-mile semicircle around Asunción. Later during the war itself, López was absent from the capital much of the time—either at the military encampment and headquarters of Cerro León or near the southern fortress of Humaitá. His vice president, Domingo Francisco Sánchez, bore most of the administrative responsibility of the directed economy, particularly food production and supply of the troops.

After hostilities began in October 1864, López determined that Paraguay needed greater financial reserves.[3] A few months later the Paraguayan Congress authorized a 25,000,000 peso loan guaranteed by yerba and land revenues. At the same time, the president attempted to raise 200,000 pounds sterling on the money markets of Buenos Aires. He found no takers for either enterprise as the turmoil occasioned by the war made potential lenders wary.[4] Some historians have cited this abortive resort to international funding after the war began as evidence of the economic incompetence of the marshal. One might also interpret it as evidence that he had no firm plans for aggression until events came to a head with the seizure of the Brazilian steamer *Marquês de Olinda* in November 1864.

The republic now had to depend solely on its internal financial reserves, which included property confiscated from the president's political rivals and seized from enemy nationals. Paraguay turned to a paper emission of 2,900,000 pesos in March 1865, more than doubling the amount of paper pesos in circulation.[5] That recourse had a precedent in the 1850s, when President Carlos Antonio López (the father of the wartime president) had taken the same action to expand the republic's money supply, and even then paper had rapidly depreciated 20 percent against gold. But in the 1850s, taxes on yerba exports and land revenues had supported the paper currency. Argentina's entrance into the war in April 1865 brought the economic isolation of Paraguay and the loss of export and import revenue to give any support to the expanded currency supply. In the same month, Solano López decreed that all government purchases would be paid solely in paper currency rather than the one-third in specie and two-thirds in paper as in the past.[6] Even greater emission of paper ensued and, as a consequence, depreciation of the paper peso and inflation.

In Asunción prices for basic commodities rose as much as 160 percent over the first nine months of the war as the government diverted foodstuffs, such as corn, manioc, and beans, to the large military encampment of Cerro León. The impressment of cart drivers into the army also contributed to food shortages in the capital, as did the confusion in the countryside when cultivators were called to service.[7] So severe was this crisis that the government at one point in mid-1865 restricted the sale of manioc flour in the capital's marketplaces. Even in the face of a strong authoritarian government, hoarding of and speculation in foodstuffs in Asunción were not unknown.[8]

Regardless of the government's attempts to control the economy, by early 1869 the paper peso had lost between 60 and 70 percent of its value relative to gold.[9] The rural barter economy may have exerted some anti-inflationary pressure, as did the operations of government-owned enterprises, such as state ranches that raised cattle to feed the troops, the iron foundry at Ybycuí, and the railroad. But price levels and inflation during the war still require much more research.

Paraguay never completely abandoned specie. Some silver coins were minted in 1866 from government reserves, and then in 1867 and 1868 gold and silver specie reappeared after an orchestrated, forced "patriotic donation" of gold and silver jewelry by Paraguayan women.[10] That wartime coinage probably prevented an even greater depreciation of the peso. In any case some specie remained in circulation, and the government retained gold and silver coinage until the battle of Piribebuí in August 1869.

## The Arms of the Republic

International problems had bedeviled President Carlos Antonio López in the 1850s, and fearful of the future, he embarked upon large-scale purchases of military equipment.[11] When war broke out in 1864, Paraguay was respectably armed, but the country had to fight with what armaments it then possessed or could produce internally. Most small arms were muzzle-loading flintlock muskets, purchased abroad or captured in the early Mato Grosso campaign. An Englishman serving in a high post in Marshal López's army stated that many were old Tower of London muskets—the "Brown Bess."[12] Foreign observers commented unfavorably upon them, given the introduction in the previous two decades of percussion-cap rifles and rifles with fixed ammunition. The marshal recognized the obsolete quality of Paraguay's small arms and took steps in 1863 to purchase more modern weaponry. Yet events overcame that plan, and the republic entered the war in 1864 with its small arms little improved over the Napoleonic era.[13] The allied blockade prevented any Paraguayan purchase of better weaponry during the war, while its enemies equipped their armies with modern firearms at will from Europe and North America.

Flintlock muskets served adequately in defensive positions. They were proven instruments of warfare with which Paraguayan soldiers were acquainted, and they were easy to maintain, given the limited industrial and technological base of the nation. Had the Paraguayans been largely equipped with percussion-cap rifles or rifles using cartridges, their circumstances would have been worse since the country possessed no mercury for the production of caps and could not have manufactured the needed cartridges. The greatest small-arms problem was the battlefield loss of muskets during the first years of the war. By 1867, even with the efforts of arsenals and workshops, it was increasingly difficult to supply shoulder weapons, and serviceable arms were stripped from local militia units to supply Humaitá.

The Paraguayan cavalry was a useful arm, particularly for reconnaissance during the fighting around Humaitá in 1866–68. About half of the cavalry units were equipped with lances, the others with swords and flintlock carbines. Unfortunately for Paraguay, the region around Humaitá was native to a noxious shrub that killed nonlocal horses that ate it. The demand for remounts, often difficult to satisfy during the winter months of flooding on the Paraguay River, was further complicated by an endemic, wasting nervous disease that afflicted horses in the republic.[14] By mid-1867 the horse herds of central Paraguay had grown so depleted that the government ordered that mounts from the far north of the Aquidabán region be driven the length of the country to Humaitá; more than 50 percent of the horses perished en route.[15]

Paraguay's artillery—both field and larger pieces—presented a strange conglomeration of different eras and calibers. Some were inherited from the colonial period, while others were purchased abroad in the 1850s and early 1860s. The country managed to produce cannon during the war, and the army also captured artillery pieces from the Brazilians in the 1864 Mato Grosso campaign.[16] The number of heavy artillery pieces at the Paraguayan fortress of Humaitá raised doubts in the minds of Brazilian naval officers about the feasibility of forcing the Paraguay River passage. Before the war the Paraguayan government recognized its deficiencies in field artillery and made attempts to purchase guns abroad. Some pieces did reach Paraguay before the outbreak of war, but Marshal López's field artillery proved woefully inadequate.[17] Given this deficiency, the Paraguayan army in field operations was essentially an infantry and cavalry force and suffered from this ill balance. For the positional warfare around Humaitá in 1866–68, however, heavy pieces in the trenches served the Paraguayan defenders well.

International problems with Brazil over boundaries and navigation of the Paraguay River to Brazil's remote province of Mato Grosso prompted Carlos Antonio López to create a navy.[18] He looked to Britain, then the foremost naval power, and in the mid-1850s a British shipyard provided the warship *Tacuarí*. At its launching this steam-powered vessel was fully modern, but progress in naval engineering was quite rapid in the late 1850s and early 1860s. Within eight years of its construction, the *Tacuarí* was obsolete as it lacked armor. Later, merchant steam vessels were armed and became components of the navy, but lacking armor and being paddle wheelers, their combat potential against the more modern Brazilian fleet was limited. This inadequacy was revealed by the Paraguayan-Brazilian fleet action of Riachuelo in June 1865. Several Paraguayan vessels were sunk, and the *Tacuarí*, badly damaged, underwent repairs in an Asunción shipyard for more than a year.[19] For the remainder of the war the Paraguayan navy essentially acted as supply fleet, and in that capacity it was quite useful.[20]

## Blockade and Economy

International trade by way of the Paraná-Paraguay river system was available to Paraguay until Argentina entered the war in April 1865. But even before hostilities commenced against Brazil, it declined due to the disruption of yerba, tobacco, and timber exports brought about by the large recruitment of workers into the Paraguayan army in 1864.[21] Nationalist historians have stressed Paraguay's ability to utilize native products and to improvise war materiel after international trade ceased. A realistic analysis of the economic blockade imposed by the allies reveals that the lack of imports severely damaged the republic's military ability. The dearth of imported medicine weakened the health of soldiers and civilians alike. The curtailment of cheap imported cotton cloth left soldiers in rags. Recourse to locally made gunpowder meant less-powerful weaponry. The dearth of high-grade iron supplies and the absence of tin and copper crippled the munitions industry. Even the short supply of writing paper caused concern.

Before the war began, López realized that political tensions in the Río de la Plata might lead to hostilities. As a precautionary measure he ordered a shipload of modern medical supplies from Europe. Unfortunately that vessel capsized off the Río de la Plata, and Paraguay went to war with only those modern medicines that it had on hand, supplemented by traditional folk remedies. These proved insufficient. Even before the onset of hostilities, an epidemic swept through the encampment at Cerro León, and for the next four years various diseases afflicted the Paraguayan army and population. The country needed large quantities of medicines but did not have them.[22] Perhaps soldiers felt most strongly the lack of calomel and laudanum. The first was a dangerous, though effective, compound used to combat internal parasites—a common problem in Paraguay. The second, laudanum, was of course the great nineteenth-century opiate and the only known treatment for dysentery, from which soldiers suffered greatly in the filthy trenches around Humaitá. The inability of Paraguay to import laudanum was sorely felt.[23] Medicinal alcohol, however, was produced in adequate amounts.[24]

The great wartime expenditure of gunpowder and the isolation of Paraguay from outside sources required an expansion of local production. For at least a century crude establishments had manufactured gunpowder, and now the government sought greater sources of charcoal, saltpeter, and sulfur. At San Juan Nepomuceno and at the headwaters of the Ypané, works processed saltpeter, but the government continually searched for new sources.[25] Sulfur supplies presented no problems as iron pyrites were reduced at Piribebuí and Paso de Santa María. New plants sprang forth in 1866–67, but consumption was always high, and several times López ordered limits on the use of powder. One must note, however, that an assessment of the quality of locally produced gunpowder was that it was of a lower grade than that made in Europe.[26]

Paraguay had its own fiber and cloth resources. Fiber from *güembe* (a common vine) and *caraguatá* (a pineapplelike bromelia), two native plants, had long served for cordage and rough cloth. In the years before the war, inexpensive imported cotton had greatly replaced the homespun variety. But Paraguay was blessed with good cotton land and had embarked upon an ambitious cotton-planting project in the early 1860s during the U.S. Civil War to take advantage of a projected worldwide shortage.[27] But by 1865 the production of raw cotton had declined greatly,[28] and the government ordered an increase in fiber production, awarding prizes for the increase of dedicated acreage, standardizing the sizes of uniforms to be produced, and establishing cloth-production quotas for the villages.[29] Not only did women raise the cotton and tend the sheep that provided raw material for ponchos, but in villages and converted workshops in the capital they also spun cotton, wove the cloth, and utilized native vegetable materials for dyes, all as in the past.[30]

Even so, by the middle 1866 there was a serious shortfall in cloth available for uniforms, and the bottleneck was the slow, laborious process of village spinning and weaving. The government recognized this problem and urged officials to accelerate the production of fiber from *caraguatá*. Common Paraguayans had used that fiber for rough clothing during the era of Dr. José Gaspar de Francia, the first great dictator of Paraguay (1814–40).[31] In anticipation of the cold winter weather in 1867 and knowing that woolen production lagged, the government attempted to utilize leather for overcoats for soldiers in the south. This effort enjoyed only marginal success as dampness and cold made the leather stiff and unmanageable.[32] At least women found no need to turn their labor to shoes since all common Paraguayans—soldiers as well as civilians—went barefoot.

Shortages in formerly minor imported items became critical to the war economy by 1867. The depletion of foreign lubricants for steamboats, for instance, caused the government to turn in desperation to grease rendered from alligators.[33] The growing scarcity of good writing paper hampered communications, and officials were admonished to preserve this precious commodity.[34] The lack of blank end pages in books surviving from this era reveals its need. Paper was needed not only for the transmission of government communications but also for newsprint. Marshal López placed great emphasis upon newspapers to bolster public morale, especially for the troops for whom papers were published even in Guaraní—the language of preference for most Paraguayans. A German telegraphy specialist, Robert von Fischer Treuenfeldt, succeeded in 1868 in establishing a paper mill utilizing *caraguatá*.[35] The product was crude, though adequate as newsprint.

The economic blockade hurt both soldiers and the civilian population. First it affected the small urban population of Asunción, who had become accustomed to imported goods such as books, fine clothing, and other manufactured items. Quickly those luxuries disappeared from shops. The mass of the population did not initially find their daily life much inconvenienced by the blockade. Traditional means of production and utilization of native resources had never ceased during the near isolation of Dr. Francia or during the more open era of Carlos Antonio López. Only as the war dragged on did country folk feel the lack of imported cotton and metal implements, such as machetes, pots, and pans. Some native products like salt, yerba, and leather did become scarce by 1866, but that phenomenon sprang from internal labor shortages, diversion of resources to the army, and transportation difficulties—not the allied blockade.

## State Enterprises and the War

State-owned enterprises served Paraguay well during the war. On the eve the conflict government ranches possessed 273,430 head of cattle, 70,971 horses, 24,122 sheep, and 587 mules.[36] Privately owned ranches probably held another 1.5 million cattle. Government employees and militia not yet called to service drove cattle and horses to soldiers' encampments in the south or on to Humaitá. The army employed oxen from the state ranches as draft animals for cartage and heavy artillery, and from sheep came wool for ponchos and blankets.

During the 1850s and early 1860s Carlos Antonio López had contracted with foreign technicians to create modern, state-owned industrial establishments in the republic.[37] Before the war a railroad was constructed from

Asunción to Sapucaí. The state founded an ironworks at Ybycuí. Foreign technicians, mainly British, oversaw the establishment of shipyards and arsenals in Asunción. A telegraph line south from the capital to Villa Franca along the Paraguay River, and then later to Humaitá, informed officials of the movement of ships into waters of the republic. Foreigners occupied administrative positions in these new enterprises, while skilled workers trained Paraguayans in new industrial techniques. The primary purpose of this modernization was to enhance the military and naval potential of Paraguay, and in this it was quite successful. All played a vital role in sustaining the republic's ability to continue the war.

For centuries Paraguay's interior depended upon two forms of transportation, oxcarts and small boats on the tributaries to the Paraguay River. The latter were important for tapping rich yerba areas and the vast stands of hardwood forests. But there was a dearth of navigable tributaries in the densely populated and rich agricultural land to the east and southeast of Asunción. There bulk commodities still moved by oxcarts over roads often impassible during the rainy months. The showpiece of internal improvements during the regime of Carlos Antonio López was the railway from the capital that skirted Lake Ypacaraí and the Sierra de los Altos on to Paraguarí and ending at Sapucaí.[38] Now people and goods moved easily to the port of Asunción or, more important for the war effort, south to the major military encampment established at Cerro León. Even so, cumbersome oxcart transport to a railhead or to a navigable stream presented a bottleneck in the supply of bulk agricultural commodities.

As the long of siege of Humaitá began, Paraguay needed more cannon than it possessed in 1864. Ybycuí had produced no artillery before the war, but it and an arsenal in Asunción met the demand. By late 1866 Ybycuí was producing large artillery pieces, both rifled and smoothbore. But the ironwork and arsenals relied upon bronze and iron stock imported before 1865, for the low-grade Paraguayan iron could not effectively be utilized for cannon, and the country had no worthwhile copper or tin deposits. Materials on hand were rapidly exhausted. In early 1867 an order went out to collect all church bells for the casting of cannon.[39] As the supplies of imported iron diminished, the munitions demand for that metal increased, and Paraguayan soldiers gathered fragments from exploded Brazilian shells to send to the ironworks for the manufacture of artillery.[40] The emphasis placed upon the production of large pieces may have been a strategic error since the Paraguayan army lacked light artillery in late 1867, when the war entered a more mobile phase. In 1868 Ybycuí turned out light artillery with great difficulty, though not enough to support adequately Paraguay's infantry in the desperate battles of maneuver of late 1868.

The arsenals of Asunción concerned themselves mainly with the repair of existing small arms. Yet the lack of copper and bronze became so great that in early 1867 the government ordered a massive collection of these metals "without ignoring any piece, no matter how small." Only necessary pots and pans were excluded from that order.[41] The shipyards of the capital repaired steam vessels and constructed small rivercraft. Workmen extracted boilers from wrecked ships and reset them into new ones, but the infant machine industry in Paraguay could not hope to supply new boilers. Even so, technicians managed to keep at least some steamcraft functioning until 1869.

The telegraph system, created and managed by Treuenfeldt, aided the war effort greatly. Marshal López, first at the military encampment of Cerro León and then at his headquarters in the south, had instant communication with his government in Asunción. Orders for supplies, demands for reinforcements, and reports of enemy movements sped along the wires. Lack of copper, however, prevented the construction of projected feeder lines, but the main line alone proved extremely valuable from 1864 to 1868.

**Manpower**

The greatest weakness in Paraguay's wartime economy and ability to prosecute the war was a growing shortage of men aged sixteen to forty-five—the most useful economic and military years. The struggle against the enemy literally consumed this human resource. An 1870 census, recently discovered in the Ministerio de Defensa Nacional, validates the traditional belief of the war as a hecatomb of the Paraguayan people—over 60 percent of the population died.[42] The first to die were young men in their teens and twenties, then men in their thirties and forties, and finally boys from thirteen to sixteen. By late 1866 the Paraguayan countryside was largely reduced in inhabitants to women, old men, and children.

The best estimate of Paraguay's 1864 population suggests around 440,000 inhabitants, of whom one-third, or perhaps 140,000 men, fit normal military age requirements. From January of that year, recruitment into the army had proceeded apace, so at the onset of war Paraguay's forces in the field numbered about 30,000 first-line troops at Cerro León and another 34,000 recruits undergoing training elsewhere. These numbers fail to include some 6,000 troops who died of disease between January and October 1864. The enlistment of 64,000 men aged sixteen through forty-five was in itself a significant loss to the nation of its most productive economic resource. It became even worse, however, as militia units were mobilized in late 1864 and 1865, so that by December 1864 one observer estimated that there were now some 75,000 men under arms—better than half of Paraguay's male population capable of military service.[43]

Months before the war began, the recruitment of soldiers for the Paraguayan army had a baleful effect upon the Paraguayan economy. The government requisitioned oxcarts and their drivers to supply the army, greatly disrupting the normal transportation of goods in the interior.[44] Riverboats lost their crews as mariners left for the army. Tobacco production in the countryside fell off as cultivators departed their fields for the ranks.[45] The extraction of yerba declined rapidly as the government called up young men for the military, so much so that by late 1865 the great enterprises, or *beneficios de yerba*, of prewar years were dead.[46] The same occurred in the timber industry. These workers could not be replaced, as the exhaustion of government yerba stores by 1867 revealed. In response the government ordered that yerba collection for the army be resumed in the Villarrica region.[47] As for civilians, they had to obtain this staple of the Paraguayan diet by what casual gathering was possible.

The disaster of the Uruguaiana expedition and casualties suffered in the Corrientes expedition in 1865 reduced the army by at least twenty thousand. The marshal ordered that more battalions be created for the defense of the southern frontier.[48] In that struggle, from 1865 to the end of 1867, Paraguay lost perhaps another twenty five thousand to thirty thousand men in combat and an unknown number from disease.

Faced with these mounting losses in the first months of 1866, the government issued a series of decrees that called for the full mobilization of the republic's male population. In February López ordered all "male citizens apt for military service" to the army.[49] Several months later this call up was repeated, but now the government ordered many formerly exempted state employees into the ranks. All employees of state ranches had to bring with them all available horses and those from private *estancias*, two horses apiece. The only exceptions to this general mobilization were a few clergy and government officials necessary for internal administration.[50] By late 1866 the only able-bodied men not in uniform were the few government employees who organized cattle drives and those in vital industries, such as the railroad, arsenals, powder mills, and the iron foundry. Children less than fourteen years of age received orders to render public service in the villages to take the place of the departed men.[51] Most of the productive male population was now removed from the internal economy.

Authorities in Asunción overlooked no available manpower for the army. Earlier, when the allies had seized the southern bank of the Alto Paraná, they conducted raids against Paraguayan fortifications on the north side of the river. Paraguay could barely defend the Humaitá region, and in March 1866 the marshal ordered that all civilians living between the Alto Paraná and the Tebicuary be moved north of the latter river. The Paraguayans destroyed all property in the evacuated region that might aid the allies and drove herds of cattle north. The misery of refugees was great as they dispersed among more northerly villages. Even so, Asunción quickly ordered officials of the districts to which evacuees dispersed to take a census of those recently displaced and commanded that all "useful citizens" among them be sent to the army. That enrollment order included officials from these abandoned districts.[52]

The losses continued. The number of those wounded and rendered incapable of further service in the army or too maimed to be of much use to the economy cannot be determined at present. But it was probably a significant addition to the twenty thousand to twenty-five thousand men killed while defending the south between 1865 and late 1867. We do know that later in 1867–68, when the manpower shortage became critical, the government ordered those crippled in combat and no longer of use to the army—as well as prisoners of war, convicts, political enemies of the regime, and even those implicated in the 1868 plot against López—to man the telegraph system, the iron works, and the railroad. Those whom they replaced went to the army.[53]

In this era the great killer of armies was not the enemy but disease. To counter that threat the army maintained a medical corps officered by Britons. The medical treatment that soldiers received owed much to Dr. William Stewart, a Scottish surgeon with Crimean War experience who played a prominent role in the organization of that corps. Paraguayan practitioners trained by these foreigners occupied subordinate positions. When the fighting stabilized around Humaitá after 1866, each division of the Paraguayan army had its own hospital while the army itself operated a larger one some distance from the battleground. Hospitals in the interior of the republic served convalescents.[54] Oxcarts evacuated casualties and those soldiers ill from disease. They were then brought aboard steamers and transported to hospitals in Asunción. Many later were transported by rail to the large military hospital at Cerro León. Steam vessels also took the seriously ill and wounded to Asunción.

The mortality of the wounded and the diseased was quite high.[55] From the battlefield to the hospitals, the highest death rate from disease came from dysentery, followed by smallpox, scurvy, and edema.[56] One Englishman stressed the effects of other diseases, claiming that measles, pneumonia, smallpox, and cholera had killed fifty thousand soldiers by early 1867.[57] Another confirmed that fact when he noted that fifty soldiers a day had died of cholera during the height of that epidemic.[58] Traditional folk medicine, utilized greatly by Paraguayan medical personnel, had no chance when faced with these killers. Considering the gaps in medical knowledge, the unhealthy conditions of trench warfare, the scarcity of food, and the lack of imported medical supplies, the fifty thousand estimated loss from disease might well have been accurate.[59]

Given all these factors, López could not maintain a large army in the field as the war dragged on. At no time during 1866 and 1867 could he mobilize more than twenty-five thousand men to hold the Humaitá area. Thus by mid-1867 at least ninety thousand to one hundred thousand Paraguayan males of the most productive age group had vanished permanently from the nation's economy; as the call ups continued, the situation deteriorated further. By late 1866 the government ordered the conscription of state and privately owned slaves as well as freed blacks bound to masters for a period of time (the so-called *libertos*).[60] Soon the marshal decreed the lowering and raising of army age limits for all Paraguayan males. The bottom of the barrel was reached in March 1867, when López ordered that all boys capable of bearing arms from the ages of thirteen through sixteen report to the army—and brooked no exceptions.[61] Immediately they gathered in Asunción for drill instruction. There the government newspaper revealingly (and slavishly) applauded "the rapid progress that in such a short time these youths have made, since in less than fifteen days they have learned to handle arms as well as veterans."[62] Following this tragic conscription of children, the forced impressment of common criminals into the army was almost an afterthought.[63]

## The Rural Home Front

During the war the government ordered the countryside to produce timber, tobacco, salt, cattle, leather, fabrics, yerba, boiler wood, saltpeter, and manioc and corn flour.[64] Prices were set for these needed items, and private contractors dared not price gouge. Nor did the government permit any refusal of paper currency for contracted war materiel. It continually warned officials to pay the fixed prices and not to strip common Paraguayans of the necessities of daily life, such as milk cows or sufficient foodstuffs.[65] The constant repetition of these warnings, however, reveals that officials felt pressure from Asunción to fill their quotas and often were more concerned about acquiring provisions than acting compassionately. Furthermore, as imports ceased by 1865, payment in currency was of little use to producers since they could buy little with paper money. Communities also felt pressure from local officials to offer "donations" of food, clothing, and other items needed for the furtherance of the war effort.[66] By 1867 the requisition and payment system for privately owned beeves—the main ration for Humaitá's defenders—had broken down, and owners dared not even ask for paper money in recompense for seized cattle.[67]

The continual drain of men for the army threw a great economic burden upon Paraguay's women.[68] The long absences of men on cattle drives, yerba gathering, or river transport had long accustomed rural women to the production of many subsistence crops as well as managing the affairs of their families. They carried produce to local markets and engaged in the barter that typified the village economy of the era. They wove much of the cloth for the rough peasant and produced alcoholic beverages. Many produced the rough pottery of the villages and performed a multitude of other daily tasks.

Food production was the most important contribution of women during the war. Several months after the large 1866 call up of men for the army, Vice President Sánchez ordered the entire rural population to concentrate on agriculture, "every day, every season, even moonlit nights . . . without distinction between the sexes":

[The government] proclaims to women, the aged, and small children the necessity to dedicate themselves to cultivation, in anticipation of the day in which the entire male population will have to abandon any pursuit that does not promote the expulsion of the perfidious enemy.

All must work, and in extraordinary circumstances such as ours, it is necessary to utilize all forces to provide the necessities of life. . . .

Peaceful days will return, and the rights of the fatherland will be assured. We then can devote ourselves to rest and the enjoyment of our possessions in the shadow of peace. Meanwhile, it is essential to work, struggling against calamities and difficulties in order to avoid the lack of food.[69]

Sánchez issued continual exhortations of this nature over the next year. Now, besides manioc root and maize, women busied themselves with the production of beans, rice, tobacco, and sugar cane as well as fruit production and the care of fowl and swine. All elements of village agriculture fell to their hands by late 1866 along with salt production.

The government's concern about agricultural production appears to have brought a significant increase of land under cultivation. Paraguay has two growing seasons a year, the summer one from October through March and the winter one of April through September. In the winter of 1866 the republic had under cultivation some 4,192,520 *liños* of food crops and had planted some 435,757 fruit trees. The area sown in food crops was some 50,000 *liños* below normal. Even so, the government deemed the harvest acceptable, though Paraguay suffered a severe drought in the last two months of the growing season. Some villages had failed to plant enough and were condemned by Vice President Sánchez for their lack of commitment.[70] In response to the government's exhortations for greater production, the reported area under cultivation for the summer of 1866–67 rose to 6,805,695 *liños* of foodstuffs and 215,189 fruit trees planted.[71] As for the winter of 1867, rural officials reported some 7,532,991 *liños* of foodstuffs planted along with some 212,997 fruit trees.[72] On the surface it appears that the women of Paraguay responded magnificently in the battle for food production. Yet these figures must be used with care. The *liño* is a vague measurement that rural Paraguayans even today have difficulty defining precisely; modern historians' estimates range from .015 to 1.85 acres per *liño*.[73] Given the vagaries of weather—droughts and extraordinary rainfall—the amount of land worked often bore no relation to actual production of food. One also suspects that rural officials may have overstated the extent of land under cultivation in order to please López. In any case, though, one cannot deny the patriotic response of the remaining rural folk—mainly women—in this vital effort, and at least until late 1867 food production for local consumption appeared adequate. The most pressing problem was distribution to the marshal's army in the south.

Never before had this society fielded such a large army, one so far from the country's center of rural population. Not only had the militia armies of the colonial and early national periods been much smaller, but their campaigns had been shorter. Now, however, the army needed manioc and maize in large quantities, and those staples had to be grown, processed, and transported to the Paraguay River for shipment south. The nation managed an adequate cultivation of manioc and maize. The bottlenecks came in processing and transportation.

Food production and consumption had been essentially that of self-sufficiency and barter at local markets. While Paraguayans did make a type of manioc flour, generally the root was consumed whole after boiling. They also consumed food made from maize flour, but again most of this crop was eaten in other forms. Now, for efficiency of transport and use by the army, both manioc and maize flour had to be laboriously handmade, bagged, and then transported by oxcarts, often in short supply, to the nearest railhead or navigable stream. If not in the form of flour, then it was baked into the country's traditional breads, which entailed much more work for peasant women at a time when so many other responsibilities had fallen upon them.

Salt production at the various licks throughout the land also became the responsibility of rural women. Yet even at the very important lick at Lambaré, near Asunción, production failed to meet demand as women were overburdened with other labor. By 1866 salt was in short supply, and the defenders of Humaitá were in dire need of it.[74]

A blow came to village production in early 1867 when cholera spread to the civilian population at the beginning of the winter planting season. The precise ramifications of the epidemic are unclear, but after it appeared at Humaitá, the disease spread north, hitting some villages hard while leaving others unscathed. The dispersal of the rural population undoubtedly contributed to the erratic nature of the epidemic. For that reason it is hard to assess its overall effect upon production. It must have been significant, however, for one observer in the countryside noted: "The plague, bounding forward, propagated itself through the country, killing many people. Its development was favored by the state of misery in which families found themselves, as they had to abandon their homes, migrating from one place to another, forming large ambulatory groups . . . which circumstance made it impossible to attend to the most elemental health precautions."[75]

Nationalists have rightly applauded the contributions that Paraguayan women made to the war effort. Yet did the government expect and demand too much of them? With all the will in the world, they faced limits to what they could accomplish. The lack of salt, the inability to clothe the army adequately, and the shortages of maize and manioc all suggest that the women who dominated the village economy by 1866 failed to meet the demands placed upon them. Women could never entirely assume the place of their men because some jobs requiring heaving, the lifting of considerable weights, and strenuous leverage were beyond them. While they did their best, Paraguayan women simply could not summon the brute force needed in cutting timber, plowing, and the management of large oxen. Efficiency and production in the villages suffered accordingly after the men departed.

## Supplying Humaitá

In the final analysis the object of all war economies is to sustain a nation's force in battle. For Paraguay the test came in the defense of the Humaitá region from 1866 to 1868. Could Paraguay withstand the ever-increasing allied pressure in that area? Much depended upon the logistical support of its army.

The need to defend the entrance to the Paraguay River was closely linked to the advent of steam power on the rivers of the Río de la Plata. In earlier times armies invading Paraguay from the south followed the classic invasion route through what is now the Argentine Misiones, across the Alto Paraná at Itapúa, then over the cattle land of Misiones south of the Tebicuary, fording that latter river north of San Juan Bautista. They then struck north through agriculturally rich central Paraguay to Asunción.

Steam changed all these strategic calculations, particularly in view of the allied decision in 1865 to utilize the powerful Brazilian navy to strike north along the Paraguay. If adequately supported by a riverine navy and supply vessels, an army could be moved by transports against wind and current and threaten the relatively long shoreline. To defend Paraguay against such an invasion, the river passage had to be held. Carlos Antonio López realized this, and ironically with the aid of Brazilian military engineers, he constructed the river fort of Humaitá in the 1850s. Situated on a bluff on the southern shore of the Paraguay River at an abrupt, narrow bend, Humaitá commanded an excellent position to block the passage of any hostile fleet with concentrated, plunging cannon fire. Yet it was also a very difficult position for the Paraguayans to supply. The Humaitá region had none of the resources that the army needed. Unhealthy marshlands and bayous almost surrounded the fortress. Camp followers of the Paraguayan army found it difficult to grow corn and manioc in the soil of this region. Nor was good pasturage for horses and cattle available.[76]

The swampy terrain essentially cut off Humaitá from easy overland transport from the Ñeembucú region to the north or the Misiones-Tebicuary region to the east. To be sure, maps do indicate a coastal road north along the eastern bank of the Paraguay to Ñeembucú and thence to the Asunción area, but it was really not fit for oxcart transport, particularly during the river's winter floods.[77] Paraguay's small steam fleet, essentially used for supply purposes after the disastrous battle at the Riachuelo, was stretched too thin to adequately provide war materiel to the republic's forces in the south. A diversion of steamboats to support forces in Mato Grosso was still necessary, and normal maintenance reduced the number of ships available. López often kept part of the fleet on patrol in the southern reaches of the Paraguay River, though they presented no threat to the Brazilian navy. Vessels left Asunción or Villeta, just to the south of the capital, laden with reinforcements, munitions, fuel, and foodstuffs, and they discharged their cargoes close to the fortress at night to avoid fire from enemy ironclads. To supplement the steam merchant marine, shipyards constructed small craft for the dispatch of troops and supply, while smaller river towns built launches and lighters. In October 1865, when supply problems to the south first became critical, the marshal ordered various districts to construct 446 cargo canoes within forty-five days.[78]

Regardless of the new concentration on the construction of river craft, the supply of food to the southern army remained a problem. The main bottlenecks were overland transportation to a railhead or a navigable stream and the winter floods. For food supplies to be transported to the railheads in central Paraguay, oxcarts were a necessity. During the winter months (June through early September) flooding of the Paraguay presented a further problem. The overflow of that river prevented small craft, and even at times steam craft, from landing at the Humaitá region; traffic between the south and Asunción might be interrupted for weeks on end. Paraguay never resolved these transportation difficulties during the siege of Humaitá, and the army suffered the consequences.

If food were landed, special parties from individual battalions received the rations at the riverside and took them to their units, for there was no regular quartermaster corps to ensure field supply; female camp followers often acted as porters. Similar special units picked up the cattle from holding areas and drove them to their battalions for slaughter. But there was never enough. Hunger continually stalked the Paraguayan soldiers, as it did the many camp followers whose essential services to the army went unrecognized and who suffered much the same fate as the men.[79] In May 1866, after the first battle of Tuyutí, allied troops observed the emaciated corpses of their enemies, and after piling the dead in alternate layers interlaced with firewood, "they complained that the Paraguayans were so lean that they would not burn."[80]

The coastal road, the main overland cattle route, passed through swampy terrain along the Paraguay. This greatly hindered the passage of large herds, particularly during the floods of the winter months.[81] Still these cattle drives from the north remained the only means of supplying beef to Humaitá, for in March 1866 the marshal had ordered the evacuation of the territory between the Paraná and Tebicuary, which might have provided an easier source of supply. Throughout Paraguay, local officials ordered beeves from state and private *estancias* to be driven to Villeta and from that point to the south. The army attempted to keep reserve herds on hand in good pasturage some fifty kilometers upriver from Humaitá along the arroyo Yacaré, but the problems of mustering cattle for regular and consistent supply often defeated that effort.

Food supply often proved erratic and rations fluctuated severely. Supply became dangerously uncertain in the winter of 1867, a year that saw a drought during the major growing season and then great flooding during the winter months.[82] Asunción issued frantic orders to the countryside in mid-1867 to get cattle and horses moving south as well as urgent demands for maize, manioc, and clothing.[83] Soldiers particularly felt the lack of warm clothing during the winter months, when the cold winds swept in from the south. It was no wonder that allied prisoners were immediately stripped of their uniforms. The Paraguayan soldier was barefoot, ragged, and usually malnourished. Normally he ate large quantities of carbohydrates—maize and manioc—but the failure to supply these starchy rations to the defenders of Humaitá contributed to widespread dysentery among the troops.[84]

By late 1867 the problems of food supply, health, and medical treatment, as well as the general manpower crisis, doomed the Paraguayan defenders of Humaitá. A British diplomat passed through the allied lines that August. His observations on the state of the Paraguayan army were very cogent: "The Paraguayan forces amount altogether to about 20,000 men, of these 10,000 or 12,000, at most, are good troops, the rest are mere boys from 12 to 14 years of age, old men and cripples, besides 1,000 to 3,000 sick and wounded. The men are worn out with exposure, fatigue, and privations. They are actually dropping down from inanition. They have been reduced for the last six months to meat alone, and that of a very inferior quality. They may once in a way get a little Indian corn, but that [*sic*] manioc, and especially salt are so very scarce, they are, I fully believe only served out to the sick."[85] Even worse than the plight of the soldiers was that suffered by the women camp followers of the Humaitá army. Although they nursed wounded and sick men in the hospitals, labored on the rudimentary supply lines, cooked food, and performed a multitude of other tasks, they received only what the soldiers gave them.

How can one assess Paraguay's response to the logistical challenge of Humaitá? Sufficient supplies certainly enabled the defenders to withstand the enemy assault for better than two years, so a verdict of "qualified success" must be made. Given the supply and transportation problems, however, one might speculate that Paraguay's resources could never have sustained any larger force than the twenty thousand to twenty-five thousand men who held Humaitá. By the end of 1867 that number could no longer withstand the ever more audacious allied army.

## Annihilation

Humaitá fell in mid-1868, but López was able to extract most of his army, deploying it to the north around Asunción. Now, with the Brazilian navy in command of the Paraguay River, he deemed it necessary in late 1868 to evacuate the capital. Civilians, war materiel, and even an arsenal dispersed into the interior while the Paraguayan army awaited the Brazilian assault. In a series of desperate battles around Lomas Valentinas in December 1868, with high casualties on both sides, the Brazilians prevailed. Marshal López and the remnants of his forces retreated into the interior, where he established his capital at Piribebuí.

The marshal's army was not yet completely destroyed. He still controlled much of the republic's remaining population, food was yet being produced, and the southern part of the railroad operated. An arsenal from Asunción had been evacuated to Caacupé and worked to repair what arms remained. Ybycuí to the south continued to provide war materiel for the army, though with difficulty. The influx of refugees into the interior caused strains upon the economy, but Vice President Sánchez struggled valiantly to reequip the army. Orders sped to militia officials to create rosters of the evacuees, with special emphasis upon all able-bodied males above the age of twelve. Sánchez demanded that refugees busy themselves with food production, but by that point internal administration was beginning to break down and there were scattered instances of noncompliance.[86] Circulars commanded the collection and dispatch to the army of all available firearms, swords, and lances.[87] Recruits—young boys, old men above sixty, and convalescents—filled the ranks. Troops and civilians constructed a defensive line barring the advance of the Brazilian army along the railroad to the southeast. By April 1869, with about thirteen thousand soldiers under his command, Marshal López felt confident enough to send raiding parties against the invaders.

Observers expressed surprise at the regeneration of the marshal's army, but it was a last-gasp resurgence. Too many young boys—often not even past the age of puberty—as well as women filled the ranks of his army.[88] What arms remained were often antique and unserviceable; many soldiers only carried machetes and spears. After the Paraguayan defeats at Piribebuí and Acosta Ñu in mid-1869, internal administration of the nation collapsed. López's army, retreating to the northeast, was a ragged, desperate band living off what food they could seize in that resource-poor region. In any economic sense, the war ended for Paraguay when its forces abandoned the hinterland of Asunción.

Paraguay should have negotiated a peace at the end of 1865. By the middle of that year the great weakness of the war economy, and hence the continuation of the war, was the lack of manpower. For the short term this was a nonrenewable, but vital, resource. The treasure spent on war industries prior to 1864, the great sacrifices and labor of the civilian population, the ingenuity in the improvisation of war materiel, and the courage and patriotic devotion of the Paraguayan soldier all gave way to one terrible, inescapable fact: too many Paraguayans were dead. By mid-1866 the republic had fallen into a war of attrition, both human and material, at too great a cost.

In a greater sense the war economy of Paraguay illustrates how the industrial revolution affected war in the mid–nineteenth century.[89] Ever-larger armies could now be equipped and supplied. One consequence was the longer duration of operations against critical strategic points. There is an eerie similarity among Sebastopol in the Crimean War, Vicksburg and Petersburg in the U.S. Civil War, Paris in the Franco-Prussian War, and of course Humaitá in the Paraguayan War. Wars now consumed greater numbers of soldiers as well as materiel. And, as these wars proved, a nation now needed an adequate industrial base or access to foreign war materiel for a sustained effort. To feed the demand for larger armies now that states could arm and supply them more easily than in the past, a reasonably large population base also was needed for recruitment and to sustain the home economy. Critical to all these economic factors were determined leadership and a population that might doggedly support the war effort.

Paraguay lacked too many of these critical elements; it could not even gain even a stalemate in the war. Both its industrial and population base were too small to sustain the demands placed upon it, especially as Brazil increased its army and acquired war materiel from abroad. Even more than the Confederacy in the American Civil War, Paraguay was overwhelmed by superior manpower and materiel. As for the improvisation within Paraguay's wartime economy, despite what various scholars have claimed, it was never enough. The South discovered the same in 1861–65 as it tried desperately to create an armaments industry, as did France when it had to recreate an army after the disasters of Sedan and Metz in 1870. Paraguay certainly possessed determined leadership in the person of Francisco Solano López, but he often used that determination more against his own people than against the allies. But historians should recognize the quiet competence of Vice President Domingo Francisco Sánchez, who worked diligently to keep the armies supplied under worsening conditions. His, however, was an increasingly difficult job. The Paraguayan people responded magnificently to the wartime sacrifices demanded of them, but it made little difference. Small states like Paraguay, with traditional agrarian economies, increasingly could not compete when engaged in sustained modern warfare.

# 3. Protagonists, Victims, and Heroes

Paraguayan Women during the "Great War"

The role that Paraguay's women assumed during the so-called *Epopeya Nacional* (Epic National Struggle) has been a point of debate ever since that devastating conflict. During the Paraguayan War President Francisco Solano López hailed their many contributions to state and society as evidence of the entire population's unconditional support for the war effort and for his government. The official newspapers recorded patriotic speeches made by women of all classes and even some offers to take up arms, such as that of the women of Areguá: "Our votes and our wishes will not be satisfied until we spill the blood of the invader with our own hands, by this reaching the heights of the sacrifices of the courageous legions of the Great López. It is with this intent, Señor Jefe, that we have united voluntarily and spontaneously to ask in the most formal manner to be enrolled in order to be instructed in the use of arms."[1]

After the war, however, women were primarily depicted as poor victims of the dictator, and their patriotism seemed more a sign of political oppression than an indication of authentic identification with the nation. As the allied forces continued their pursuit of the fugitive president, an Asunción newspaper asked: "Who has not sensed both horror and compassion [when faced] with these unfortunate women? . . . Who has no delicate sentiments for the unlucky Paraguayan woman covered with the sheets of misery, lying on the hard soil, and revealing on her bitter visage some mysterious and dark resemblance to Egyptian mummies and living cadavers? . . . Poor victims! . . . They have seen evil incarnate in the satanic figure of an unchristian. . . . They even have lost sensibility, because tyranny has had more power over them than God."[2] Whether victims or heroes, Paraguayan women, like Mexican *soldaderas*, have entered the realm of national folklore, but even more than their Mexican counterparts, women in Paraguay have become synonymous with the national identity.[3]

The official account, however, stresses not so much the economic contribution of women during the war, but rather their activities in the army camps and in their public support for the national cause that implies no change in gender roles. Despite transgression of these roles during the war, women are still described as sacrificing and supportive wives in the standard historiography. Paraguayan historian Olinda Massare de Kostianovsky endorses this conventional interpretation: "With unmatched abnegation and innumerable sacrifices, she formed the nascent Paraguayan nationality. . . . The role assumed by the Paraguayan woman during our epic [struggle] is enormous, given that she was a protagonist in it, revealing her virtues and the shining brilliance of her strong and sincere personality in all the efforts that demanded firmness to uphold the nation's dignity and sovereignty and to sustain its heroic defenders."[4] In addition to the question of what motivated Paraguayan women to support the army until the bitter end not only at home but also at the front, many others can be asked. How was it possible for women to run the Paraguayan economy when almost all of the men were either dead or in uniform? What did this mean for gender relations and the political status of the country's women? Did the active role that women assumed during the war lead to their acceptance as citizens with full political rights?

## The Economy

In the early 1860s, Paraguay still maintained a largely subsistence economy coupled with the export of a few cash crops, such as Paraguay tea (yerba mate), cotton, and tobacco. The economic role of women in the *Epopeya Nacional* was shaped by their gender-specific insertion into this system. Men traditionally worked in the export and market sectors, while women cultivated the manioc, corn, and beans used by the family. Women had handled heavy fieldwork since pre-Columbian times, and this custom prevailed throughout the colonial period, while men commonly worked in yerba production and in the downriver transport of cash crops. (I have elsewhere concluded that women managed at least half of the agricultural subsistence work at this time.)[5] They were also heavily involved in petty trade, and travelers who came to Asunción left vivid descriptions of a picturesque marketplace dominated by women in impeccably white dresses (*typois*).[6]

Paraguayan women did not limit their marketing to the Asunción plaza during the war; they also sold their surplus to households and to the military. Indeed, while the *estancias de la república* (government-owned ranches) provided the troops with meat, the women of nearby villages became their chief suppliers of fruits and rum.[7] Washerwomen and female cooks also lived from the services that they provided in the army camps. Many were migrants who traveled to Asunción, Cerro León, or Humaitá when a male family member enlisted. They accompanied the relative and provided him with many of his daily needs, cooking his meals and doing his laundry.[8] For many girls or young women this camp work ushered in a more independent life, leading to similar occupations in the civilian sector after the war.

In this narrow sense the outbreak of the war brought good business to many Paraguayan women. Their commerce with the army increased, prices rose, and women could donate part of their surplus (in cigars, food, or clothes) to the soldiers. If we are to believe the Paraguayan newspaper reports, the greater part of such contributions came from the women.[9] The state, though, helped widows or single women whose sons were in the army by exempting them from paying rent on their land and providing them with seeds and other items. No wonder then that women initially favored the war and its material consequences.

President López had managed to convince the majority of the population that national honor was at stake, and women heartily concurred. In the early campaign in Mato Grosso, they had something to gain. French consul Émile Laurent-Cochelet noted that the women who accompanied the army north supposedly went to aid the wounded but then stayed on to participate in the plunder.[10] The bad news of the Paraguayan defeats at Riachuelo and Uruguaiana and the concomitant problems within the army camps only spread at the end of 1865 after the army withdrew from Corrientes. Women from all over Paraguay then tried to get permission to go to Humaitá and Paso Pucú to see their relatives, provide them with food and tobacco—and engage in some additional business.[11] Whether prostitution also played a role is not clear; nowhere in the documents does this matter come up explicitly. The impression is that organized prostitution did not exist in prewar and wartime Paraguay, but this should not imply an absence of venal love.[12] Something similar to formal prostitution certainly accompanied the concentration of soldiers in the camps.

We cannot easily determine when support for the war and López began to wane. Certainly experiences like those of Ybytymí's Patricia Acosta became more common as the conflict wore on. In 1867 she wrote Vice President Domingo Francisco Sánchez to ask for assistance, asserting that she had been "left alone with her insolvent mother who [was] sick and half-blind." Sánchez noted: "Her six sons have been called to arms, and four of them have died with the army in the south; she works on the land in order to subsist and maintain herself and her old mother, and, for this reason, she requires a yoke for the oxen, an ax, a knife, and a plow. She also needs one or two cows in order to feed her mother with the milk, and someone to help her restore the hut in which she lives; she herself will supply the necessary straw."[13] We cannot know whether the loss of four sons made Acosta doubt the wisdom of the war, but it is clear that, under ever more difficult circumstances, women like her had to do the work hitherto left to men. When imports of cloth stopped due to the allied blockade, women had to turn first to home-spun cotton and later on to local fibers taken from coconuts and *caraguatá*.[14] They also had to work in the traditionally male fields of salt processing and livestock butchering.[15]

Throughout the war the civilian population continued to support the army, but how much of this resulted from patriotic enthusiasm and how much came from social and political pressure cannot be determined. In the countryside local justices of peace and other authorities periodically summoned the people to hear the news from the front, and usually thereafter the offers to help the army increased. In the beginning of 1866 the marshal ordered not only the total mobilization of the male population but also the coordination of "spontaneous" and "voluntary" donations by the civilian population; another decree specified in detail the items needed.[16] These orders clearly did more than simply coordinate the donations.

Even more significant than the women on the home front were those in the army camps. These women provided the soldiers with food and kept the camps clean. As nurses they became indispensable, and every family was obliged to send one daughter to serve in that capacity. Such nurses received a small salary. Their service and knowledge of local plants became vital when imported European medicines ran out early in the war.[17] The central role of women in the camps and their growing numbers eventually prompted authorities to name *sargentas* (female sergeants) who supervised every aspect of the life in the camps, from the provision of food and the laundering of clothes to the organization of dances in the evenings.[18]

The more desperate the situation of the Paraguayan army became, the more important the agricultural and medical knowledge of the women and the more crucial the emotional comfort they provided soldiers. Authorities required women to participate in weekly dances, held with rum in abundance. In addition to these scheduled diversions, López ordered dances for Paraguayan soldiers to celebrate not only victories but also battles in which the army had shown its mettle.[19] Dancing surely played an important role in the nation's culture, but such fetes turned into grotesque propaganda exercises when mandated by the marshal to celebrate the troops or the arrival of new cannon at every railway station on their way to the front. In 1867 *El Centinela* reported an especially striking celebration for a newly founded artillery piece as it passed through Luque on the way to the front: "After some time of dancing and a lively banquet, where there were enthusiastic toasts to the Supreme Chief [López], to the Army, and to the Paraguayan cannon, [it] continued on its journey accompanied by the fair sex of Luque."[20]

## The Patriotic Acts

Dances and festivities were not confined to army camps. They also constituted an important instrument in the regime's war propaganda. In the beginning the departure of the soldiers from Asunción was accompanied by music at the square in front of the railway station, where Madame Eliza Alicia Lynch, López's consort, distributed cigars. As the wartime situation became more critical, these joyful celebrations gave way to political manifestations in Asunción, which were often accompanied by dances. These acts apparently started after the publication of the Triple Alliance Treaty's secret clauses in August 1866, which brought a wave of indignant nationalism, even among the upper classes, which were generally critical if not hostile to President López. The terms of the treaty—the transfer of more than one-third of Paraguay's territory to Argentina and Brazil, the country's total disarmament, and the requirement that López be removed from power before any peace—were too much to stomach.

Confronted with this apparent menace to national survival, women of all classes offered their jewelry to the state to help cover the costs of the war. After the first "spontaneous acts" in the countryside, assemblies of the "fair national sex" (as *El Semanario de Avisos y Conocimientos Utiles* called them) were organized systematically in 1867. In Asunción upper-class women led the effort, with individuals offering their jewelry and declaring that hence-forth the national colors would constitute their only adornment. López at first declined these offers, but then accepted a portion of the jewelry with "heartfelt gratitude," declaring that the state could still finance the war on its own. The real reason for his reluctance, however, may have been that allied blockades after 1866 made it nearly impossible to procure new war materiel on the international market; specie and jewelry were thus virtually useless to the government. Nevertheless, women continued to demonstrate their loyalty with patriotic gifts to the president, such as a sword bedecked with precious stones, a diamond-studded triumphal cap, and other symbolic items.[21] The final stage of these acts were offers by women to take up arms. Along with the supposed existence of a company of women soldiers, these offers provide either absolute proof of Paraguayan nationalism or, as López's

1. Elite women making a patriotic presentation to President Francisco Solano López (*El Centinela* [Asunción], 12 September 1867)

detractors have put it, manifest evidence of the regime's tyranny. A closer look at these shows of support reveals a rather different story. They were neither so voluntary as the official sources depicted, nor were they entirely coerced.[22]

The women's assemblies that offered their jewelry and symbols of glory such as jewel-encrusted swords and caps were not as spontaneous as the newspaper reports suggest. Significantly the Asunción lists of contributors were headed either by Madame Lynch or by the president's sister, and many letters reveal that the women who organized these gatherings had been obliged to do so.[23] Encarnación Bedoya, a young woman from a prominent elite family, recounted later:"When the tyrant López wanted the families to give up their jewelry for the maintenance of the war, the gold that was gathered was for him alone and Doña Fulana [Madame Lynch] asked for the jewelry. Nobody gave anything except rings from wire and old earrings. . . . When this Doña Fulana . . . was uttering the wish for the gold and jewelry, an innocent man stepped forward to say that this was her second thought, but none of us was mistaken: We all knew who had asked for the jewelry and nobody gave anything save those pieces that they could spare anyway."[24]

The oft-cited tale of the women of Areguá who offered to fight looks different upon closer examination. First, offers to take up arms had already been made by women in the countryside when it became apparent the Paraguayan army lacked men to guard the rivers and to conduct mail. Women volunteered to do these tasks as early as 1865, and the justice of the peace of Villeta reported that local women "would even take up arms, not only to guard the coast of this place but also to join the army voluntarily."[25] Such proposals poured in from all over the country in 1867, and they show that the notion of taking up arms was a symbolic act that evolved from the emotional assemblies and a wish to protect one's own village, though preferably with less-aggressive methods. The most famous of these offers—that of the women of Areguá—was far from a spontaneous desire to help the army. It owes its fame to a song subsequently published in the Paraguayan newspapers that lionized the bravery of the town's women. In fact, the entire demonstration was orchestrated by Madame Lynch, who took up the emotional displays of popular support and fashioned them into formal statements that had propaganda value.[26]

López turned down all these offers, but rumors of Paraguayan women fighting in regular companies persisted and circulated abroad. The *Baltimore American and Commercial Adviser*, for example, reprinted a report from the *Buenos Aires Standard* with rumors about women defending the rivers, adding: "The guerilla portion of the campaign—or what is termed here the '*guerra de recursos* [struggle for supplies]'—is entrusted to the women of Paraguay; and reliable data have been received that the troops to the north, near Tranquera Loreto, are exclusively composed of women." The report listed the different tasks performed by women since the outbreak of the war, concluding that "with Satanic power, they are dragged to the front, and placed in the breach to fight the whole Allied army! . . . If, as the news goes, the Allies, in attempting to cross the Tebicuarí, have to fight the girls, then the honor of Europe is at stake in at once stopping this horrible war."[27] It seems, however, that notwithstanding some individual cases (and the self-defense of women against allied soldiers after the fall of Piribebuí in August 1869), organized female units never existed in Paraguay. Tales of companies of women soldiers were wartime propaganda, nothing more.

Paraguayan propaganda made extensive use of contemporary gender stereotypes in pursuing its aims, and did so quite skillfully. Bilingual Guaraní and Spanish newspapers directed at the lower classes appealed to the martial and patriarchal values of Paraguayan men when they warned against the Brazilian "monkeys" and "black hordes" anxious to rape Paraguayan women. Or they told stories of brave women who defended themselves against jaguars with only a knife, concluding, "if Paraguayan women are capable of this, what potent mother's milk to feed the legions of López."[28]

*El Semanario*, a newspaper directed at both the Paraguayan elite and foreign residents, used a different language and addressed different topics. It covered extensively the assemblies of "the fair national sex" and their contributions to the cause. It also described the dances and festivities that accompanied these manifestations in the same way that it had reported social events before the war. By 1867, however, new notions of women's roles surfaced in these reports. *El Semanario* began to address women as "fellow citizens [*conciudadanas*]" and stated that their participation in the patriotic assemblies elevated their position in society. It drew a direct and explicit line from the women of ancient Sparta to those of modern Paraguay: "The Paraguayan woman this evening has given the most outspoken expression of her patriotism, and her great and noble soul has entered into the full rights that heaven has given to her. She participated in public affairs and formed the first American assembly, which is more important than the antique ones, reunited by the inspirations of the sovereign people." This newspaper described the assemblies of 24–26 February 1867 as "magnificent, since for the first time we saw women taking [their] place at the grand banquet of civilization to enjoy the public rights of which society has deprived them with unjustified egoism. The fair sex has taken one more step on the road to progress when it positioned itself on the tribune of the popular assemblies."[29] Thus the role of women became a yardstick for the degree of civilization; Paraguay could rank among the most civilized of countries, for the marshal had given women rights and opportunities that even European countries denied them. Just as twentieth-century Latin American dictators (like Rafael Trujillo of the Dominican Republic) granted women suffrage to give their regimes a democratic veneer, so López used the officially organized female assemblies.[30] Whether this really appealed to the elite women was no doubt another matter. Most had long opposed López and even more so his Irish-born mistress. The pressure on them to give up their jewelry was not well received, as Encarnación Bedoya's diary shows, and postwar memoirs of elite women express nothing but contempt for the dictator and his consort.[31]

It is doubtful that López had more success with lower-class women. He evidently courted them, praising their role in agricultural labor, and arranged for government newspapers to reflect his admiration. Judging by Vice President Sánchez's reminders in 1866, however, not all were eager to labor in the national cause. He exhorted women and children that "everywhere in the world it is necessary to work in order to live," and, "though these orders [for increased field labor] leave little room for rest, it can never match the fatigue and sleeplessness of our brethren now in the theater of war, with a close threat to their lives, while here after work is done all go to their homes and sleep quietly."[32] After 1867, when women's subsistence activities became even more vital to the country's survival, their efforts again received attention and recognition. And yet even in April 1869, official discourse rarely gave women credit and tended to turn even this small portion into a praise of the country and its government: "How lucky are our countrywomen because they were born in a free country that Providence has provided with a very rich soil where the seed repays the laborer with a tenfold product, and more than this, in a country where [women] are appreciated and loved, and where those who merit it always receive praise."[33]

## The Last Years of the War

By the time that sentence was written, praise in the newspapers was all that was left to the hardworking Paraguayan women. Until mid-1867, food supply was still relatively good, but the situation worsened by the end of the year. Improvisation became the order of the day. Women started to make use of local plants to get fibers for cloth, paper, medicine, and food. Oil was produced from a small indigenous coconut, and newspapers gave tips on how to use local produce to manufacture soap and other items. Oranges grew wild all over the country, and when sugar cane became sparse, women made alcoholic beverages from orange juice. At the very end women even made a kind of sweet from bitter oranges (*apepú*), a fruit detested by Paraguayans, who considered the plant fit only for the oil present in its leaves.[34] Because of the heavy agricultural labor, women neglected the salt deposits of Lambaré, which brought severe consequences for the health of the population. The incidence of diarrhea increased, and by the end of the year cholera and other epidemics started to affect soldiers and civilians alike.[35]

The situation of women worsened in late 1868 after the marshal evacuated Asunción and his army lost the battle of Lomas Valentinas in December. López then ordered all women to evacuate the lands he had abandoned to the allies and to follow the remnants of the Paraguayan army as they escaped east and later north. While such tactics served the purpose of leaving only scorched earth to the enemy, the marshal's army still needed the foodstuffs that only the female labor force could provide. Agriculture received even more supervision than before: Women worked literally day and night (or at least nights with full moons), and every aspect of civilian life took on a military character. Overseers might have been old men or invalid soldiers, but women performed all the labor and increasingly took on administrative tasks as justices of the peace and other authorities.[36]

As the war came to an end, displaced women, known as *residentas* and *destinadas*, came to constitute a large part of the population. The latter were internal exiles, while the former were displaced women who, willingly or unwillingly, had left their homes and defended themselves against the allies advancing on Piribebuí, the new seat of government. Many *residentas* later followed the army on its retreat into the northern forests. The term *residenta* derives from the formula with which these women declared their identity, giving their place of origin and their temporary residence after the evacuation, *"vecina de . . . residente en,"* or "[permanent] inhabitant of . . . [now] resident in." The *residentas* were later declared national heroes, and at the beginning of the 1970s, Gen. Alfredo Stroessner dedicated a huge monument in a central Asunción square to an anonymous *residenta*; her deeds were presented as proof of women's strong and unconditional nationalism.

*Residentas* certainly performed some heroic acts, but oddly their efforts to ensure army subsistence have received little attention. In any case it is doubtful that their motivations were stirred by pure patriotism. After all, they had little choice but to obey the evacuation orders that were brutally enforced. Moreover women had other reasons for remaining with the army. They had always cared for their menfolk, even before the war, and it was part of their family obligation to do so. Who else would feed and nurse their brothers, husbands, lovers, or sons if they did not? Remaining with the army, then, was more an act of solidarity with the men closest to them than an act of love for country. It can thus be best understood as an extension of the traditional female role in the family. Furthermore, falling into enemy hands held few attractions, given that the allies offered no succor to noncombatants (and not all reports of atrocities and rapes by the occupation army were lies).[37]

Such reasons in themselves might explain the loyalty of the Paraguayan women to the army, but they in no way preclude a more developed political sentiment among women of all classes. Women as well as men had learned since the time of Dr. José Gaspar de Francia, Paraguay's first president, that independence represented the highest good for the republic, and after all the war threatened the country's existence. But even if women had developed a national consciousness and saw their defense of the fatherland in terms of serving the army, they still became increasingly critical of the López regime. The French consul Laurent-Cochelet had written as early as 1865: "The popularity of President López has diminished considerably among the lower classes since the events of the war woke them cruelly from the golden dreams into which the easy capture of Coimbra and the profitable pillage of the cities of Mato Grosso had drowned them. The women, who form almost exclusively the rest of the population, began to speak with considerable freedom by Paraguayan standards, and they say that the President is responsible for the hand of Providence falling so precipitously on the country."[38] Reports from the justices of the peace for the first trimester of 1868 have survived almost in their entirety, and they confirm the consul's impression. More than half of the crimes prosecuted fell into the category of "treason"; while there was little difference between men and women in overall crime rates, women outnumbered men by three to one among those charged with political crimes. Women apparently spread defeatist news about the bad conditions in the camps, the abuse of alcohol to maintain soldiers' fighting spirit, and the rumor that López and Lynch had secretly fled the country. Others complained about their private situation or said that they would prefer their men at home, even wounded or invalid, than to see them die for their country.[39]

Does this mean that women had more political wisdom and more courage to criticize the regime than men, as one modern author has suggested?[40] Probably not. A more likely explanation lies in the fact that men accused of disloyalty or of undermining the war effort simply received orders to deploy to a more dangerous sector of the front, where their chances of survival were nil. There was no need to put them on trial and consequently no record of any proceedings against them. What the justice of the peace reports do show, however, is that Paraguayan women (and men) never followed their president so unconditionally as certain foreign observers and some later historians have argued.[41] Of course it was dangerous to utter even the slightest criticism of the regime. Those women found guilty of treason were frequently whipped before being dispatched to the remotest of internal exiles, thereby becoming the so-called *destinadas*, those destined or sent into such banishment.[42]

Some *destinadas* were real opponents of President López, but others were simply relatives of men out of favor with the marshal. As he became increasingly repressive toward the end of the war, resistance among even his former supporters increased. In 1868 a supposed conspiracy was unearthed, involving several individuals in the Paraguayan elite, including members of López's own family (it may have been the product of the president's paranoia). The wives of the men involved were obliged to distance themselves publicly from their husbands, but this did not save them from prosecution. Even women like Susana Céspedes de Céspedes, who had been among the founders of the assemblies of the fair national sex, ended up as a *destinada*.[43] At the beginning only women found guilty of political or common crimes were destined to remote villages, where they were obliged to work in the fields. Later the mere fact of belonging to the family of a presumed traitor or the close association with one provided sufficient grounds for conviction and internal exile. No one dared help these women or even their children because they feared compromising themselves. [44]

The *destinadas* came from all classes of Paraguayan society, but upper-class women stood out decidedly among them. López considered the men of these elite families as potential collaborators with the enemy, and he regarded any show of disloyalty on their part as much more dangerous than similar displays from the lower classes. For this reason even the slightest muttering of disapproval led to conviction, and most elite women saw the end of the war, if they survived it, as *destinadas*. This explains the many pathetic accounts of the horrors that these women suffered. [45] Unlike their sisters in the lower classes, elite wives and daughters were not used to working under a blazing sun and walking for long distances over difficult terrain. They (and some foreigners) tried to maintain their social distance from the lower-class *destinadas* as best as they could, but during the last two years of the war such class distinctions lost all meaning; the lives of women of all classes, *residentas* and *destinadas*, became increasingly similar. Only those closest to the president still had wagons with oxen to pull them. The wealthier families eventually sold all that they had of value. Fancy clothes and jewelry, which had once seemed so valuable, lost their importance. All had to work to feed the remnants of the Paraguayan army and state. Women tilled the land with old wooden plows and knives. One *destinada* related that they sometimes used their bare hands or ox yokes to cultivate the ground. [46]

Scarcely had they built huts for shelter in their new destinations when the *destinadas* in Yhu, Ygatymí, and other places in that area received marching orders again in late 1869. A large number were led along a tiny path through the forests of eastern Paraguay. About three thousand women found themselves in a place called Espadín (today Brazilian territory), where most immediately realized that they were sure to starve. Not even bitter oranges were available, and after having eaten the last mules and horses, they had to live on herbs and reptiles. Although they were guarded by only twenty prepubescent soldiers, flight proved difficult; they had nowhere to go, and the marshal's troops still patrolled the surrounding territory. Some women nonetheless tried to escape with the help of local Indians, but most were caught and brought back. Death swept through the group, striking down children especially. At the end of December 1869, a Brazilian force rescued about eight hundred surviving *destinadas* from Espadín.

The *residentas* who had stayed with the army were not much better off in late 1869. Forced to leave the fields they had planted in the villages to which they had been evacuated, they marched north at the hottest time of the year. While López still hosted parties and celebrated holidays (including his own birthday), the women in his camp had to live on thin soup cooked with herbs, leather, and bones. When the marshal finally departed from Zanha Yhu (near Panadero) with those troops still capable of marching (on 28 December 1869), the weak and wounded, the women, and the children were left to starve while López went on to Cerro Corá and a "glorious" death.[47] The remaining women, children, and sick men apparently starved, and nobody bothered about them, least of all the allied forces who were pursuing the marshal-president. In 1873 a Brazilian-Paraguayan commission charged with settling border questions found the region's paths strewn with bones.[48]

## The "Land of Women"

Those women who survived the war (and their first more-or-less good meal) tried to walk to Asunción, where they hoped to find better conditions and at least something to eat; the countryside, full of deserted fields and villages, offered few attractions. But in the capital, where the occupation army had installed itself at the beginning of 1869, the situation of these refugees was indescribably bad.[49] Half-naked women and children scrambled for crumbs thrown to them by the Brazilian soldiers. Death, rape, and prostitution were daily scenes in the streets. In the countryside, if anything, the situation was worse.[50]

Improvements came slowly. The allies installed a provisional government that tried to bring some order to society, and the Paraguayans who had survived the war—mostly women, invalids, children, and old people—began to work the land once more. The provisional government's measures often proved inadequate and sometimes even ridiculous: It forbade the use of Guaraní in public, the afternoon siesta, and the custom of bathing naked in the rivers, all cultural traditions of long standing in tropical Paraguay.[51] Other decrees made more sense, such as the creation of public schools for both boys and girls, the regulation of burials and markets (urgent sanitary measures), and the efforts to return the rural population to their villages and fields.[52]

With the borders open again, women who had worked in agricultural labor and petty trade before the war could again travel up and down the river to Argentina and to Mato Grosso to earn a living as street vendors and

2. Market women after the war (Wilhelm Vallentin, *Paraguay: Das Land der Guaranís* [Berlin: Verlag von Hermann Paetel, 1907], frontispiece)

domestics. They came to dominate the markets and streets of Asunción and other towns even more than they had before the war. One foreign observer concluded some ten years later that not even the National Bank dared do anything without the approval of the Asunción market women.[53]

In the aftermath of the war, Paraguay became famous as the "land of women," attracting adventurers who wanted to see a country in which women did almost all the work and in which they were said to outnumber men ten to one. One Russian traveler, Alexander Jonin, wrote that when he "prepared for the journey to Paraguay, a Frenchman praised the country and said, 'There are only women,' and meaningfully smacked his lips. And he was right."[54] In some villages in the interior, few men were left apart from the local officials, and the average number of women to men in the general population (higher estimates notwithstanding) was at least four to one, an extremely unusual figure.[55] During the postwar decades this imbalance slowly righted itself, but not before it entered the national psyche as part of a nationalist myth.

What consequences did these developments have for the position of women and, more broadly, for gender relations? Did women's economic and political importance during the war bring any changes to their role in the

Paraguayan state and society? If one considers that by the 1870s women in Europe and the United States had begun to claim political rights and that these ideas soon reached Argentina and Brazil, and if one takes into account the fact that López had raised the political consciousness of women, addressing them as fellow citizens, then one might ask whether the new liberal constitution improved the lot of women. Modeled after the Argentine, United States, and French charters, the constitution took no account of Paraguayan realities. The allies never allowed Paraguayans the necessary political freedom to make it work. In addition many of the members of the new government had lived in exile for years and adopted attitudes and values modeled after bourgeois European examples.[56] But even among those men who had survived the *Epopeya* in Paraguay, mentalities regarding women's places in society had undergone few modifications, and in the end few changes came as a result of the war.

The new, modern newspapers tried to propagate the bourgeois ideal of the loving and caring housewife who raises her children but abstains from all public affairs—an idea that before the war had appealed only to the upper class. If women now protested certain political decisions, the press dismissed them as either silly or the ingenuous tools of evil men. In September 1871, after a group of women condemned the appointment of Father Manuel Vicente Moreno as the new bishop of Paraguay, *El Pueblo* wrote: "If we did not know the motives of these pious women, we might suspect something adventurous. In our society women are destined to other occupations, and they are not allowed to leave this circle. It is ridiculous to see how the Paraguayan woman clings to the customs of yesterday. López had formed assemblies among the female part of society, had them give speeches, in which they demanded the blood of other people. And these customs today still serve some irresponsible [men], even if the demands have changed."[57] On another occasion, after women protested to the Brazilian occupation authorities against actions of certain members of the provisional government, *La Libertad* asked in an article entitled "Ridiculous":

> Who has suggested such a nonsense to the women? Why are some people ridiculed by abusing their ignorance? . . . Do they not know that according to our laws and customs women have no civil rights? . . . The task of the woman in our society is housework and tenderness; the rough work of politics and war-making should be left to the men. Our women have the tasks of ruling the domestic affairs of the households and safeguarding the gentle children, serving the Lord in order to serve mankind, sewing or ironing and washing, cooking soup, fermenting

cheese, caring for their husband's clothing, and [should] not meddle in things best left to the President or to the justice of the peace.[58]

Aside from the fact that most women no longer had a husband or a man to care for, such articles about women's political protests show that they continued to voice an interest in public affairs and intervened when they thought that something of importance to them was at stake.

Women never insisted on suffrage or formal political rights, however, until well into the twentieth century. This was probably due to two factors, both rooted in Paraguayan history. First, the country had no democratic tradition, and men could claim few political rights during the governments of Dr. Francia and the López dynasty (and women none at all). Political parties and general elections were unheard of until the 1880s, and even thereafter Paraguayan "democracy" was far from perfect. Why bother, therefore, to demand a right that was largely meaningless even to those who actually had it? There were more important and more immediate things to do. Second, women's mentality had not significantly changed with the war either; most Paraguayan women also held the opinion that formal politics was not their concern. They had learned, however, that they could make their grievances heard even under authoritarian regimes like those of Francia and Carlos Antonio López. So they protested and intervened if they thought it necessary, but they did not demand the franchise.[59]

Perhaps a Swiss traveler, J. B. Rusch, was right when he wrote in the 1920s:

It is the woman who governs the Paraguayan lower class. . . . Slim and tall, delicate and with natural grace in all her movements, the mestizo women of Paraguay are probably the most beautiful American women. . . . They are all Amazons, who move around with male freedom and ability, smoke their big strong cigars and give orders to the men. It should not be forgotten that this able kind of women, without whose stubbornness the Paraguayans would have remained a rather neglected folk, has emerged from the sixties and seventies of the past century when almost all manhood of the country was wiped out. . . . This dangerous time gave rise to the image of the Amazon, which, once established, never allowed men to gain a newfound importance. The Paraguayan man is of no importance in the family and in commerce. Only in [his capacity] as citizen does the woman allow him [a voice in] the affairs of the country, and making politics is the only occupation that can make a Paraguayan man impulsive. It even seems that these strange women want nothing more than that their men are somewhat lazy and disdainful of any kind of work. Apparently, they feel better in their male role.[60]

Rusch was not the only foreign observer who considered Paraguayan men lazy and thought that women did most of the work as a consequence of the war. Paraguayan men explained this by claiming that, with so few of them left, women necessarily fought over them and for that reason did everything to coddle their menfolk.[61] That this was the case seems rather doubtful. While we can never determine whether Paraguayan women in the late 1800s preferred to let the few men lay in hammocks or debate in the plaza, today's Paraguayan women clearly do not, though they still do a large part of the work. Women perform much of the agricultural labor, still dominate the marketplace, and are still the ones who offer stability to the (often incomplete) Paraguayan family. All of these customs have a long presence in the country. The war and the subsequent demographic imbalance aggravated women's disadvantages, though it did not create them.[62] The war and the postwar years only made more visible the important role of women's work, not just to foreign observers but also to Paraguayans themselves. The only conclusion that men could draw from this was that it was absolutely necessary for the well-being of the nation to improve female education at all social levels. Before the war even many upper-class women were illiterate, but those who could read and write actively promoted women's education after the war.[63] This was perhaps the conflict's only significant and lasting positive consequence for women, and it helped change attitudes in the following generations. Today the gender gap in illiteracy rates is comparatively small in Paraguay, 7.8 percent for women versus 5.6 percent for men; in contrast, in Bolivia these rates stand at 20.6 and 7.9 percent respectively.[64]

In the immediate postwar years, circumstances for women in Paraguay did not improve but worsened. The country became famous as "the land of women," but this did not make it a "land *for* women." Female social standing and political rights were neglected in Paraguay until quite recently. That the female contribution to the *Epopeya Nacional* was less appreciated than feared by Paraguayan men is evident from the traditional historiography, which prefers not to celebrate the women who plowed the fields as much as those who gave their husbands and sons for the cause. This traditional portrayal is harmless to gender hierarchies. It keeps women subordinate to men and thus avoids any direct challenge to the old patriarchy. It also provides a more attractive backdrop for the nationalism propagated by subsequent Paraguayan governments, especially the military dictatorships of the twentieth century.

# 4. Patriotic Mobilization in Brazil

## The Zuavos and Other Black Companies

Shortly after allied troops crossed the Paraná River and invaded southern Paraguay (mid-April 1866), the Brazilian plenipotentiary to the allied governments, Francisco Otaviano de Almeida Rosa, exulted to the war minister: "A warm embrace [*abraço*] for our triumphs. Long live the Brazilians, be they white, black, mulatto, or Indian [*caboclo*]! What brave men!"[1] Otaviano's enthusiasm for the military feats of his mixed-race countrymen raises the question of the war's effect on racial politics in this racially diverse society. Brazil was then the largest slave society in the Americas, with some 1.5 million black men and women in bondage. But at least 4.25 million Afro-Brazilians were free, and they accounted for two-fifths of the total population of just over 10 million.[2]

The significance of the war's massive mobilization for these Afro-Brazilians remains a controversial, but relatively unstudied, topic. Certainly black men dominated the rank and file arrayed against Paraguay, though the republic's propaganda that portrayed all Brazilian soldiers as slaves or "monkeys" exaggerated this feature in playing on racial stereotypes. For many, notably the popular historian of the 1980s, Júlio José Chiavenato, the large number of black men in the ranks is evidence of a deliberate genocidal policy, for commanders used these soldiers as cannon fodder, especially after the start of slave recruitment in late 1866.[3] Others echo Otaviano and see the war as an experience that forged a common nationality in battle.[4] But Eduardo Silva's well-known biography of Cândido da Fonseca Galvão, better known as Dom Obá II (the name that he took in Rio de Janeiro in the 1880s), a black man who served in one of the all-black Zuavo companies raised in Bahia, reveals some of the complexity that the war experience assumed for black Brazilians. Deeply monarchist, Obá clung to his service to the emperor as evidence of his membership in the nation, yet he also published sophisticated critiques of the racial discrimination from which he and his fellow Afro-Brazilians suffered.[5]

In 1865, however, the future Obá II was but a minor figure in the mobilization of black men in Bahia and Pernambuco. In the provincial capitals of Salvador and Recife, several all-black companies, known variously as Zuavos, Couraças, and Sapadores, were organized in 1865–67. Well over a thousand men headed to the battlefields sporting distinctive uniforms and bearing an identity as black defenders of the empire. This ideology drew on a long tradition of black men's service to the monarchy and the state and on patronage networks that incorporated free black men into the political order. The experience of these soldiers, and particularly that of their officers, reveals the complex racial politics of a state that resorted to such recruitment but ultimately proved unwilling to countenance the distinct identity implied by the all-black units. Wartime mobilization invoked old traditions of black men's service, but the Brazilian government and army soon rejected them, abolishing their separate units, and in the process undermining black men's identification with the state. In the aftermath of the war few spaces existed in Brazil for black men to pursue collective interests or claim citizenship, and they, like most other veterans, remained marginalized.

## Patriotic Mobilization in Brazil, 1865–66

The outbreak of war sparked an unexpected surge of patriotism throughout Brazil. On Christmas Eve 1864 João Batista Calógeras, a civil servant in the capital, wrote of the "patriotic effervescence" that had reached "36 degrees." "God help Brazil," he added in a note of worry.[6] While much of this "militant patriotism was," as Richard Morse has suggested, "the perquisite of a Europeanized elite," it reached more deeply into society than most historians have acknowledged, tapping into what Eduardo Silva has called an unrecognized vein of nationality.[7] Thousands of men (and even a few women) volunteered to take up arms or otherwise serve their country while national and provincial governments were inundated with donations in cash and in kind for the war effort. The creation of black companies in Bahia and Pernambuco formed part of this massive patriotic mobilization.

To facilitate recruitment the Brazilian government created the Voluntários da Pátria (Volunteers of the Fatherland) in the first week of January 1865. The soldiers in this elite corps would receive a substantial enlistment bonus, higher salaries than the regulars, and land grants and preference in the civil service after the war. These terms were soon extended to national guardsmen called up for service, and fully 75 percent of the ninety-one thousand men enlisted (according to army figures) claimed the status and benefits of Voluntários (though only a small fraction of them ever received the promised benefits).[8] Thousands signed up in 1865. A clerk in the Bahian treasury naively requested three months' leave with pay to participate in the war against the "despot of Paraguay"; a public school teacher more sensibly sought an indefinite leave.

Medical students volunteered en masse to serve in army hospitals. Most of those who volunteered as individuals were members of the middle class with close ties to the state, and Calógeras wondered what would become of such men who had never handled rifles.[9]

Soon patronage networks began to produce "volunteers" as rural land-owners mobilized their clienteles and led their followers to provincial capitals, just as they marched them to polling booths on election day. A historian of Pernambuco has noted that most volunteers in that province enlisted in groups, often under a patron's guidance.[10] Those who collected such recruits expected to command them in the field. A National Guard major from Curralinho, João Evangelista de Castro Tanajura, offered land on his ranches and sugar estates to the families of the volunteers who would join him. He insisted, however, that these men would only march under his command, a request that the Bahian president (governor) denied. Dionísio Cerqueira, at the time a young lieutenant, records that Tanajura, his cousin, subsequently died of "cerebral fever, certainly caused by the bitter disappointment at seeing his battalion given to the command of another." An officer and several soldiers from another such volunteer battalion deserted rather than serve under the officers whom the president assigned to their unit.[11] However the Voluntários da Pátria had been recruited, all assumed that they were different from army recruits, and the first battalions embarked from Salvador amid great fanfare in March and April 1865.

Along with voluntary enlistments, donations for the war effort began in late 1864, when Brazil invaded Uruguay, and their number soared after news of the Paraguayan invasion of Mato Grosso reached the empire. Salary deductions by civil servants and army officers led the list of donations, but clerks in commercial houses also contributed part of their monthly pay. Wealthy merchants and planters offered sometimes substantial sums of money to the government; after a meeting with more than one hundred of Salvador's merchants in August 1865, the Bahian president reported that he had received donations totaling 20,000 mil-réis (US$40,000) to help outfit Salvador's battalions. The owner of a printing press offered to produce war-related proclamations and circulars for free, while railroad lines and shipping companies agreed to transport recruits at no charge to the government. Musical and dramatic societies put on benefit concerts and patriotic performances. Principals of private schools opened their doors to the children of volunteers.[12]

Women also participated in the mobilization. Wives and mothers of men in the service sewed shirts for soldiers and later prepared linen bandages for field hospitals. Even elite women took up needle and thread. Calógeras,

ever critical, offered a "smidgen of comedy" to his son and described the
ostentatious manner in which the "great ladies" of the capital stitched pillows
for the wounded. To ensure maximum visibility they gathered around open
windows between 5:00 and 7:00 p.m. [13] Elite women also joined in a more
symbolic campaign led by the Viscountess of Tamandaré (the wife of the
Brazilian fleet's commander) who called on *senhoras* to contribute jewels
to decorate a sword to be presented to the emperor. One Bahian woman
offered "the best stone from the best bracelet" that she owned. [14] Others
volunteered to serve as nurses, while Jovita Alves Feitosa, a young woman
from Piauí, became a minor celebrity for disguising her sex and enlisting
in the Voluntários from that province (though authorities in Rio de Janeiro
refused to let her go to the front). [15]

Most of those who contributed to the war effort had some connection to
the state. Merchants and civil servants might have been subject to sanctions
had they failed to do so, and they saw their contributions as services that
would later earn them reward. Thus, like the ladies of the court, they sought
as much publicity as possible. The first Bahian to offer his services in 1864, at
the outset of the crisis in Uruguay, was an honorary army major, a lieutenant
colonel of one of Salvador's National Guard battalions, and an employee of
Salvador's customs house. He explicitly requested that his offer be presented
to the emperor and proclaimed his pride at being the first Bahian to step
forward to stop the "vandalism" of the Uruguayans. [16] These were "middle-
class" patriots, respectable individuals, whose aspirations differed little from
their counterparts in France or Germany.

Such patriotism contrasted with what many perceived as a disturbing
deafness to the country's call. From remote Monte Santo a National Guard
commander complained to his superiors that the local populace "does not
know what patriotism is and will only march if impressed," the time-honored
solution to the problem of filling the ranks. [17] Indeed the first reaction of most
provincial governments to the Paraguayan invasion was a forced recruitment
drive. As news of the Voluntários' creation reached provincial capitals, the
dreaded *recrutamento* subsided but never disappeared entirely in 1865. [18] In late
1866, when the defeat at Curupayty heralded a manpower crisis, impressment
resumed in full force.

This mix of voluntarism and coercive recruitment led to no small confusion. Bahia's commander of arms complained of the "anti-military manner in which the organizers of forces are proceeding" and of a "civilianism
[*paisanismo*]" that threatened to exclude him, "head of the military class in
this province," even from the appointment of army officers (men subject to

him) to posts in the Voluntários. Officers' memoirs contain laments about the "incompetent citizens" who received commands in reward for raising units, which led to many unnecessary battlefield losses. All this confirms Gilberto Freyre's observation that Brazilians rushed to defend their country "more in the spirit of the warrior than the professional soldier."[19] Given the importance of patron-client ties in recruitment, however, it was essential to adopt this manner of mobilization. By March 1866 Bahia's 10,189 soldiers had embarked as thirty-seven separate battalions or companies, ranging in size from 12 to 598 men; only 593 were recruits for existing units.[20] Indeed the president was extremely reluctant to send *recrutas:* "It looks bad [*É feio*]," he explained bluntly.[21]

Although reorganizations of the army in the field erased many of the distinctions between Voluntários and regulars, the key theme in the 1865–66 mobilization was its voluntarism. This was, on one level, a myth, for many—perhaps even most—of the Brazilians who served against Paraguay did so against their will, but such myths proved crucial to portraying the war in an acceptable manner.[22] Moreover it had a significant basis in reality, as the very real voluteerism of 1865 that extended deeply into society shows. The example of the Zuavos, furthermore, raises questions about the origins and nature of that identification with the state and the nation.

## Zuavos and Couraças: The Independence War's Legacy

Why the Bahian government resolved to recruit Zuavo and Couraças companies in 1865 remains something of a mystery. To create separate black units flew in the face of longstanding military policy. The last segregated units in the Brazilian army (the black and mulatto militia battalions) had been abolished in 1831, when the National Guard was created to replace them. The remaining legal racial preferences in recruitment for the army rank and file (which barred the recruitment of black men) were lifted in 1837 as part of the military buildup of the conservative Regresso administration.[23] After that the army maintained a formally color-bind policy regarding its personnel, one that it carried to remarkable extremes: the standard service-record form contained no information on enlisted men's phenotype, so the army normally could not provide this information to the police authorities charged with tracking down deserters.[24]

The original proposal to create all-black companies came from outside of the army, like so much of the rest of the patriotic mobilization of 1865–66.

3. Capts. Quirino Antônio do Espírito Santo and João Francisco Barbosa de Oliveira (*Bahia Illustrada* [Salvador], 7 July 1867)

Quirino Antônio do Espírito Santo offered, on 26 January 1865, to organize "creole citizens" into a "respectable volunteer corps which, through its daring, courage, and love of homeland will recall, once again, the valorous combatants under the command of the celebrated Henrique Dias." Quirino invoked the patriotism that he had felt during the Independence War (1822–23) and proclaimed, "impelled by a supernatural force, I come to offer myself to the government to fight for the honor, integrity, and sovereignty of the empire, which vile gauchos insanely seek to offend."[25]

The proposal gained quick approval, and on 1 February Quirino took up quarters in Fort Barbalho, where he began raising the company. Within days it had taken the name "Zuavos Baianos," the president having approved a subscription to outfit the new recruits with the distinctive uniform of the French colonial troops of Algeria.[26] No less than eleven Zuavo companies, numbering 638 men, along with one company of Couraças, 80 strong, sailed for Rio de Janeiro and the southern battlefields by March 1866.[27] No satisfactory explanation is known to exist for the decision adopt the name and uniform of these French colonial troops. By the 1860s the French Zouave fashion of baggy red pants, decorated vest, and small cap or fez (based on North African dress) had spread widely among armies as diverse as the Union and Confederate forces in the U.S. Civil War and the international papal troops.[28] Marco Antônio Cunha argues that the heroic death of a Rio-born French Zouave during the storming of the Malakof Tower in the Crimea inspired the creation of Zuavos in Bahia a decade later, but this man—Eduardo de Villeneuve—

was never invoked in the Bahian mobilization.[29] Moreover Zuavos were only raised in Bahia, and the sole other all-black company created in 1865–66 (in Recife, Pernambuco) only took the name when it joined the Bahian Zuavos at the front.[30]

In Bahia the rhetoric and personal networks surrounding the Zuavos' creation drew on other thoroughly Brazilian traditions, some of which they shared with the larger mobilization in the country. As Quirino's leadership suggests, veterans of the Independence War played a central role in the early mobilization. Bahia had seen the most significant fighting of the independence struggle in Brazil—a year-long siege of Portuguese troops in Salvador (mid-1822 to mid-1823)—an episode that had profoundly marked Bahian society.[31] In the 1860s the province witnessed an upsurge of interest in this heroic episode. The youngest veterans of this struggle were approaching sixty years of age, and in 1862 they founded the Sociedade Veteranos da Independência (Independence Veterans' Society), a mutual-aid organization that undertook to promote the commemoration of independence heroes by celebrating annual masses for them. The society played a significant role in the annual celebrations of Dois de Julho (2 July), the date on which Portuguese troops evacuated Salvador.[32] It raised independence veterans' status in Salvador society, and its members figured prominently in many aspects of the Paraguayan War mobilization. Elderly veterans formed honor guards to send off Bahia's troops in 1865 and 1866; late in the war the society raised funds for the eagerly anticipated victory celebrations.[33]

Numerous leaders of Bahia's early mobilization had fought in the Independence War. When Quirino embarked as a lieutenant commanding the First Zuavos Company, his commander was Lt. Col. José da Rocha Galvão, another independence veteran. So was José Eloi Buri, captain of the Couraças. Indeed the Couraças, raised between August and November 1865, recalled the leather-clad cowboys of the interior who had joined the patriots in the independence struggle.[34] To this list we could add Lt. Col. Domingos Mundim Pestana, commander of the Third Voluntários Battalion, who had first joined the army in 1821 at the age of fifteen, as had Col. Joaquim Antônio da Silva Carvalhal, the driving force behind the society and the key figure in the Zuavos' organization (whose role is examined below).[35] The commanders of Bahia's police (quickly converted into a Voluntários unit) and the local infantry (the Batalhão de Caçadores da Bahia) were also independence veterans.[36]

Independence service provided these men with contacts and connections that proved useful. During their brief stay in Rio de Janeiro en route to the south, Rocha Galvão and Quirino received a courtesy call from Antônio Pereira Rebouças, the mulatto statesman who, along with Rocha Galvão and his brothers, had led the defense of Cachoeira against Portuguese attack in 1822.[37] Few of the elderly veterans lasted long at the front. Quirino died in November at Montevideo, and in February 1866 a sick Pestana was back in Salvador, where he died two years later. Others soldiered on. Rocha Galvão perished during the battle of Tuyutí, while Buri passed away shortly after being invalided out in late 1867.[38] As long as they could serve, however, age ensured these men respect, at least judging by a description of Quirino during a brief stop in Desterro (today Florianópolis), Santa Catarina: "an old black, a truly good man, whom his soldiers respect as a father."[39]

Not only did the Zuavo and Couraças leadership hark back to the independence struggle, but their mobilization also recalled an older tradition, that of the black militia abolished in 1831. Quirino's proclamation invoked Henrique Dias, a black man who had led a troop of free blacks during the seventeenth-century struggle against the Dutch in Pernambuco. After this war his men had been converted into a militia unit. Such regiments, dubbed "Henriques" in honor of their first commander, proliferated in the eighteenth century and constituted a key linkage between Afro-Brazilians and the colonial state; their officer corps formed a black elite. In Bahia the Henriques distinguished themselves during the independence struggle, but liberal reformers in the 1820s undermined their status in the armed forces. With the creation of the National Guard in 1831, the government abolished the black militia. Its officers and soldiers played a large role in the 1837–38 Sabinada Rebellion, which restored their status, but many of their leaders were killed in the massacre of rebels that followed the defeat.[40]

In Pernambuco a provincial patriotism that looked to the seventeenth-century expulsion of the Dutch as the province's foundational moment kept the Henriques' memory alive.[41] By contrast the Henriques seem to have been wholly absent from Bahian discourse between 1838 and 1864. Nevertheless the creation of the Zuavo companies prompted an outpouring of patriotic rhetoric that recalled the black heroes of the independence struggle. Carvalhal sent off the Second Zuavo Company with a rousing speech that called on the men to "fight bravely against the Paraguayans just as the intrepid and immortal Henrique Dias fought in the past against the Dutch, and as in the glorious epoch of independence, the courageous Lieutenant-Colonel Manoel Gonçalves [da Silva] led those of your color in valor and bravery."[42] In time for the embarkation of the First Zuavos, Francisco Moniz Barreto, then Bahia's greatest poet (and also an independence veteran), dashed off a bit of bloodthirsty doggerel, the "Hino dos Zuavos Baianos" (Hymn of the Bahian Zuavos), whose first verse and chorus ran:

Sou crioulo: da guerra na crisma
Por *Zuavo* o meu nome troquei
Tenho sede de sangue inimigo
Por bebel-o o meu sangue darei
   D'*Henrique Dias*
   Neto esforçado
   Vôo ao teu brado
   Patria gentil!
   Mais que o da França
   Ligeiro e bravo
   Seja o *Zuavo*
   Cá do Brasil

I am a Creole: christened in war
I changed my name to *Zuavo*
I am thirsty for enemy blood
To drink it, I will shed my own
   Of *Henrique Dias*
   Valiant grandson
   I hasten in response to your call
   Noble homeland!
   More than those of France
   Light and brave
   Be the *Zuavo*
   Here from Brazil

Subsequent verses recalled Gonçalves's distinguished service during the Independence War and warned Paraguayans and Blancos to fear the Zuavos' wrath.[43]

This was not just symbolic rhetoric. Several direct connections can be drawn between the Zuavos of 1865 and Salvador's pre-1831 Henriques. For a brief period in February and March 1865 Capt. Joaquim José de Santana Gomes held a commission to raise the Second Zuavo Company; until 1831 he had been adjutant of the Henriques.[44] Among those who marched with the First Zuavos was First Cadet Constantino Luiz Xavier Bigode, son of the black battalion's last commander.[45] Although no troop registers from the black regiment have survived to confirm this, it is quite likely that some of the Zuavo officers had served in the Henriques' enlisted ranks in the

1820s. Similarly the organizer and commander of the black company raised in Recife, Felipe José da Exaltação Maniva, had enlisted in the black militia there in 1817 and was promoted to second lieutenant in 1821.[46]

Little information has come to light on the civilian occupations of the Zuavo officers. According to the Count of Eu, the heir apparent's consort, many had been sergeants in the National Guard, which suggests that they enjoyed at least a modest degree of economic success and social standing. Both Buri and his second in command in the Couraças, João Capistrano Fernandes, had been lieutenants in the guard before 1850. Officer ranks in that corporation then required a minimum annual income of 400 mil-réis (US$250), while rank-and-file members needed to demonstrate half that income.[47] There are at least three passing references to black officers' occupations: Maniva was a carpenter; Bigode a cabinetmaker; and Capistrano a typographer. Capt. André Fernandes Galiza owned a small farm (*roça*) on the outskirts of Salvador.[48] In short, this evidence suggests that the Zuavo and Couraças officers came from the ranks of the skilled-artisan class, a profile quite similar to that of the Henrique officers before 1831.[49] In this respect the Zuavo leaders were of more-modest social origins than the civil servants and professionals who rushed to the colors in 1865 and dominated the Voluntários da Pátria officer corps.

The rhetoric surrounding the mobilization of the Zuavos, as well as the background of key individuals involved in their organization, suggests that they embodied a vibrant tradition of patriotic service to the state on the part of Afro-Bahians. Elderly veterans led much of the early mobilization and saw themselves as successors to the black heroes of past struggles against foreign invaders. That such men should have enthusiastically taken up arms in 1865 is not surprising, for they (or their fathers) had done so four decades earlier. The younger ones had likely grown up hearing about the black heroes of earlier wars.

### Recruiting for the Black Companies: Race, Politics, and Patronage

Not surprisingly, less information is available on the Zuavos' rank and file than on their officers. What exists suggests that they consisted of a mix of more or less willing volunteers and unwilling draftees, which would make them typical of Brazil's recruitment in 1865. Quirino proudly declared that the First Zuavos consisted only of "spontaneous volunteers," but this declaration was prompted by the refusal of one of these "volunteers" to swear his oath to the flag.[50] The classic example of volunteering comes from outside of Salvador: Cândido da Fonseca Galvão (the future Dom Obá II), a freedman from Lençois, brought thirty volunteers to the capital, where they were promptly enlisted in the Third Zuavos, with Galvão named second lieutenant.[51]

Considerable prestige accrued to those who, like Galvão, could collect volunteers. André Fernandes Galiza complained that his commission to raise the Third Zuavos had suffered by the simultaneous appointment of João Francisco Barbosa de Oliveira to raise a competing company. Barbosa enjoyed more success than Galiza, embarking in command of forty-eight men in what became the Third Zuavo Company (though most of them were Galvão's recruits), while Galiza's Fourth Zuavos set sail shortly thereafter with only twelve men (but with a full stock of eighty uniforms).[52] Joining a unit was rarely an individual decision, and volunteers typically presented themselves in groups, often under the auspices of a patron. The role of prominent individuals in organizing the Zuavos and the Couraças, particularly Carvalhal but also Abílio Cesar Borges, the educator and future Baron of Macaúbas, suggests such patronage networks. (Borges acquired eighty Minié rifles for the Fifth Zuavos, whose organization he oversaw.)[53] Other recruits apparently succumbed to peer pressure: in November a Zuavo volunteer regretted his decision to enlist, claiming to have been tricked into doing so by some friends during a party.[54]

Enlisting in the Zuavos differed from signing up for other units, for it meant joining a black company. Presumably Quirino's "spontaneous volunteers" shared a racial identity that led them to join that service rather than one of the several other battalions then being organized. Some designated guardsmen also requested to serve in a Zuavo company in August 1865, which may indicate similar views. Authorities apparently worked to maintain the racial profile of Zuavo units. The commander of arms normally selected *crioulo* (Creole) recruits from among the volunteer contingents that arrived from the interior and once excluded a man from the Zuavos "for being of brown [*parda*] color."[55]

Indications of forced recruitment for the Zuavos increased in frequency in the middle of 1865. In August *O Alabama* recommended the discharge of one Veríssimo, who suffered from insanity and disturbed the peace with his shouts as he fled the barracks to escape military duties. Later that month the same newspaper reported that the companies then being organized had lists of national guardsmen destined for conscription into their ranks. The chief of police sent another guardsman to the Zuavos as a new recruit after arresting him in an illegal gambling house. On 26 August Zuavo soldiers sought to impress Simão, a mulatto slave, who eluded his pursuers by diving into the sea, where he drowned.[56]

Two other instances of slave recruitment suggest solidarity between the Zuavos and the slaves, who apparently joined willingly. A young slave, João, sent out to purchase banana leaves, turned up two hours later outfitted as a Zuavo, ready to serve his country rather than his annoyed master, who began proceedings to reclaim him. When the owner of another slave, João Gualberto da Silva, sought to reclaim his property, he was insulted by the Zuavos; returning the next day, he found his slave already enlisted, which meant that he would have to file a more detailed claim for the man's return. Moreover João Gualberto had been conditionally freed, which weakened the owner's case. The president ordered him to provide further documentation, and a month later João Gualberto was still in prison.[57] In both of these cases it is likely that the slaves were complicit in their recruitment and that the Zuavos willingly helped these men in their efforts to escape bondage. After this flurry of complaints about Zuavo impressment, most of which resulted from excesses on the part of one officer, their recruitment practices ceased to provoke complaints.

A few other sources suggest that the Zuavo rank and file were both a disorderly lot and thoroughly integrated into Salvador's urban popular culture and street life. *O Alabama* complained in early June 1865 that the Zuavos doing guard duty outside their quarters spent their nights "provoking disturbances, cavorting with black women, and setting off fireworks" at passersby. Street children joined in the soldiers' diversions, earning the nickname "zuavinhos."[58] The fireworks suggest that the men were celebrating St. John's Day (24 June) a bit early.

The degree to which Brazil's mobilization followed partisan political lines—Liberal versus Conservative—has received little attention, yet partisan considerations shaped recruitment in wartime as much as they did in peacetime.[59] Liberals controlled government and administration from 1862 until 1868, and Conservatives regularly denounced their rivals' excesses. In one such case the *Jornal do Comércio*'s Conservative correspondent bitterly condemned Marcolino José Dias's appointment to command the Second Zuavos, describing him as a freedman who "has done nothing to elevate himself." The journalist claimed that Marcolino earned his living as a police spy and had received his commission as a National Guard sergeant "for the terror that, during the [last] election, his head-butts [*cabeçadas*] instilled in everyone." Shortly before his Zuavo appointment, Marcolino led a "bunch of thugs" who gathered in the visitors' gallery of the provincial legislature to intimidate the sole Conservative deputy.[60]

The sergeant's skill at *cabeçadas*, one of the characteristic moves of *capoeira*, the Afro-Brazilian martial art, tied party politics to the rough-and-tumble, largely Afro-Brazilian, world of the street. While *capoeira* gangs were a constant and often lamented feature of life in Rio de Janeiro during the nineteenth century, there are almost no contemporary references to this martial art in Salvador. In the Brazilian capital *capoeiristas* faced police repression but sometimes incorporated themselves into political networks (as did Marcolino).[61] Manoel Raimundo Querino, the chronicler of Afro-Bahian history, wrote in the early twentieth century that the Bahian government packed many *capoeiristas* off to the front, where they proved themselves valuable in hand-to-hand combat, such as during the storming of the Curuzú fortifications in September 1866.[62] While there are no specific references to the impressment of *capoeira* practitioners in Bahia during the war, Marcolino in fact distinguished himself at Curuzú (see below).

Regardless of the truth of any accusations against Marcolino, they clearly show his partisan ties. Others viewed him favorably; back in Salvador on leave in 1867, he was apparently a highly popular figure: "Wherever he goes, he is accompanied by a multitude of the people," reported *O Alabama*.[63] The 1868 change in government (prompted by a ministerial crisis over the war's conduct) rendered Marcolino's position considerably more difficult. In September he narrowly escaped assassination at the hands of unknown assailants. The *Jornal do Comércio*'s Liberal correspondent doubted that the police would find the culprit, for the intended victim "was one of those who has taken the most active part in elections for his party. The rulers [of this province] have long sworn to teach him a masterful lesson."[64]

As long as they were out of power, Conservatives could do little more than rail against what they perceived as inappropriate appointments during the patriotic mobilization of 1865–66. Liberals ensured that the Zuavos enjoyed a high profile in Bahian society. During the 1865 Dois de Julho celebrations, dapperly dressed Zuavos stood on guard at the decorative stage that was the centerpiece of this civic ceremony.[65] The Liberal *Bahia Ilustrada* opened its front pages to Zuavo and Couraças officers, four of whose portraits joined those of the other Bahian patriots that the newspaper featured in 1867–68.[66] While they were being organized in Salvador, the Zuavo companies were always included in the celebrations of Brazil's early victories, including the fall of Montevideo and the battle of the Riachuelo.[67]

The central figure in the organization of the Zuavo companies was Colonel Carvalhal, who personally embodied many of the networks already analyzed. He was a retired National Guard superior commander and long-time customs official who had served as a cadet during the Independence War.[68] He enjoyed considerable prestige among those recruited for the Zuavos, overseeing the training of several companies and looking after dependents. He allowed Sgt. Inocêncio da Costa Lima's family to live in one of his own houses (which he was later reported as planning to give to the family after Inocêncio's death at Tuyutí), and he acted as tutor for Marcolino José Dias's son; in 1869 he looked after the funeral of Captain Barbosa's son. Marcolino and Inocêncio publicly thanked Carvalhal for his assistance to them.[69] The colonel presented Buri and Capistrano's proposal for the Couraças company to the provincial president. He witnessed the marriage of one Couraças volunteer on the eve of the soldier's embarkation and wrote in support of his wife, who a year later had not received a promised salary consignment. *Bahia Ilustrada* asserted that he personally arranged the enlistment of many more soldiers.[70]

The source of Carvalhal's influence among these nonwhite officers and soldiers is not clear, but many had served under him in the National Guard. He was a Liberal Party stalwart, and *O Alabama* proposed him as the "popular candidate" for city council in the 1868 elections, swept by the Conservatives who then controlled the electoral machinery.[71] His ties to Captain Marcolino underscore this Liberal connection. Moreover, as a leader in the Sociedade Veteranos da Independência, Carvalhal had connections to many of the veteran commanders of Bahia's units. And he had links to Afro-Bahian organizations. In 1859 he served as "protector" (*sócio protetor*) of the Sociedade Protetora dos Desvalidos (Society for the Protection of the Needy), a black mutual-aid society; a number of other men involved in raising the Zuavos sat on this society's board.[72] A decade later he figured among the founders of an abolitionist society that met in his spacious house. In 1870 Carvalhal drew a direct connection between the Zuavos and abolitionism when he gave Captain Barbosa the honor of presenting the letter of liberty to a slave child on 7 September (Brazil's independence day).[73]

But Carvalhal also had his share of enemies. His independence from the regular chain of command rankled military authorities. In January 1865 the garrison's commander censured him for addressing dispatches directly to the provincial president instead of through the military hierarchy.[74] Sometime in 1866, after the last Zuavos had embarked, Carvalhal offered to organize companies or even a battalion of African and Creole freedmen, adding that he wanted to do so as a direct agent of the president, not as a subordinate to the commander of arms, who might subject him to "unreasonable admonitions." The president denied this request, but in early 1867 Carvalhal organized the Sapador companies, which consisted mostly of former slaves whose freedom the government had obtained by compensating their owners. The commander of arms complained that Carvalhal had exceeded his authority by issuing promotions, granting leaves, and naming cadets, all without consulting him. In this way the recently freed sappers received training "better for ruining them than for turning them into good soldiers."[75] Perhaps most remarkably, even at this late date, the networks over which Carvalhal presided could generate volunteers. Francisco Antônio de Carvalhal Menezes e Vasconcelos, a former army cadet dishonorably discharged in 1856 and who returned to the colors to serve as sergeant in the First Sapador Company (and possibly a relative of Carvalhal), presented twenty-one volunteers to the unit.[76]

Despite Carvalhal's ability to organize companies and find volunteers, the president refused to place him in charge of provincewide recruitment in late 1867, a task that he had offered to undertake without pay. For a month *Bahia Ilustrada* railed against this decision, praising Carvalhal and accusing the man appointed instead of cowardice for having turned his back on the Paraguayans and of incompetence for having earlier been removed from the post of inspector of the army arsenal.[77] Other newspapers joined in this clamor, but Carvalhal failed to obtain this commission, which carried a handsome monthly stipend of 300 mil-réis (US$138).[78]

The organization of the Sapador companies in early 1867 (along with Maniva's appointment to raise an "Henrique Dias" company in Recife in the middle of that year) were the last attempts to recruit racially distinct units for service in the Paraguayan War.[79] By this time the country needed recruits for its existing battalions, not more independently organized companies. An increasingly desperate government undertook ever more coercive impressment, ordered levies of designated national guardsmen, and resorted to the purchase of slaves to be freed and enlisted. By this time too the Zuavos had long ceased to exist as separate units in the forces arrayed against Paraguay.

## Zuavos at the Front

It is not easy to follow the Zuavos after their departure from Salvador.[80] The companies, attached to Bahia's Voluntários da Pátria battalions, left Bahia separately, usually stopping at Rio de Janeiro en route to the south. In the capital they sometimes underwent reorganizations; Marcolino José Dias, for example, received his promotion to captain there.[81] The first Zuavos to pass through Rio de Janeiro caused something of a stir, at least judging by *Semana Ilustrada*'s cartoon suggesting that black men in the capital were eager to emulate the Bahians' patriotic example. Stopping briefly in Desterro, Santa Catarina, the First Zuavos stood out for their "robust physique and discipline."[82] At some point the First and Second Zuavos were joined, and both were rushed upriver from Montevideo in August. They distinguished themselves on the improvised flotilla that disrupted communication between the two Paraguayan columns advancing on opposite sides of the Uruguay River. After the Allied victory at the battle of Yataí (17 August) put an end to the enemy column on the river's right bank, the Zuavos headed for Uruguaiana, arriving in time for the Paraguayan surrender on 18 September. There the Count of Eu judged them to be "the most handsome troop . . . of the whole army." He was particularly impressed by their officers, who were attentive to their duties and "proud of their battalion [*sic*]."[83]

During the next months the First and Second Zuavos spent some time attached to the navy; Quirino fell ill and passed away in a Montevideo hospital. On 1 December 1865 the Baron of Porto Alegre (Manoel Marques de Souza) organized the four-company Provisional Zuavo Corps at São Borja as part of the Brazilian army's II Corps. It consisted of the First, Second, and Third Companies from Bahia and Maniva's black company from Pernambuco, which until then had not taken the Zuavo name (soldiers and officers from the tiny Fourth Zuavos Company probably joined them at this time). Captain Marcolino received temporary command of the Zuavo Corps, but Porto Alegre replaced him on 1 January 1866 with a regular-army captain granted a brevet commission as major.[84] Both the death of the respected Quirino and the reorganization of the Zuavo companies prompted, according to Francisco Otaviano, the Brazilian plenipotentiary, "some disturbance in the Zuavo Battalion [*sic*], and from São Borja, I am receiving constant complaints." One of the bearers of these complaints was 2d Lt. Cândido da Fonseca Galvão, then in Buenos Aires to beg the minister to intercede on his behalf. He had faced two courts-martial, unjustly, according to the minister, and sought reincorporation into the army.[85] There are indications of other abrupt personnel changes in the Provisional Zuavo Corps at this time, but despite these difficulties it remained with Porto Alegre's II Corps.[86]

A second contingent of Zuavos, consisting of some of the later and generally smaller companies from Bahia, was gradually organized in the I Corps under Manoel Luiz Osório (the future Marquis of Herval). On the eve of

4. The Zuavos' influence in Rio de Janeiro. In this illustration, a black man, dressed in a Zuavo uniform, volunteers in Rio de Janeiro, accompanied by his wife. He declares that black men in the capital are no less patriotic than their Bahian counterparts. In fact, there is no indication that a black company was raised in Rio de Janeiro. (*Semana Illustrada* [Rio de Janeiro], 2 April 1865)

the invasion of Paraguay he assigned them to the health service, where they worked in hospitals at the rear. Salvador's *O Alabama* lamented that these men, "worthy of a better fate, were reduced to hospital janitors and other such occupations."[87] Like other Brazilian commanders, Osório had little use for small independent units at a time when it was crucial to maintain battalions at full strength. Back in January he had dissolved the Couraças almost as soon as they arrived at his camp at Laguna Brava, assigning the soldiers and officers to other units.[88] This was likely also the fate of the last Zuavo companies raised in Bahia, which embarked in early 1866. Turning the Zuavos into janitors, however, smacked of traditional slavocrat attitudes about menial service as an appropriate role for black men. Cerqueira, a Bahian, later lamented that Osório had failed to take advantage of the Henrique Dias tradition of separate black units.[89]

Meanwhile the Provisional Zuavo Corps remained with Porto Alegre's II Corps in Corrientes; this force finally crossed into Paraguay on 1 September 1866 to move against Paraguayan fortifications in conjunction with the fleet. On 25 August Porto Alegre had ordered the Zuavo Corps dissolved and its personnel distributed among the rest of his II Corps; by this time it may have received reinforcements from some of the other Zuavo companies. There may not have been time to implement Porto Alegre's order before the battle of Curuzú (3 September), in which the Bahians and Pernambucans led the charge against the Paraguayan trenches and ramparts. Sixty-six-year-old Pernambucan captain Maniva was one of the first into the enemy trenches, while Captain Marcolino was reportedly the first to scale the enemy earth-works, scrambling up on the back of one of his soldiers. There he engaged in a hand-to-hand struggle over the Paraguayan flag, knocking down the enemy standard, raising the green-and-yellow Brazilian flag, and according to Manoel Querino announcing, "Here is the black Bahian Zuavo!"[90] His *capoeira* skills must have come in handy. At least four other Zuavo officers received recognition for valor during this battle.[91] Cándido López, the artist who arrived at Curuzú with Argentine reinforcements a few days afterward, later recalled the Zuavos and their "showy uniforms," including them in his 1891 painting of the camp.[92]

By the end of September the Zuavo Corps was definitively disbanded, part of the constant reorganizations necessitated by massive losses due to disease and combat, particularly the Curupayty defeat (22 September), in which four Zuavo officers fell wounded (one fatally); one more was decorated for bravery in that battle.[93] The distinctive uniforms noted by the Argentine painter gave way to standard military dress—there are, in fact, no contemporary portraits of Zuavos in the peculiar attire of 1865.[94] As the conflict wore on, many Zuavo officers joined the long lists of casualties that accumulated from the grinding trench warfare around Humaitá and in the unhealthy Allied camps. Others, like Captains Marcolino and Maniva, were invalided out. Few made it through the war. Captain Barbosa, commander of the Third Zuavos, managed to serve for the entire conflict but failed to receive a promotion. Wounded twice, he never took leave, as he proudly explained in a postwar petition; he was among the troops that finally caught up with Francisco Solano López at Cerro Corá (Aquidabán).[95] Cadet Bigode fell into Paraguayan hands shortly after the battle of Curupayty and spent more than two years as a prisoner of war, working at the Ybycuí foundry. Liberated in 1869, he returned to his post, earning a promotion to second lieutenant in March 1870.[96]

In 1870 three Bahian Voluntários da Pátria battalions returned to their home province. They were received with great fanfare, after which authorities quickly disarmed and disbanded them. Many of the soldiers mustered out without receiving the salaries still owed to them.[97] Few Zuavo officers or men were, however, among the veterans who returned home that year. Carvalhal prepared an elaborate wreath to welcome back Captain Barbosa, the only Zuavo officer noted in the surviving press coverage of these celebrations. A nostalgic poem addressed to Carvalhal lamented the passing of "our old friends" Rocha Galvão, Buri, and Quirino, the independence veterans who had served as examples for Bahia's youth and then gave way to the next generation.[98]

No doubt Zuavos found the return to civilian life difficult, as did other veterans, whether they returned home in 1870 or earlier. Bigode, rewarded for his services with an unpaid honorary commission as army second lieutenant, unsuccessfully sought a pension in 1875, claiming that he could not support his family because of war injuries.[99] Like Bigode, Marcolino remained in Salvador; according to a later memorialist, he found himself reduced to working as a street sweeper until he received a sinecure as doorman at the public library. Until his death in 1888, Captain Marcolino was a well-known figure in Salvador, heavily involved in local patriotic activities, regularly leading celebrants on the Dois de Julho holiday. He also served on the Sociedade Protetora dos Desvalidos board in 1886.[100] Others joined Galvão in the emigration from Bahia to Rio de Janeiro traced by Eduardo Silva. Like the newly named Dom Obá II, Maniva, Barbosa, and another Bahian Zuavo lieutenant spent time in the capital's Asilo dos Inválidos da Pátria (the old soldiers' home); their petition files in the army archive reveal that they doggedly pursued further rewards, pensions, and promotions in compensation for their wartime service, of course underscoring their patriotism and service to the pátria.[101] Obá went further and created a record of military service for himself, which contemporaries gradually came to accept, though he failed to present any documentation to corroborate his claims.[102]

Unfortunately none of these men left any documentation affording insights into their postwar political views in the way that Obá left through a series of newspaper articles. Like the majority of Brazil's veterans, they melted into the free poor population from which they had been recruited. In Salvador's black community, memories of the Zuavos endured. In the early twentieth century Manoel Querino recorded their names and military feats, drawing on oral tradition.[103] By this time there was no place for black soldiers in the public imagery of a republican regime that looked to Europe as its model. Even the late empire offered little to its black defenders, as Eduardo Silva makes clear in his biography of Galvão (Obá II). To be sure, Emperor

Pedro II regularly received the Prince of the People at court, but when the monarchy seemed to take a populist turn in the aftermath of abolition, it was overthrown.[104]

Black soldiers may have returned home with a "new spirit" and a "much greater ability to analyze Brazil's slave society," as Nelson Werneck Sodré has argued, but the empire (and much less so the republic) offered them little and provided them with few avenues for membership in the nation for which they had fought and died.[105] Ultimately, as Miguel Angel Centeno has observed for Latin America more generally, "a too active or fervent sense of nationhood," such as that expressed by the Zuavos in 1865, "could actually backfire and create conditions inimical to elite domination."[106] Brazil needed such patriots in 1865, but after the war the country's narrow political culture offered few opportunities for black men like the Zuavos to make their demands known, much less exercise full citizenship.

# 5. Benjamin Constant

## The "Truth" behind the Paraguayan War

The Paraguayan War was still raging when pundits identified Benjamin Constant as the author of an article on the conflict published anonymously in a Rio de Janeiro paper.[1] In a letter to the newspaper's editor the recently returned veteran denied authorship but instead offered to publish under his own name "the truth that I know of what has taken place in the current war with Paraguay."[2] There is no indication of this promised article in his private archive, but his correspondence during the time that he was at the front certainly contains elements of the "truth" that he would have told about the war.[3]

Born in 1837, Benjamin Constant Botelho de Magalhães reached the rank of lieutenant colonel in the Brazilian army. A professor of mathematics in military and civilian schools and one of the most important advocates of positivism in Brazil, he acted as the principal organizer of the military coup that overthrew the monarchy in 1889. In the subsequent provisional government (1889–91) he served as second vice president, war minister, and head of the Ministry of Education, Post, and Telegraph. After his premature death in January 1891, the republic's constituent assembly bestowed on him the title "Founder of the Republic."[4]

During his eleven months in Paraguay (October 1866–September 1867) Benjamin Constant corresponded with several people, including his wife, his father-in-law, his brother, and several close friends. The approximately sixty extant letters are but a fraction of this correspondence. Several have been lost, and most of those that he received during this time have not come to light.[5] These losses do not, however, diminish the value of the surviving letters. That they were not written for publication distinguishes them from the wartime correspondence previously available to researchers—official dispatches and isolated letters. It also distinguishes them from the classic war memoirs written for posterity in different political contexts. These letters resemble the sources used by Bell I. Wiley in his classic studies of the U.S. Civil War based on the private correspondence of Confederate and Union soldiers.[6]

Benjamin Constant's correspondence can also be read as a counterpoint to the war narratives that repeat the official government or army view.[7] Explicit criticisms of military and civil authorities occasionally appear in his writings, especially when he and his friends question official reports. The letters thus offer important insights into the war's influence in forming the worldview of the generation that fought in it and whose members later played important roles in Brazilian society and politics. [8]

The author emerges as the product of his time, a man caught up in events whose importance for the development of Brazil's society and polity would only become clear much later. The letters reveal how an individual lived through social and political processes set off by the war, whose significance neither he nor his contemporaries recognized. Benjamin Constant did not, of course, consciously see himself as part of historical events later perceived as central to the foundation of Brazil's national army. But his letters contain many indications of how this overwhelming process took place on the individual level: the experience with other peoples and other forms of social and political organization, the contrasting values of allies and enemies, the relationships of subordination and loyalty between soldiers and national leaders, and the construction of images of the enemy and of altruistic service to the nation.

It is important to recognize at the outset that Benjamin Constant's dual role as soldier-professor shaped his understanding of the war. As a youth he had enlisted at the rank of cadet in order to gain an education and to enter a profession that enjoyed some status in Brazil. But he was not strongly committed to his military career; in Paraguay he described himself as an officer without a military vocation. Rather, before the war he dedicated himself to teaching and to his family. This goal echoed the career of his father, a low-ranking Portuguese naval officer who remained in Brazil after independence and combined his military career with that of primary-school teacher. The need to provide for his family in case of his death prompted Benjamin Constant to join numerous public and private mutual-aid societies and even led him to create one himself. Before being called up he planned to write a mathematics textbook and to donate the profits from its sale to the asylum for disabled veterans. In a bitterly ironic turn of fate he would return to Brazil, like many other veterans, sick, unable to work, and lacking a means of support.

## The Individual and the War

When the Paraguayan War broke out in 1864, Benjamin Constant was in dire financial straits. He supported a relatively large family, consisting of his wife, one daughter, three brothers, a sick mother, and an elderly aunt. His mother's condition was particularly burdensome, for she had suffered from mental illness since the death of her husband in 1851. She never regained her emotional equilibrium, and young Benjamin, the eldest son, found himself responsible for his family at the age of twelve. All of this was apparently too much for him, and during a subsequent attack of delirium he tried to drown himself in a river, surviving only because a slave washerwoman rescued him. To support his household and pay for his mother's medical treatment, Benjamin Constant counted on income from several sources in 1864: his base pay as an army lieutenant, a salary as assistant engineer at the National Imperial Observatory, his pay as a teacher at the Commercial Institute and at the Imperial Institute for Blind Boys, and the payments that he received for tutoring students from the Army College. It appears, nevertheless, that the income from all of these occupations did not cover his expenses, particularly those for his mother's treatments, which frequently forced him into debt.

Several times he tried to obtain a more secure public-school teaching position but failed in the competitions because he lacked the necessary connections. These difficulties accentuated his cynicism about Brazilian society. He repeatedly complained about his hard life and the many adversities that he had faced. Although he claimed to have come to terms with himself, he recognized that repeated suffering undermined his most solid beliefs. He once admitted that being "a shameless rogue" sometimes seemed a necessary condition for human happiness, though hastening to distance himself from the logical conclusion—that he too should become one in order to attain happiness.[9]

Benjamin Constant experienced the first months of the war in contradictory fashion. In the face of the wave of patriotism that swept through the country, he showed little personal enthusiasm for the war and did not let himself be carried away by the belligerence that many of his fellow citizens expressed at that time. Like many of his comrades, generally of modest social origins, he lacked a military vocation. Financial difficulties certainly colored his view of the war. He explained his neutral position to a friend: "The government has not bothered me, nor have I volunteered, for in the circumstances in which I find myself, offering my services would amount to offering poverty to all of my family."[10] Yet such a stance could appear as cowardice, which explains his almost obsessive concern to avoid anything that could be taken as a refusal to endanger himself while he was at the front.

5. Benjamin Constant at the time of the Paraguayan War (Museu Casa de Benjamin Constant, Rio de Janeiro; reproduced by Aníbal Sciarreta)

The young officer received promotion to captain in the general staff in January 1866. He was carrying out his duties in the imperial astronomical observatory when, on 25 August, he received orders to depart for the battlefield. He left considerable emotional and material baggage in Brazil and sailed south with high hopes. With luck he could return from the campaign with improved prospects. To do so he would need to obtain a well-paid post and win promotion for distinguished service. Returning alive and healthy would at least not worsen the situation of his many dependents.

He arrived in Paraguay at the beginning of October 1866, a critical juncture for the Brazilian army. A few days earlier the allies had suffered their greatest defeat of the war at the battle of Curupayty (22 September). The imperial government blamed this failure on poor coordination between the Brazilian army and naval commanders and consequently began significant reorganizations of the army in the field. Command was centralized under the Marquis of Caxias, and Admiral Tamandaré, commander of the fleet, was replaced by Joaquim José Ignácio, the Viscount of Inhaúma. Nevertheless the defeat represented a significant setback. The allies spent a year without making any progress against Paraguayan positions. Benjamin Constant's stint in the field coincided almost exactly with this long standoff.

Once at the front Benjamin Constant seemed chiefly concerned with obtaining a well-paid position. To this end he used his father-in-law's connections among the political elite. This was, for example, what he did when he met with Francisco Otaviano de Almeida Rosa, the minister plenipotentiary for Triple Alliance matters in Argentina and Uruguay: "I spoke to him with complete frankness about my main concern which in this case is getting a good commission."[11] He soon worked his way into the complex social networks that existed in the field camp that was increasingly becoming a permanent army encampment. There he found most of his generation of officers, with whom he strengthened ties of friendship and corporate solidarity, building up his social capital. He confidently wrote that he was cultivating positive connections in the military world, declaring to his wife that he lived "in good harmony" with his superiors, a concern that would become another feature of his career. In this same letter, however, he also reminded her of his positivist views regarding the army hierarchy: "You know that I only pay attention to superior virtue and superior intelligence, as far as officers' seniority [*superioridade*] is concerned, I hate it."[12] This stress on merit was positivism's response to divine-right and hereditary principles in the establishment of social hierarchies.[13] Regardless of his ideological views, Benjamin Constant could not avoid the need to cultivate ties to the army's higher ranks. He once visited the Brazilian naval squadron. On each of the ironclads he met numerous officers and commanders and was surprised at the hearty welcome that they gave him: "I never thought that I would meet so many friends and well-wishers [*afeiçoados*] and receive so many and so varied proofs of the most sincere friendship during the campaign. If the purpose of my coming to the campaign were satisfying my vanity in this way, it would be more than satisfied."[14]

## "The Miserable Life of an Officer on Campaign"

These connections paid off. Within days of his arrival Benjamin Constant joined the First Division's staff as an assistant quartermaster. In December he received command of a supply post at Itapirú and was charged with inspecting all of the army's supply depots in that region. A month later he transferred to the army's engineering commission, where he oversaw the difficult and dangerous task of constructing advanced trenches, earthworks, and artillery emplacements on the "Linha Negra (Black Line)." He soon caught malaria. Commanders evacuated him to Corrientes in late March 1867 to carry out lighter duties while he recovered. Despite having lost much weight and suffering two additional malaria attacks, he returned to the front lines in late April, supervising several construction and surveying operations as the army prepared to tighten the siege around Humaitá.

Besides facing the dangers inherent in war, Benjamin Constant labored under difficult conditions that undermined his health. While at the front lines he worked day and night, always "in the most dangerous places, not even having time to sleep."[15] His daily routine was murderous: He worked until 3:00 or 4:00 in the morning, resuming at 6:00. He ate his meals in the lines, where he also rested in a comrade's tent or under the open sky, with his poncho as mattress and blanket against the cold; he often slept in the open air because of the great heat, even when it rained. To slake his thirst he had only the muddy water from wells dug "on the edge of swamps and pools in which one can see piles of rotting horses, cattle, and Paraguayans."[16] Other combatants, such as Dionísio Cerqueira, confirmed this testimony, also sharing bad memories of the flies that joined with the Paraguayans to torment those who lived in the Brazilian camp. These insects covered soldiers' and officers' food and laced their coffee and cheap wine. While Cerqueira felt "like a fakir [*faquirizado*]" in this situation,[17] from which he had no hope of escape, Benjamin Constant at first adjusted to the filth without getting sick: "As the saying goes—what doesn't kill you makes you stronger [*o que não mata engorda*]—and so it is," he assured his wife.[18]

In such circumstances the Brazilian army's medical service could not have been anything other than insufficient. André Rebouças reported the troops' bad health, blaming their illnesses on the change in climate, the smallpox epidemic brought by volunteers from the North, and the lack of hygienic measures in the camp. The "ignorance and the revolting indifference of the majority of the army's doctors" greatly aggravated the problem.[19] In Mato Grosso, where the war had begun, the situation was no better when, in 1866–67, a Brazilian column attempted unsuccessfully to open a second front. Alfredo d'Escragnolle Taunay described the inadequate medical services that accompanied that force. He bitterly condemned the medical commission, led "by a head as poorly prepared as he was lazy and indolent, who only aspired to retire and live comfortably with his wife and children": one of its members was "intelligent but careless," another "not very intelligent," and "the rest stood out for the ignorance of and indifference toward their specializations." They had no skills beyond treating fevers and individual cases of malaria, for which they prescribed sudorifics, purges, or quinine. In the face of more serious epidemics, "the degree of incompetence and careless of the medical commission was clearly revealed."[20]

Given the hospitals' locations, the treatment of the sick and the wounded often worsened their condition. Charged with conducting wounded soldiers to the hospital on his first day of service, Dionísio Cerqueira was shocked by "the nauseating odor that emanated from that improvised sanitary establishment," set up on the grounds of an abattoir, "where large numbers of steers were slaughtered and where dried meat was prepared."[21] The "predilection for unhealthy locales for hospitals and barracks" already seemed well-established, and sick soldiers often preferred fighting the enemy to being hospitalized. To get to the infirmaries soldiers faced long marches under heavy rains across flooded fields, enormous swamps, and fast-flowing streams. Thus, asked Taunay, "what comforts could the unfortunate sick [soldiers] expect? They preferred a thousand violent struggles of the battlefield to the agonies of the infirmaries."[22]

The sight of sick soldiers deeply troubled Benjamin Constant. While convalescing in Corrientes in March and April 1867, he experienced the cholera epidemic and witnessed the arrival of two ships carrying more than three hundred cholera victims, transported "in the most complete state of abandonment, almost naked . . . , without a single doctor or any nurses, with no one to conduct them, [and] with no medicine or food at all." He survived the terrifying outbreak of a disease for which medical science then had no effective treatment. In Corrientes cholera had already killed fifteen thousand people, the majority soldiers. To his father-in-law, a doctor who well understood the gravity of the situation, he described conditions that worsened because of the local population's ignorance and terror. Families fled to the countryside, leaving the city almost completely deserted. The relatively well-off Correntinos headed for their country properties, while the poor sought shelter under trees, certain that they could thus escape the disease. Benjamin Constant described hellish scenes that they left behind: "When cholera strikes a Correntino, the house in which he lives is completely abandoned, all flee in terror and the unfortunate victim remains helpless, with none to find him a doctor, medicine, food, etc. . . . After the individual's death, the local police, charged with burying him, with great difficulty dare to enter the house. The laments and bitter cries of those from whom the pest has taken a loved one are heard at every turn. To pass through this scene in the streets of Corrientes is to run the risk of returning home with one's heart covered in sorrow." He acknowledged that Brazilian army doctors offered some assistance to the civilian population but deemed it insufficient. The officer recommended that local newspapers advise the population to adopt hygienic measures and take medicines. Although there was no scientific certainty about the degree of cholera's contagiousness, "doctors, in the face of the inhumane scenes that have taken place . . . , should attempt to convince these people that the illness is not contagious, so as to diminish in some way the calamities that are taking place here."[23]

### Beyond Allies and Enemies—Human Beings

Perhaps the most radical human experience that Benjamin Constant underwent during the war involved his contact with the people of the Plata region. Biased and defensive attitudes on both sides reproduced the rivalries of the colonial period, when Spaniards and Portuguese fought over this region, agreeing to boundaries only to violate them soon thereafter. A certain naiveté appears in his early letters from his conviction of the friendly and disinterested character of Brazilian diplomacy in the Plata region. This attitude reflects the age and life experience of most Brazilians engaged in the war. Benjamin Constant was then twenty-nine and had never left the empire. A large proportion of the Brazilian contingent had even less experience of the world. Dionísio Cerqueira later described himself and his companions as lads of eighteen to twenty anxious to take on the Paraguayans in a search for glory.[24] It was thus difficult for Benjamin Constant to accept that the supposed beneficiaries of Brazil's Platine policy lacked enthusiasm for the allied cause. Not surprisingly he also parroted the official Brazilian image of

Francisco Solano López as a "monster" who deserved "just revenge" for the war that he had started.[25]

From the Argentines he expected very little. For example, although he spent only a single day in Rosario en route north, he left with a negative impression of its inhabitants. He saw in them the worst, both in their appearance and in their relations with Brazilians, for whom they displayed open hostility and ingratitude when they should have been thankful to "the sons of the country that has done so many good things for them." Passing through the town of Paraná, he condemned its population: "a mix of Spaniards and Guaraní . . . , a people inferior even to those of Rosario," who treated Brazilians respectfully to their faces but insulted them behind their backs, calling them "monkeys, little monkeys."[26] Scarcely had he arrived at Corrientes when he wrote his wife about the city: "I have no time to tell you anything about it. Just that it is the worst that can be imagined."[27]

Benjamin Constant nevertheless had a tendency to look benevolently on the common people of Argentina—"Far from inspiring in us hatred and ideas of vengeance, these folk prompt compassion"—for he perceived that their hostility to Brazilians derived from the situation in which they were kept: "Without education, without industry . . . , burdened with taxes and without entertainment, they are merely blind instruments of those who govern them." He saw the contradictions in the alliance against Paraguay, which led some Argentine provincial governors to turn the population against Brazil: "They fill them with false notions about Brazil and consider us their enemies, despite the many proofs of its good faith that the empire has given and its favorable intentions toward these bad neighbors." He regarded the Triple Alliance as entirely favorable to Brazil's two allies and disadvantageous, even harmful, to the empire: Despite the "true generosity and . . . good faith [that we] have shown them, . . . many newspapers insult us, and attribute to us evil intentions that we do not have and have never had."[28]

The traditional hostility between Brazilians and residents of the Plata region, papered over by an alliance between politicians, frequently surfaced. The cholera outbreak sharpened the "very old and inveterate" hatred that Correntinos felt for Brazilians. In addition to all the "evils" that the Brazilians had brought them, the locals now accused them of bringing cholera—were it not for the "monkeys," the epidemic would never have struck. Benjamin Constant perceived this hatred among Argentines, and in Corrientes even heard rumors of attacks planned against the Brazilians, writing that "they tried to fire all of our hospitals and other departments. Fortunately, as of today, nothing has come of it."[29]

As if this were not enough, the allied command used Brazilian soldiers to suppress opposition movements against local authorities in Corrientes. Shortly after the alleged arson plots, rumors circulated that large forces were gathering on the outskirts of the city to overthrow the provincial governor, burn the Brazilian hospitals and supply posts, and attack the battalion in which Benjamin Constant was serving. The movement's main goal was reportedly to force the imperial government to accept peace with López without simultaneously forcing his departure, a major condition stipulated in the 1865 Triple Alliance Treaty. The Brazilian military command in Corrientes quickly took measures to forestall the alleged insurrection. Four hundred soldiers reinforced the three thousand already stationed there. The naval squadron sent four gunboats, which anchored in front of the city and prepared to bombard it upon receipt of orders from the land forces.[30]

Although much weakened by malaria, Benjamin Constant volunteered to aid in the repression. In his "position of honor, waiting for the storm to come," he felt his dislike of the Argentines growing. Overcome by a desire for revenge, he wished "from the bottom of my heart for the revolution to grow and for it to provide us with an opportunity to violently break this miserable alliance that our diplomats contracted through their lack of patriotism, bad faith, and imbecility." He believed that these feelings were reciprocated, given of the alliance's lack of legitimacy among large segments of the Platine population. The Argentines were worse enemies than the Paraguayans, "for there is no greater enemy than he who pretends to be our friend." By this time Benjamin Constant considered the alliance absurd, given the unequal contributions of its members. From his perspective Brazil sacrificed herself practically alone, bearing most of the war's costs, providing personnel, weapons, supplies, munitions, and money. Nonetheless "all the Argentine and Oriental [Uruguayan] newspapers unite in continually slandering her, in throwing up obstacles, and in attributing to themselves the little or nothing that we have done." Not only was the alliance unable to diminish "the racial hatreds that existed between Brazil and these miserable republics," but it also wound up exacerbating them. He only hoped that "before we return to Brazil, we erase [this hatred] here on the battlefields."[31]

Disillusioned with Brazil's allies, he perceived virtues among the enemy. He acknowledged the Paraguayan soldiers' valor and loyalty to their leader, though he considered them "fanatics and victims" of López's "despotism." The account of a "little action" that he witnessed in July 1867 well expresses the respect felt for his adversaries, framed by the tragic wartime violence:

A Paraguayan picket composed of ten soldiers under the command of an officer was completely surrounded by a cavalry platoon from Osório's [forces]. They closed and tightened the circle and the commander told them to surrender and that they would not be killed. Our soldiers' lances and swords reflected the sun's rays and in each one they saw the death that awaited them if they resisted or if they refused to surrender. In the midst of that ever-closing circle of swords and lances, facing death, those heroic men did not forget the oath that they had sworn to their despotic leader, nor the orders received; this oath and these orders had, for them, more value than life itself and they responded that they would not surrender for they had no [such] order from the supreme government. The commander of our troops repeated that they would be killed and they responded with the greatest of calm, "Well, we'll see," and their commander, waving the flag in circles, shouted, "Don't surrender, be Paraguayans to the grave." Then began the most horrible scene that one could witness—the heads of some were ripped from their bodies with sword blows, those of others were split open, their brains splattering out; some were pulled from their horses, impaled on lances and in their death throes they bit the [lance] handles, twisting themselves in terrible convulsions, blood pouring from their wounds and spraying on our horses. In no time, there was nothing more on the horizon than cadavers, or rather, body parts, because most of our soldiers took pleasure in killing and cutting up [enemy] bodies.[32]

On another occasion, Benjamin Constant had personal contact with Paraguayan officers. While working on his artillery battery, a cavalry picket bearing a white flag sought him out and requested authorization for a U.S. diplomat in Paraguay (Charles Ames Washburn) to meet with Caxias. While waiting for the officer who would issue the safe-conduct pass, Benjamin Constant chatted with the Paraguayans—a captain, a lieutenant, and a second lieutenant—and considered them "very courteous." They exchanged cigarettes and conversed pleasantly for some time, but Benjamin Constant did not reveal the subject of their conversation. The next day, however, when he returned to work on the fortifications, the enemy "fired furiously" at him and his men. He tried to respond, leading his soldiers to the trench where he had conversed with the Paraguayan officers. The captain was still there, but this time their contact was hardly friendly. As the Brazilians approached, they received two volleys. They fired back three volleys and retreated.[33] Conversations with Paraguayans were better conducted under white flags!

## A Professional's Complaints

Benjamin Constant also had strong views about the Brazilian side. Upon arrival at the front in October 1866, he immediately felt indignation at the way in which military authorities and newspaper correspondents twisted the information they sent to the capital. Upset at the effects of the Curupayty defeat on the troops and at the generally low morale in the army, for which he blamed the minister of war, he condemned the false newspaper reports that repeatedly promised an imminent decisive battle: "The truth is something quite different. The hoped-for decisive battle is a holy grail [*pérola dourada*] with which they will delude the people's good faith."[34] Morale could not have been lower, and many soldiers engaged in activities that did not further the allied cause. In Corrientes, Brazilian military men looked foolish: "Soldiers serve as pages, slaves to the prostitutes of this city, many sent by officers; others work in private houses, avoiding military duties and frequently earning money for those who sent them."[35]

Not surprisingly, the high command did not escape Benjamin Constant's critical eye. He considered the Marquis of Caxias, commander in chief of the allied forces, to be the epitome of all that was wrong, not just with the army but also with Brazilian society. Caxias's standing among the troops approached that of veneration, as Dionísio Cerqueira later recalled: "Such prestige surrounded him that no one could see him except through an aureole of glory. Who did not believe in his omnipotence? . . . It was not just respect for his high position in the hierarchy; there was a further religious veneration and admiration without limits."[36] Although Benjamin Constant gave no indication of a personal grudge against Caxias, he held such rancor against the commander in chief that in all likelihood it can only be explained by some private incident.[37]

Benjamin Constant insisted on morally distinguishing himself from those who surrounded Caxias—the "toadies"—responsible for the deliberate misinformation on the war's course sent to Rio de Janeiro: "In their correspondence to our dailies, they do their miserable best to take advantage of the people's good faith to advance their personal interests."[38] His friends endorsed these criticisms, which echoed the Liberal Party's position vis-à-vis the Conservative Caxias.[39] A positivist advocate of merit as the sole measure of a man's worth, Benjamin Constant considered the marquis "a nobody stupidly perched at the peak of our official positions, offending all the men of true merit and causing shame to the century in which we live with the continual and dreadful scenes of the most brutal despotism," in sum, "truly a deviation from all social laws."[40] For a positivist this was a severe indictment indeed.

In contrast to Caxias, Benjamin Constant considered himself impelled only by the "recognition of merit." Notwithstanding his efforts early on to obtain a commission that would increase his salary, he disdained all that he did not consider just. On one occasion he received praise from the director of the engineering commission for a mission he carried out, which to him seemed insufficient acknowledgment. He responded to the director's letter in a way that bordered on petulance, declaring that he had done nothing more than simply his duty, that he did not serve any superior, and that he had no desire for praise or other reward: "I served my country, or better, my conscience and . . . keeping it clear was my only goal."[41]

This reaction embodied a rejection, shared by many in the army, of the ways in which the corporation recognized and rewarded meritorious service. No doubt many military men were motivated by the patriotic sentiments that the government had managed to stimulate among the troops. A favorable assessment of services rendered, however, weighed heavily in consideration for promotion and appointment to posts that carried extra remuneration. Injustices resulted from the rarity and brevity of combat, and as Cerqueira explained, "sacrifices were frequently rewarded with praise in orders of the day, honorific decorations, and promotions." Nonetheless he admitted that this was not always the case: "Many brave men had to satisfy themselves with a good reputation among their comrades and the faith that soldiers, impartial judges, had in them. This was worth more than anything else. Justice could not be done to all, because generals could not be at all places at all times, and many acts of bravery went unnoticed."[42]

There were, however, other explanations for this. Concerns about slow promotions were in fact general in the army at this time. John Schulz notes that such complaints were particularly acute among "young skilled officers who had to wait [for promotion] in the junior ranks, while older officers, despite lesser professional qualifications, held the senior ranks."[43] As a recently promoted captain, Benjamin Constant could see his future in the careers of his colleagues: nine years to make major and thirteen more to lieutenant colonel. Obtaining official recognition of merit was more difficult than performing good services. He knew this, but he refused to pay the price: "I don't trumpet the few services that I have done, nor do I, nor will I, officially report in writing what I do. . . . I know that this is not what one ought to do, but this is what I have [done]. I don't know how to flatter generals; I [only] know how to carry out my obligations, loyally and serenely, and fortunately no one doubts or could doubt [this], for the proofs of it that I have given are many, and many have witnessed them."[44]

The deeply rooted rivalry between *tarimbeiros* and *científicos* in the officer corps shaped recognition of services. The former were officers who had risen through the ranks and took their moniker from the *tarimbas*, or barracks bunks, on which soldiers slept; the latter, like Benjamin Constant, generally younger, had received a technical or "scientific" education in the military academies that had expanded greatly in the 1840s and 1850s. Their rivalry exemplified the contradictions of an army that still harbored prejudices against formal education. The competition between these two groups turned on the relative merits of scientific education and experience acquired in the daily labors at the barracks. Given that Brazil's commanders were generally *tarimbeiros*, not *científicos*, they tended to attribute little value to the likes of Benjamin Constant, perceived as more of a bureaucrat than a soldier. Ultimately he understood that, appearances notwithstanding, this was really not deliberate persecution and that the problem derived from his attitude toward his military career: "[It] is a natural consequence of the conduct of those who do not see the uniform as the guarantee of their future, but nevertheless religiously do their duty."[45]

### Waiting for the Great Offensive

The prospect of the war's end reassured Benjamin Constant, at least early on in his time at the front. Whether to allay his wife's worries or out of naiveté or a need to believe in the allies' victory, he repeatedly asserted that Paraguay's defeat was imminent. In the face of the Brazilian army's lack of progress, he concluded soon after arriving in Paraguay that the war "was only rhetorical": "We're in an armed peace that promises to last until hunger and lack of resources forces the enemy to surrender. . . . Rest assured that within two or three months at the most the war will be over without any further loss of life."[46]

But he did not tell his wife all of the truth that he gradually learned about the war. References to the lack of danger and the conflict's imminent conclusion eventually became ways to put her at ease in Rio de Janeiro. Rumors about the war's end were common, but Benjamin Constant, serving with troops encamped almost on top of enemy trenches, came to believe less and less in that eventuality. Disgusted at the loss of life, he reflected on the number of "unfortunate families produced by this delay in our operations." At times he despaired: "I don't know why the government will not pay more attention to these things. Why are we not preparing for a decisive battle? They want to kill us without glory."[47] The birth of his second daughter brought him a measure of sadness, for he had no idea when he would see her: "And I still haven't kissed her, I have not blessed her up close as I want to and I don't know when I will be able to do so!! This boring war looks like it will never end."[48]

His despair worsened amid all the false rumors, which he saw as a deliberate policy of Brazilian commanders. The constant tales about the start of peace negotiations left soldiers confused and uncomfortable. The high command sometimes intimated that it was pursuing this goal. Immediately afterward, however, came the denials: There was no possibility that López would accept the peace conditions demanded by the allies and leave the country. On other occasions commanders laid plans for an offensive, "a sort of frenzy of preparations for combat." "Orders are issued to bring up munitions, uniforms, etc., to lighten baggage, etc. Then, the orders are cancelled and so we go on (these are intermittent fevers)."[49] Uncertainty about the resumption of offensive operations weakened the troops' morale, "even the bravest and most fanatic about the uniform."[50] As part of the engineering commission, Benjamin Constant had access to discussions on strategy. During a preliminary meeting of the commission to give advice on plans for a strategic offensive, he "told some hard truths." In fact he mistrusted his commanders' intentions when it came to offensive operations. Likely, he concluded, rumors about them were merely "practice for some masked ball that they intend to give in order to take advantage once again of the country's good faith."[51]

While at Corrientes in April 1867 (and therefore somewhat removed from the front lines) Benjamin Constant struggled to understand the reasons for the army's long spate of immobility at Tuyutí, facing an enemy that he judged "already demoralized and exhausted." Since the generals failed to present convincing explanations, he offered his own: "We don't attack because we have no generals worth anything; we don't attack because the generals are afraid." There was no better time for an offensive, especially because conditions were rapidly worsening for the Brazilians in early 1867. The number of cholera and malaria victims was steadily increasing, and the region's harsh winter was approaching. The reasons for the delay seemed even more puzzling when he considered that, "with the resources that we still have, an energetic and decisive operation would bring us total victory."

The army's lack of forward momentum was "more than laziness, more than a crime, more than a lack of patriotism; it was treason against the country." He was certain that the politicians and officers who "so clumsily and stupidly" steered "the ship of state" that it ran aground "before the insignificant walls of Tuyutí and Curupayty" and who "shamelessly go about well-protected from danger" would escape blame for their crimes: "They are certain to be received with applause and cheers. They will be judged the homeland's only martyrs! Wretches!"[52]

By this time (April 1867) even Benjamin Constant himself had given up trying to reassure his wife that the war would soon end. He admitted that he was sick and tired of the delays in offensive preparations, which left him even more skeptical about the prospects for an early peace: "There is no intelligent management and this poor army that has already sacrificed so much will go on dying uselessly. . . . It could be that all this will end soon, but given our lethargy we must assume that this war will last for a long time."[53] Gradually he too began to question the purpose of the war, finally coming to a definitive conclusion: "I am convinced that, far from serving my country, I am rather doing my . . . bit for its ruin."[54] He was certainly ruining his health. After suffering from malaria for several months, Benjamin Constant finally left Paraguay in September 1867 for treatment in Brazil. Having failed to improve his financial situation, he returned home with the war deeply marked on his body, his soul, and in his pocket book.

## Conclusion

Benjamin Constant's role in the Paraguayan War was short lived and had little military significance. Its importance lies elsewhere. His involvement in the fighting was crucial to his emotional, intellectual, and political development. On a strictly individual level the war had important consequences, some of which would become part of larger collective historical experiences. The image of his mother suffering from mental illness; the separation from his family, increased by the birth of a daughter during his absence; and the poor conduct of the war and its attendant horrors all left profound impressions on his understanding of life.

On an ideological and philosophical level the war strengthened his identification with the positivism of Auguste Comte, to which he had been drawn through his studies of mathematics. His family difficulties quite possibly also underlay the attraction of this philosophy, which privileged affective relations over other aspects of human existence. He set issues as diverse as his love for his faraway wife and criticisms of Brazilian leadership in the philosophical context of "the wise and honorable Auguste Comte."[55] The triad of positivist values—family, homeland, and humanity—offered him a rigorous political yardstick. Benjamin Constant's eventual rejection of the monarchical order derived from this worldview, especially its emphasis on moral virtue as the key point of reference for public life. At that time the desire to moralize public life was one of the common routes to republicanism.[56]

Furthermore his disagreement with administrative practice and the war's conduct (which had been characterized by clientelism and incompetence) led Benjamin Constant to his highly critical view of Brazilian political elites. But his experience in Argentina and Paraguay also contributed to an image of the popular classes that weighed heavily on his political outlook. He considered the Brazilian people immature and incapable of grasping elite actions, letting themselves be exploited, not unlike the Argentine folk he described in his letters.

Benjamin Constant approached a certain, if limited, critical understanding of the war's political significance, linking its course with party politics. There is no evidence in his letters that he went much further than that in his questioning of the moral or political value of the conflict. While he certainly recognized its disastrous effects, he ultimately blamed them on the Paraguayan president, whom he perceived as the war's cause. In this way, at certain points, he joined in the anti-López political climate that swept Brazil, demanding that the generals prosecute the war more aggressively.

He was clearly not among the group of officers who were influenced by the republicanism of the Plata.[57] To be sure, while en route to the front in 1866, he claimed to favor "an American policy, an alliance among all the states of the two Americas to raise up strong barriers to the unrestrained ambitions of Europe, principally England."[58] Most likely this argument constituted a response to the aggressive British position in the recent Christie Question (1862–63), a diplomatic incident that had prompted Brazil to break off relations with that European power. At no point in his subsequent correspondence is there any reference to the question of republicanism. On only one occasion did he refer to the countries of the Plata region as republics—and then it was to speak ill of them.[59]

After the war his trajectory was closest to those "degree-holders who advocated positivist pacifism," gave little importance to military activities, and considered the Paraguayan War a fiasco.[60] In fact the positivist worldview was a civilian one, which saw armed forces as part of a stage of human evolution that would give way to a positivist order, guided by scientific and technical rationalism. Once humanity reached that point, weapons would go into history museums. Nonetheless, Benjamin Constant never failed to praise the heroism and courage of Brazilian soldiers in Paraguay.

The war experience had powerful effects on his personal trajectory and his future political role. Several men from his circle of friends served with him, and Benjamin Constant's letters reveal how important it was to connect with colleagues as he carried out his duties. His experience of the war ultimately became part of the ideological patrimony of the generation that in 1889 destroyed the regime responsible for their country's involvement in the tragedy of Paraguay.

## Appendix: Letters from Benjamin Constant to His Father-in-Law

*Paraguay, Itapirú, 23 January 1867.*[61]

*My Father and dear friend*

The bearer of this one is the captain from the Sixth Battalion of Voluntários whom I met here for the first time, although I knew him by reputation for his acts of valor and patriotism. He has been in all the battles and has been cited with distinction. On 16 July it was he who captured an artillery piece and an enemy trench. He says that he knows me well from the Court.

My dear father, a short while ago I wrote to you via Lieutenant-Colonel Esaltino and via Major Pinheiro Guedes and now I am sending you a long letter via the mail; I wanted to take advantage of the bearer to write you this little letter to learn of your health, about Dona Olímpia[62] and Dona Mariquinhas.[63] You must have already passed through the worst period of your work at the Institute which is from late December to early January. I am glad that you have been successful, as always, in all of your work and in your praiseworthy love for your little blind charges [*ceguinhos*] [but] do not forget that you should not exhaust yourself with too much [work], that you should pay attention to your health, not only for your children who regard you highly but also for the blind ones whom you guide, with so much dedication and love, acting for them like a good father. Here the war continues in the same way, with little change. It is true that, strictly speaking, one cannot anymore repeat the nauseating old saw:

"The army occupies the same positions," for the day before yesterday, two companies from the Sixth Battalion entered Potrero Pires via the bush and took two small enemy trenches. Thus, we have advanced another little bit. Now we are going to rest and give the enemy time to fortify himself so that we can later advance another bit (Brazilian chivalry). What seems bad to me is that in this *tortoise*-like pace our soldiers and officers will keep on disappearing under fire from the skirmishers and advanced guards, for the Paraguayans hidden in the bush behind tree trunks mock the courage with which we attack from the open [*a peito descoberto*]. But who knows whether this is part of some important and transcendental plan? The Count of Eu is working on the army's organization and will put an end to our (truly bad) system of recruitment and replace it with Conscription—nowadays, Conscription is incompatible with the organization of our army, [and] maybe for this reason they are trying to finish it off, gloriously throwing it into combat. In truth, I have seen and heard so many things here that nothing causes me surprise. Orders to retreat were played when the army had crossed enemy trenches (16 and 18 May). You see that closed columns are the favored method of attacking fortified points, advancing on artillery that spits out shells, grenades, grapeshot [*cachos de uva, lanternetas*], etc. (the brilliant feats of Curuzú and Curupayty); that the infantry flees in terror at the shout of "there comes cavalry" which replaces the terrifying cries that the Count of Lippe imagined[64] (one sees this every day) (tactics in action); the division corps's camp with its flank or rearguard turned toward the enemy (castramentation!); an invading army that doesn't want to provoke the enemy, always first receiving fire from the invaded enemy and responding mildly by superior order (energetic action!)[65]; a complete indifference to offensive operations, but a great fuss over parades, inspections when the General comes by, processions during the gala for his excellency, the "Acting Emperor"[66] (not adulation but a tribute to his merit!); two armies that come from peoples who could not hate each other more, who antagonize each other on the same battlefield, refusing bread and water to each other in the presence of the common enemy (allied armies!); orders for officers to not wear their insignia on days of battle (bravery!); a sutler selling supplies to the army for a much higher price than he could obtain from any other [purchaser] and even from the petty merchants who accompany that very army (administration!); ships that spend days sailing from one point to another without knowing for sure where they should leave the cargo, which finally spoils or fails to arrive on time (planning!); men in charge of uniform and supply depots who take it easy and live loosely, letting everything spoil or disappear (activity and zeal!); officers who hide behind [tree] trunks and even dig holes in the ground to hide themselves on the days of battle and bombardments (we have many of them among us, Drago, for one); others who don't even come here (condemned for services performed in the war); and others who perform acts of true heroism [that are] completely forgotten (acts of justice!); some of the bravest commanders, the most scrupulous, censured and undermined (formally) in front of their men just because a private didn't have his pants properly pressed (as happened here to some commanders from the First Division, some of the most distinguished [men] of the whole army) (stimulating enthusiasm!), etc., etc., etc.

Doctor, it seems to me that things here go by the opposite of their name?! . . . Or then I am moonstruck (as one would say). They say that His Excellency (the Acting Emperor) will now lead a resounding attack! May the wind fill his sails. The evil tongues, however, say that what he wants to do is to fool [*embromar*] us, as the Castilians say, that what is being planned is a new and massive attack [to take advantage of] the good faith of the country which gapes in wonder [*está embasbacado*] with its eyes turned toward Paraguay, but which grasps [*capisca*] nothing of what is going on in this hornets' nest. Come what may in the end! As I already reported to you, I left the First Division when General Argolo[67] went to command the army's II Corps [and] I was named engineer of the army's I Corps and was immediately charged with undertaking a general inspection of the Itapirú and Paso de la Patria depots and writing regulations for these departments. Within two days I will wrap it up and go to Tuyutí. Your second granddaughter, my daughter, will be just as pretty and fun-loving as the first one. I already asked Nhanhã[68] for a picture; [from her] I have recently received many letters and long ones (of the sort that I want her to write to me). Tibúrcio[69] sends you his greetings. This distinguished officer is becoming ever more distinguished and is taking giant strides toward the great tasks that the future, smiling [on his fortune], holds for him. We are becoming ever closer friends. I request that you give my regards to Dona Olímpia, Dona Mariquinhas, Dona Maria Marcelina, Dona Maria Texeira, Mr. Rocha and his wife, and to my good friends Guimarães, Veiga, Honório, Coimbra (when you speak with them). The bearer is already leaving and so I'll stop here. Adieu, my good father and true friend, accept a warm embrace and the loving heart of your son

*Benjamin Constant Botelho de Magalhães*

N.B. I ask you to go with my wife when you can to Malaquias and Tibúrcio's home so that she can thank them on my behalf for the numerous favors that they have done for me.

*Corrientes, 11 April [1867][70]*

*My dear Father and friend*

On 23 March I wrote to you from the army. In the month of April I have also written two letters to you from this city: one dated the second, carried by the first lieutenant of our navy, Pedro Antônio do Monte Barros; the other dated the fifth, carried by Captain José de Cerqueira Lima. Now I am writing you this little letter with the purpose of finding out about your health and that of Dona Olímpia and Dona Mariquinhas and all of the people of our family, and to tell you my news at the same time. Inside the letters that I wrote to you were letters to my wife. Besides these, I wrote three more to her, which went by the mail and by the same bearer. Everything continues in the same criminal [state of] apathy, and so there is little news to tell you about what is going on here. Nevertheless, I'll always tell you something. Happily, the cholera [epidemic] is diminishing in intensity; however, it did much damage in this city, taking 1,400 and some men up to today, among them some officers. The captain of the General Staff, first class, Manoel Feliciano Pereira de Carvalho (son of the Medical Corps's head), my colleague, married with three children, died here from cholera. Among the natives, the casualties have been great; however, the terror that has seized the population is greater than everything else. Families have abandoned the city which is almost deserted. There are entire streets along which one finds not a single house inhabited by Correntinos. Where do these poor victims terrified by the pest go? Those who have places in the country (*La campaña*) go to them; those who lack [such places], who are much more numerous, seek shelter under trees two or three leagues from the town and think that they are free from danger. The stupidity and ignorance of this wretched people is the cause of the panic that has taken hold of them. It causes pity to see entire families abandoning everything to go and live under trees in the countryside, without the slightest protection, exposed night and day to rain and sun, etc. The day before yesterday, the police register recorded that almost 8,000 Correntinos have left the city. These are official figures (note that the population of the entire province of Corrientes doesn't exceed 16,000 souls). The city of Paraná ([in the] Republic of Argentina) was also attacked. I don't know what happened there. It tears the heart to see how much suffering the pest has caused here and the scenes of inhumanity that have taken place (I am now speaking to you about the Correntinos), all having their origin in ignorance and terror. When cholera strikes a Correntino, the house in which he lives is completely abandoned, all flee in terror and the unfortunate victim remains helpless, with none to find him a doctor, medicine, food, etc. Rare are the exceptions to this cruel practice. I have seen many such scenes and have done what I could. After the individual's death, the local police, charged with burying him, with great difficulty dare to enter the house. The laments and bitter cries of those from whom the pest has taken a loved one are heard at every turn. To pass through this scene in the streets of Corrientes is to run the risk of returning home with one's heart covered in sorrow. In this midst of this general conflagration, it is true, our doctors have performed some services, but I consider them (with few exceptions) far from deserving praise. In the face of the extraordinary terror which has seized the population, no one has thought to publish newspaper articles recommending the health measures that should be taken to attempt to avoid the worst, the medicines that one should have and which should be applied as soon as the familiar symptoms appear, while one sends for the doctor, etc. While medical science has not yet definitively resolved the question of whether cholera is contagious, I think that doctors, in the face of the inhumane scenes that have taken place and which I have told you about above, should attempt to convince these people that the illness is not contagious, so as to diminish in some way the calamities that are taking place here. In the end, the medical corps (as I see it) has not given such advice, has not performed the services that humanity demands from its skills. With cholera's invasion, the hatred that these people have for us has increased sharply. They talk here [about], and have taken measures with the local authorities to forestall, the plans that are contrived against us; they tried to fire all of our hospitals and other departments. Fortunately, as of today, nothing has come of it. Besides this, our situation is worsened by the revolution being prepared with the aim of removing the current governor, Don Evaristo López, from the government of this province. The Provisional Corps commanded by Tibúrcio always has men armed and ready to aid any point attacked when the revolution breaks out. In short, everything is going marvelously. Communications, or at least the movement of troops, between this city and the army's I Corps is cut because of the epidemic: There are express orders from Caxias that no soldier or officer come to Corrientes from the I Corps and vice versa, so I will be here until the epidemic ends entirely. If I had not encountered Tibúrcio here I would have found myself in dire straits because everything here is extremely expensive and I brought no money when I came here. Now let's turn to the ways in which our wretched soldiers have been treated under these circumstances. The soldiers who comprise the Provisional Corps and those attached to it, who are many, amount to more than 4,000. Well, except for those few who are officers' orderlies, or servants, the majority of these poor folk don't [even] have a tent under which to seek shelter; they sleep in the open exposed to the drizzle and the rain, many without blankets or ponchos; for this reason too, the pest has been much more severe here. Tibúrcio, zealous and active as he is, has ordered tents in vain; there are none is the response that is given, and it is true, there are no tents. Our army administration goes so well! . . .

The I Corps has still not been attacked by this pest; there is a lot of disease there, but it is another kind; three or four days ago, however, the II Corps has suffered much. Yesterday the steamer *Dona Teresa* arrived here from Curuzu with 300 cholera victims. These wretched sick men arrived in the most forlorn state, almost naked (for some wore shirts but no pants or leggings, some had on pants but not shirts, few came with full uniforms and hardly any brought a blanket to cover themselves), without a single doctor or nurse, nor anyone who was in charge, without any medication at all, without food, etc. Sixteen arrived dead and others were almost dead. At midnight on the same day, the steamer *Dona Francisca* came with cholera victims from Curuzú treated in the same way. These facts are true and a doctor from the cholera hospital, by the name of Macedo, dared to file a protest. Now, is it necessary to say more? Moreover, is he the only one who reveals the inhumanity with which sick soldiers are treated? It will be hard to believe all the truths that I am telling you! . . . The newspapers of the Court praise everything that is going on here (as I have read several times) so that I am [presenting] an absolute contrast to all the official and private correspondents of these papers; however, I have a clear conscience and I am telling the purest of truth [and] I am satisfied. According to the newspapers of the Court, the army's health is most satisfactory, the number of dead is insignificant, but the truth is this and it is revealed in official figures that don't turn up there; before cholera's invasion, the number of sick from various diseases rose to almost 12,000 men, and in Corrientes alone, in the various hospitals, the death toll always exceeded

300 men per month and the number of sick has increased ever since. This is the truth, you can believe it. I spoke of the number of dead here in Corrientes, for I don't know for sure what has happened in the hospitals of Cerrito, Itapirú, Chacarita, Paso de la Patria, nor in the field hospitals.

Fortunately I have avoided [getting sick]; it appears that the intermittent fever has left me completely for it has not returned for six days. I am, however, very thin and very weak.

I cannot now give you news about your son, João, because, as I have said, communication between the I Corps and this city has been cut, but when I came here he was in good health. It would take too long to describe all of the evils that surround us here, and besides, I don't want you to take me for a pessimist, an unbeliever, an exaggerator or something like that, and for this reason I am only writing about what is going on and even this only superficially. Corrientes is the most corrupt city that I know and, in general, our officers, soldiers, etc., cut a most ridiculous figure here. There are, fortunately, many exceptions, many Brazilians worthy of praise for their rectitude, for their conduct; the majority, however, are a disgrace. Soldiers serve as pages, slaves to the prostitutes of this city, many sent by officers; others work in private houses, avoiding military duties and frequently earning money for those who sent them, etc., etc., etc. Tibúrcio does not rest when it comes to his battalion; he has taken energetic measures to overcome the evil that is already well-rooted and has done much, but much still remains for him to do; but, one swallow doesn't make a summer. Adieu, my father and good friend, many greetings to Dona Olímpia, Dona Mariquinhas, and to all of our friends. Accept a warm embrace and the loving heart of your son and friend

*Benjamin*

# 6. The Paraguayan War and Political Culture

## Rio Grande do Sul, Brazil, 1865–80

For the people of Brazil's southernmost province, Rio Grande do Sul, the Paraguayan War represented a potential source of political capital. Indeed, so aggressively did Gaúchos (the inhabitants of the province) seek to turn the war to their political advantage that Joaquim Nabuco, writing some thirty years later, contemptuously likened them to speculators who "abandoned everything to make their fortunes." Rather than patriotically serving the empire, these men interested themselves only in amassing wealth and influence, with which they could then acquire a "clientele avid for money." Gaúcho leaders ultimately turned the glorious national cause into a veritable "California," or gold rush—as the slang of the time had it—of patronage.[1]

Not surprisingly, the men who were the objects of Nabuco's disgust described their actions in starkly different terms. Throughout the war years and afterward, propagandists of all major political parties in the provincial capital of Porto Alegre argued that Gaúcho participation in the war constituted yet another example of the "tribute of blood" that their region had regularly paid to the fatherland. Always sensitive to allegations that their geographic and cultural proximity to Spanish American republics somehow made them less Brazilian than their peers from the Northeast or the central South, partisan leaders in Rio Grande do Sul emphatically claimed that their military contributions made them the very bulwark of the Brazilian nationality. In 1868 Antônio Eleutério de Camargo captured this sense of Gaúcho sacrifice in a particularly romantic formulation: "It is true that the traditions of our wars are inscribed on our lands, but it is also certain that the Riograndense abandons his labors, his home, his family when the fatherland calls; uncomplaining and proud, he fulfills his duty out of patriotism, he does not go . . . to seek the satisfaction of his aspirations and desires in the vicissitudes of war."[2] In contrast to Nabuco's later portrayal then, Gaúcho elites depicted Rio Grande as the site and source of disinterested heroism, which not only proved the *brasilidade* (Brazilian-ness) of their province but also justified its rise to a position of greater prominence in the highly centralized imperial political system.[3]

It was not only members of the regional elite, however, who sought to transform the defense of the fatherland into a mark of honor. In Porto Alegre and throughout the province, commoners also struggled to turn wartime service into improved social and political status. The initiatives that these plebeians exhibited were, however, more than a vague (if vigorous) desire to improve their social standing. Having patriotically carried out hazardous duties, returning veterans in Porto Alegre felt that they should now move out of dependent positions in the clientelistic social hierarchy. Like their comrades in other areas of Brazil, such veterans claimed rights normally out of reach for plebeians dependent on paternalistic patrons.[4] What these survivors of the war demanded, in effect, was recognition as independent and active members of their nation.[5]

What made possible this new discourse of status and rights in Rio Grande's popular political culture was the particularly intense experience of the war in the province, which suffered a Paraguayan invasion in the winter of 1865. Indeed, even after enemy forces surrendered at Uruguaiana in September and the war shifted out of Gaúcho territory, the front remained close to Rio Grande do Sul. Officers and men—including Emperor Pedro II—moved between cities like Porto Alegre and the fields of battle. Some civilians even traveled to army camps to visit relatives stationed there.[6] More significantly, Rio Grande do Sul provided a critical portion of the imperial military effort, supplying 33,803 fighting men, more than any other province of Brazil, and serving as a vital launching area for campaigns into Paraguay through 1869.[7] Like the rest of the empire, Rio Grande do Sul was also subject to the patriotic propaganda that accompanied the first truly national mobilization in the country's history.[8] Even if the average soldier had gone into war against his will—as had many of the so-called Voluntários da Pátria—authorities hailed them as essential elements of a great national victory.[9] Together with efforts to modernize and "moralize" the military—to turn the armed forces into a more effective corps of honorable men—this propaganda provided new terms for a discourse on plebeian action in Gaúcho political culture.[10]

### Wartime Evasion of Dependence

The war's most highly visible consequences for popular political culture did not involve plebeian claims on effective citizenship so much as the simple intensification of conventional strategies by dependents in this seigniorial society. Even when the province served merely as a staging ground for battles elsewhere, the war disrupted normal social relations and threatened to recreate the scenario of "insubordination and dissolution . . . of obedience and respect" that one official had observed during the Farroupilha Rebellion

(1835–45).[11] The arrival of thousands of outsiders of various ethnic, racial, and regional backgrounds and the departure of other groups to the front brought new contacts and new chances to slip away from one's *senhor* (master). The reconfiguration of the forces of order—as when units of the provincial police corps went off to battle early in 1866—also created confusion that plebeians turned into opportunities to press their own agendas.[12]

This upheaval in day-to-day relations of domination fueled an apparent increase in efforts to escape bonds of patronage. Rio Grande do Sul witnessed radical challenges to the dominant system of social relations in the nineteenth century and particularly in the years immediately preceding and during the Paraguayan War. Chief among these was slave revolt. The 67,791 slaves in the province (according to the 1872 census) amounted to nearly one-fifth of the provincial population of 367,022 and lived under the most extreme forms of dependence.[13] After the Farroupilha (during which three planned insurrections were reported), the province experienced its share of actual, planned, and rumored uprisings. By the count of historian Helga Piccolo, nine revolts of varying size came to authorities' knowledge from 1848 to 1863.[14] When tensions in the Platine region led to war in 1864, rumors of slave rebellions multiplied. Elites across the province shared the trepidation of the U.S. consul in the city of Rio Grande, who asserted a few months later that "a slave insurrection [was] imminent, and [that] the people [were] much alarmed."[15] Indeed in Porto Alegre the provincial chief of police ordered his men to follow slaves suspected of plotting uprisings.[16]

Particularly troubling for elites was the possibility that foreign infiltrators might incite or assist slave revolts. When the Paraguayans invaded the Rio-grandense border district at São Borja in 1865, stories of *Orientais* (residents of the Estado Oriental, present-day Uruguay) and Paraguayans "inviting" slaves to rebel abounded; similar reports continued until the end of hostilities.[17] The disorder that the war threatened led elites to fear the worst about their control over the province's slave population.[18]

One must treat such wartime rumors of servile uprisings with a healthy degree of skepticism. Some of the panicked calls for arms or men to put down imminent rebellions doubtlessly reflected more the fears of understaffed police departments than actual slave conspiracies. Few of the anticipated revolts actually took place; in some cases the authorities who had originally reported them later explicitly recognized the rumors as false alarms. In a confidential message to the ministry of justice in Rio de Janeiro, for example, provincial president José Marcelino de Souza Gonzaga described the actions that he had taken when word reached him of a slave conspiracy in the provincial capital at the end of 1864:"There is news circulating that a plan for slave insurrection has been discovered in Porto Alegre. I have not yet received official communications but am inclined to believe those reports exaggerated. The province's public spirit is so impressed with the gravity of the situation that it is easily frightened and exaggerates the smallest happening." The provincial executive had, it is true, quickly dispatched the chief of police, one hundred policemen, and more than two hundred national guardsmen in case the rumors proved true. So ready were citizens to believe in this insurrection that fifty German immigrants—perhaps also eager to reassure local authorities of their loyalty to Brazil—quickly offered their services to help restore "order and public peace." Gonzaga was soon convinced, however, that the scare had begun with the whisperings of "some freedmen, and among these many ex-army soldiers." His proposed solution was a well-tested one:"Recruit them for the navy."[19]

Not all of the anxieties about slave conspiracies proved to be so illusory. Steep though the odds against their success might be, dramatic plots to flee once and for all from masters' overwhelming power or to rise up and destroy slavery itself emerged during this period, thus justifying elite worries. Paraguayan forces apparently did carry off, by force or with promises of freedom, slaves from Jaguarão and other Riograndense communities.[20] In one of the most notorious conspiracies the plotters apparently aimed to win liberty by demanding it directly, arms in hand, in the middle of the provincial capital. The rebellion failed to materialize because of the most common reasons in such cases—a slave privy to the conspiracy betrayed it to his master, who then informed the authorities in June 1868. The national government eventually authorized the proper funds, and the informer, Antônio Maria, received his freedom (and his master, a fair cash payment for the loss of property).[21] Antônio Maria, in fact, provided few details about the conspirators' intentions. Clearly afraid of having his betrayal discovered, he had refused to act on the police chief's orders to infiltrate the conspiracy as a way of learning the plotters' timetable.[22] His brief testimony, however, led to several arrests and to worries about a possible international dimension to the conspiracy.

The story that the police wrung out of the slaves Dionísio and Patrício, the conspiracy's alleged ringleaders, was complicated and incomplete, though not without a certain logic. According to Dionísio, they had made careful preparations. After initially wanting to act on the night of Espírito Santo (Pentecost), a major holiday, Patrício had changed the plan, "considering that many unnecessary misfortunes could result on that night (such as the deaths of women and children), since great confusion would reign when the insurgents took the Praça do Palácio [the city's central plaza], which would be full of people watching the fireworks and festivities."[23] To ready their movement the leaders set out to invite "many other slaves." Patrício and Dionísio provided different versions of the plan to the others, based on the leaders' level of confidence in each new comrade. The most trusted received full information about the plan, while those of dubious loyalty were told that the invitation "was simply for a dance." An exceptional role fell to a slave who lived on the Caminho do Meio; they charged him with supplying 144 lances on which blades could later be mounted. After distributing those weapons at a rural site, the insurgents would then proceed in separate groups to the quarters of the National Guard, "where it was known that few people slept"; the munitions plant; and the army arsenal. With the better arms obtained from those strategic depositories, the slaves would then march on the city "to obtain their freedom." According to Patrício's confession, they were not to act alone in this uprising; he claimed that they counted on the help of some Paraguayan prisoners in the city's jail. The evidence in this regard is shaky at best; police officials interrogated four Paraguayans, who admitted that Patrício had mentioned the "noise" that he and the other slaves were organizing but said that they had dismissed him as a drunk. Despite the lack of proof of their collusion, the chief of police considered the Paraguayans "of bad faith" and ordered them removed from the city. Even without a demonstrable foreign connection, the conspiracy certainly seemed a grave matter to the police, strapped as they were for manpower during the war. As noted, betrayal and subsequent police repression crushed the plot before Patrício and the others had a chance to put it into effect. For their participation in the conspiracy the slaves mentioned in the interrogations were "punished in accordance with [the wishes of] their masters."[24]

Despite its failure, the 1868 conspiracy suggests how near the military frontier could be for plebeians in Rio Grande during the war years. In fact, during not only the Paraguayan War but also the other military conflicts that hit the province (the Cisplatine War of 1825–28, the Farroupilha Rebellion, the campaign against Argentine leader Juan Manuel de Rosas in 1852, and the Federalist Rebellion in 1893–95), the relative proximity of a strategically important border proved a mixed blessing for Gaúcho plebeians seeking to flee from dependency on a patron. The mere existence of a nearby international border raised the possibility of escape. Unlike the United States before the 1857 Dred Scott decision, Brazil had no internal zones of potential freedom to which slaves might escape until the last five years before abolition. Throughout the country, of course, slaves and the free poor often opted to flee conditions of oppression; the opportunities for complete evasion of masters' control that a relatively close frontier presented, however, existed in few other populous areas of Brazil.[25] Even before Uruguay definitively abolished slavery in 1842, Brazil's neighboring countries lured Gaúcho slaves away from their masters.[26] The onset of the Paraguayan War brought waves of letters to provincial authorities from slaveholders. *Senhores* wrote to provincial officials about the loss of slaves who had fled to those countries—and they did so repeatedly, bitterly, and often with little hope of recovering their servile workers. So common was flight over the border that even masters who had no direct knowledge of a runaway's location would frequently assume him or her to be in Uruguay. Often, however, masters heard rumors of a runaway slave's presence in Montevideo, Salto, or other towns, or even in foreign armies. Whatever their final destination then, some Gaúcho slaves clearly hoped to follow the formula that the Afro-Brazilian brothers Leopoldino and Adão expressed in 1878: "they would go to the other side of the line, where they would become free."[27]

When captured, some runaways constructed sophisticated arguments against their re-enslavement (or had such arguments constructed on their behalf), reasoning that their time in free countries had made them free. Protesting against the auction at which she had been sold following the death of her master, for example, the slave Júlia took one such case to court in 1866. A witness explained that eleven years earlier she had sought to establish her freedom on the basis of her residence outside of Brazil. At that earlier date, the former municipal judge testified, Júlia had approached him "saying that she was free because she was residing in the Estado Oriental in the company of her owners, who wanted or were trying to sell her." Unfortunately for Júlia, her case disproved the observation that Michael George Mulhall would make seven years later. Seeing the punishments meted out to captives near Pelotas, the English merchant wrote, "These slaves very often escape across the frontier to the Banda Oriental, and return again in two years, after which period no master can claim them." In fact Júlia's efforts to achieve liberty failed, and she found herself sold to a new master.[28]

Another case from 1866 sparked heated debates in the provincial assembly. This time it was a woman named Claudina who used judicial means to push her claims of freedom. Saying that she had been born in Uruguay, she managed to convince a local official to accept her complaint against her widowed mistress. News of this prosecution led several provincial legislators to decry unjust persecution of decent slaveholders. While offering different accounts of the complicated legal history of abolition in the neighboring nation, Pedro Maia and other deputies argued that the Uruguayan government had continued to respect the status of Brazilian-owned slaves, even those born in that emancipated territory. For Maia the case centered on simple corruption; he insinuated that Claudina's Portuguese lover had through illicit means persuaded the local police to torment the "large and invalid family" that depended on the rents that their legitimately held slave brought in. For the Liberals Gaspar and Silvestre Silveira Martins the question touched on property rights. Silvestre in particular declared that, though he was no "apologist for slavery," he had to support the slaveholders' rights over Claudina. To accept her freedom merely because of the place of her birth, he denounced, would be an "anarchic doctrine" that could even lead to revolution. The outcome of Claudina's case remains obscure; what is clear, however, is that slaves' efforts to use the frontier to win freedom set off heated debate among some of the highest political officials in the province.[29]

Legislators' prejudices against accepting a slave's assertions aside, Claudina's example reveals how some slaves used the frontier in their resistance efforts in Rio Grande do Sul. The legislators here accepted Claudina's Uruguayan birth; their debates revolved around the implications of that fact and the behavior of local authorities. Other slaves tried to turn less impeccable claims of birth in free nations into tools with which to gain freedom. In early 1866, for instance, the authorities arrested the Creole Manoel Antônio Soares in the city of São Gabriel. Adopting a Spanish accent, he simply tried to pass himself off as a free native of Uruguay. Eventually, however, Manoel confessed to being born a slave in Rio Grande do Sul and having run away to the neighboring country some fifteen years earlier.[30]

As one of the most frequent regions to which fugitives escaped, the border region could also be an area of subjugation. Illegal enslavement clearly made the poorly policed frontier a potential threat to free persons of color.[31] The considerable military presence that the empire maintained in Rio Grande do Sul provided not only another source of danger but also one of potential liberation for the province's plebeians. The negative side of the province's militarization derived from the injustices of conscription and horrible living conditions that made military service "tantamount to slavery" in public perceptions.[32] Service in the army, National Guard, or navy was technically required of all Brazilian men. The law provided so many exceptions, however, that the raising of forces largely depended on forced recruitment. In practice the wealthy and powerful manipulated this system to keep themselves, their sons, and their dependents out of the army and the lower ranks of the National Guard. Military service thus fell mainly on the unprotected poor.[33] Even members of the police, however, could be targeted for recruitment when their behavior threatened social peace. The police delegate in Conceição do Arroio informed authorities in Porto Alegre of one such soldier in 1870: "Graciano Dias da Costa, because of his deplorable qualities, has become absolutely incapable of continuing here, or even in any other place in the province, whether as a policeman or simply as a private citizen, so that it is recommendable that he serve the nation, in the army or principally in the navy. His precedents and habits are the darkest possible, and have already led him to be taken twice before the tribunal of the jury, where he was unfortunately absolved."[34] More dangerous (and thus more recruitable) were those individuals whose unruly behavior seemed to threaten social hierarchies. When a group of slaves ran through a city of the interior shouting "subversive cries," local authorities quickly recommended that Porto Alegre authorities recruit the leader, a freedman, who unlike his followers could be impressed.[35] As this correspondence makes clear, officials not only let conscription weigh most heavily on the poor but also used it as a means of punishing "vagrants" and disobedient plebeians.[36]

Brutal though army life may have been—and however much many men tried to avoid it—for other plebeians the military represented not something to escape from but rather a haven.[37] Although they might themselves later desert, at least initially such men found some liberation in the army. Undiscriminating, at times voracious, recruiters often paid little attention to the status of new conscripts. Many either neglected to ask for the letter of emancipation that freed recruits were supposed to present or did not subject possible forgeries to great scrutiny.[38] This indiscretion created an opening for slaves who hoped to escape their legal captivity. Taking advantage of the opportunity, slaves like Martiniano José de Alencastro declared themselves freedmen and enlisted. When owners learned that their slaves had enlisted, they complained to authorities. Often masters managed to discover not only the unit in which a captive was serving but also the alias under which he had joined. When no one attempted to reclaim a known slave, as in Martiniano's case, military officials were content not to lose the soldier.[39]

The poverty and discipline that military service entailed failed to turn conscripts into models of order and subservience.[40] In fact the military encountered tremendous difficulties merely to keep recruits within its ranks, and the outbreak of war in 1864–65 severely aggravated this problem. Judging from the reports of civilian officials, desertion became a major problem across

Rio Grande during the war, rivaling slave rebellion as a potential threat to the social order and lingering on after the final victory. In July 1865, for instance, a police official in Cruz Alta expressed his qualms not only about the imminence of a Paraguayan invasion but also about the "insults" that deserters and allied criminals might carry out against the families unable to flee that border city. Five years later another police subdelegate, this time in Arroio Grande, requested outside assistance in controlling both slaves and free peons, calling the latter "a generally turbulent class." Throughout these years then, authorities across the province called for action against clusters of deserters said to be infesting various districts.[41]

Particularly ominous in elites' eyes was the formation of *quilombos*, runaway slave communities, that might include plebeians who had fled not only slavery but also the army. Benedito Santana de Arruda, a deserter arrested in 1867, related to police the story of his flight from the army and his integration into one such *quilombo*, Pedras Brancas. Led by a former slave known as Camizão, the community Arruda described boasted elaborate political structures and plans for its defense.[42] Authorities expressed horror at such fraternization between deserters and runaway slaves, two social types that should have remained bound to their superiors by ties of dependency—and even of property in the case of bondsmen—and their union only seemed to multiply the danger of their breaking out of such positions. If not as openly confrontational as insurrections, *quilombos* like Pedras Brancas still threatened the established regime since they provided an alternative order that explicitly rejected traditional social boundaries.

### From Service to Citizenship?

Like rebellion and definitive flight (over the border or into the military), the formation of *quilombos* occupied the radical side of popular political culture. Even during the war years projects to destroy or permanently evade seigniorial power were infrequent in Rio Grande do Sul; instead plebeians generally worked within the prevailing paternalistic model of elite-plebeian social relations. It may be more useful to think of these strategies as working *with*, rather than *within*, paternalistic relations; the latter preposition implies a greater degree of restraint than plebeian actors exhibited. The Fortunatos and Felipes, Luizas and Leopoldinas who made up the *povo* (common populace) insistently and creatively pushed the limits of paternalist models, flirting constantly with danger by moving in and out of what masters would consider acceptable behavior for plebeians. Common strategies involved the assertion of certain rights for the less powerful parties in paternalist relationships. These alternative readings of paternalism accepted terms set by elites only up to a point; they also continually offered interpretations of those terms that at times threatened to transform the very character of the social relations that they seemingly embraced.[43]

When veterans made their claims for a new status then, they were acting in the context of a rich plebeian political culture in which aspirations to diminished dependency and strategies of claiming rights already existed. The terms in which veterans expressed their demands for recognition and rights thus represented a significant extrapolation from core elements of the region's popular political culture. Rather than seeking to improve their lot as relatively autonomous clients, these veterans wanted to throw off dependence altogether. Although these initiatives built on longstanding tendencies within popular political culture, they turned out to be no less radical than the strategies of revolt against seigniorial power or evasion of it.

Four years after the end of the Paraguayan War, in which he had served in the Twelfth Infantry Battalion, Antônio da Costa e Oliveira was still trying to gain status through military action in the streets of Porto Alegre. That attempt would, according to later court testimony, end in Antônio's violent death in late March 1874. Ironically the site of this bloody affair was a tavern on Voluntários da Pátria Street, the busy commercial avenue that had been renamed to honor his Paraguayan War comrades.[44]

Entering the establishment shortly before the curfew bell rang, Antônio "began to recount the deeds that he had performed in Paraguay." When the volume and bravado of his stories started to irritate other patrons, the tavern owner, Felipe Lopes de Bittencourt, tried to silence him. Likely nervous about losing business, Bittencourt heeded the wishes of several English customers and repeatedly ordered the troublemaker to stop his harangue. Antônio bristled at this perceived challenge. As four witnesses recalled afterward, he accused the tavern owner of being "a false Brazilian since he stood up more for the interests of the English than for those of a soldier who had gone to Paraguay in defense of the fatherland" and added menacingly, "there [in Paraguay] he had committed many murders and here he could kill one more." Not content to issue such threats, Antônio then vaulted the bar to attack Bittencourt; his advance fell short, however, when the bar's clerk grabbed a pistol and shot the veteran, first in the abdomen and then in the forehead. The resulting wounds proved fatal and brought to a close Antônio's prolonged campaign against enemies foreign and domestic.[45]

One might at first dismiss Antônio's rage as one man's "evil instincts," as a lawyer in the case put it, or as yet another example of the violent behavior for which "forces of order"—soldiers of the police and military corps—were notorious in nineteenth-century Porto Alegre.[46] Antônio, however, was far from the only veteran to carry his experience in the Paraguayan War back to the streets, taverns, and residences of the city. So too did other men, such as João Alves Pedroso, who returned from the war to stir up life in Aldeia dos Anjos (present-day Gravataí). Indeed witnesses in Pedroso's 1874 trial for murder said that the defendant had come back from the front a changed man. One of João's lifelong acquaintances explained that, whereas his friend "until going to Paraguay was worthy of esteem . . . for his beautiful qualities," he had now taken to provoking police and neighbors alike. The witness further averred that Pedroso's "behavior has been such that today in the Aldeia there is no one, except perhaps some relative, who has not been offended by him." The defense lawyer in the case, while attempting to soften Pedroso's image, pointed out the key—and for residents of Aldeia dos Anjos the most problematic—characteristic of this and other veterans' behavior: their experience had left them with an "independence of spirit" that caused friction with the bosses (*mandões*) who dominated peacetime society.[47]

In the complex encounters of daily life in Porto Alegre, however, these bids for recognition only infrequently brought overt confrontations with elite power. Pointing to one's military service was a common device for claiming honor and rank in the established social order of the 1870s and 1880s; since state war propaganda represented military service as an "act of patriotism" rather than "a humiliation," a military record could support claims to respectable status within terms set by a dominant discourse.[48] This was true even of men whose disciplinary records were less than immaculate. To demonstrate his orderly nature, for instance, the former cavalryman Salomé Suzano Escalara presented a judge with his discharge papers, which indicated that he had suffered "just two correctional arrests" and thus showed that "he was never disorderly nor [had] committed any criminal act for which he had been punished."[49] Others to whom the postwar years had not been particularly kind tried to make similar use of their service. Manoel Francisco da Cunha, for instance, lamented that a "lack of means" had led him to become "the *agregado* [dependent, resident peon, or servant] of Fermino Martins de Oliveira Prates" but still considered his "many years" of service "to the state" a source of status.[50] In more explicit fashion Propício José de Magalhães used his military past to position himself above other plebeians. Magalhães had been arrested for using a whip to beat a black man, Pedro Luiz de França, who had clambered through the outer fence of the truck garden that Magalhães owned near the Guaíba River. Unlike França, insisted the defendant, he did not "live loitering on the street" but was a hardworking former army soldier; even though he held "a mediocre position" since his properties could not place him "on a par with the highest entities," he still stood "well above the alleged victim, so that the intention of injuring him must be absurd."[51]

Other veterans used their military service to try to overcome racial hierarchies. Former sergeant Manoel Florêncio da Conceição referred specifically to the war to explain the assault on his supervisor, for which he had been imprisoned in 1874. Working as a carpenter—again, on Voluntários da Pátria Street—Conceição received instructions to remove dirt from a hole in the street. Antônio José Martins accompanied the instructions with an insult, calling Conceição a "*negro* [black]," a racial term that carried connotations of slavery.[52] This was more than the veteran would stand for, as he testified: "It is true that he hit Antônio José Martins, because the latter directed at him a calumny that he, in his capacity as a soldier who had defended his country in the war against Paraguay, could not tolerate."[53] Similarly in the case of the Afro-Brazilian ex-soldier Leocádio Ferreira de Lacerda, heroic sacrifice in the war failed to free a veteran from racial discrimination. He was refused service in a bakery in 1880 for being "of color," despite having lost one arm and three fingers on the hand of the other in Paraguay.[54] Such examples suggest then the potentially powerful use that veterans could make of their military service as well as the difficulties they faced in doing so.

In part because of the potential power that veterans' discourse of service to the fatherland represented, men of the armed forces and civil authorities felt particularly appalled by the fraudulent use that some plebeians tried to make of the war. The illicit distribution and sale of military gear had long been part of the contraband trade for which Porto Alegre's shops and taverns were notorious.[55] Between the 1870s and the 1890s this commerce took on new meanings as men who had never served in the military sold and wore army uniforms in the streets of Porto Alegre and other Gaúcho towns.[56] The provincial chief of police felt it necessary to warn his block inspectors of such practices shortly after the war ended, and notices of individual desertions at times made the obvious point that men escaping the military took their uniforms and arms with them.[57] Authorities could not, however, stop such abuses. Perhaps hoping to share in the prestige that his friend enjoyed as a soldier in the light cavalry, for instance, an unemployed clerk, Pedro Firmiano da Silva, appeared in 1878 "dressed in military clothes without being a soldier."[58] Even slaves attempted to take on the power of the uniform; that same year one such slave, Guilherme, was said to have fled his master in a soldier's "pants and shirt of blue cloth."[59] For military men like the commander of the Sixth Infantry Battalion, of course, only soldiers deserved to wear such symbols of honor; in late 1871 that officer ordered his men to arrest any civilians found wearing military uniforms, "principally black slaves, belittling the military class."[60]

This particularly strong reaction to slaves in uniform is far from surprising; the degradation and dishonor of slavery were the opposite of the discourse of heroism and service to the country on which veterans in this period hoped to capitalize. With even greater vigor than the Sixth Infantry's commander, rank-and-file soldiers tried to protect their new status from both frauds and rivals in uniform after returning from Paraguay. Members and ex-members of the military, for instance, strove to construct boundaries between themselves and the police forces. At one level, of course, tensions between the military and the police reflected an understandable competition between two "forces of order," each of which claimed authority over the general populace. For men returning from the campaigns, however, there existed another level of meaning. For army and National Guard veterans wanting to turn their past service into recognition and status, the daily vigilance that policemen carried out was not merely an irritation but more importantly a threat to their honor and autonomy. As a result soldiers and guardsmen often challenged or refused to recognize the legitimacy of police authority. After taking part in a fight at the Teatro São Pedro, army cadet José Vieira Pacheco proclaimed that "he could not be arrested by members of the police" but assented to arrest by army soldiers guarding the theater.[61] Especially telling was the declaration of Pvt. Joaquim Álvaro, who arrived on the scene of one encounter between the police and three of his fellow members of the National Guard in Porto Alegre. Supporting his comrades' resistance to arrest, Álvaro declared that "the police lacked the power to arrest National Guardsmen—citizens—and that, if they drew their swords, they would have to tangle with him."[62] Since the National Guard had long conferred status on its members—particularly in the militarized pampas of the Gaúcho interior—Álvaro's position in that body gave him special grounds on which to explicitly claim citizenship.[63] Such assertions, whether direct or indirect, revealed the political and social aspirations of military men (army soldiers and national guardsmen) after the start of the Paraguayan War.[64]

In a way roughly parallel to the veterans' efforts, the *mandões* of Rio Grande do Sul also tried to turn the Paraguayan War to their political advantage. Gaúcho elites felt themselves unjustly marginalized in the imperial polity, dominated as it was by the coffee interests of the south-central provinces of Rio de Janeiro, São Paulo, and Minas Gerais.[65] While other regions had offered a weak and hesitant defense of the empire, the men of Rio Grande do Sul had proven themselves true sons of the nation, even if, as one Gaúcho lawmaker put it in 1873, the court (Rio de Janeiro) acted like a (presumably unaffectionate) "stepmother" to the province.[66] Soldiers and veterans—and other plebeians pretending to be soldiers or veterans—also sought more-central positions within the nation during and after the Paraguayan War. The telling difference, of course, is that elite projects envisioned only shifts of power between regional ruling blocs, not between classes. The plebeian initiatives, however, contemplated an empowerment of at least some of the popular classes through their inclusion into the nation. Antônio da Costa e Oliveira, João Pedroso, and their fellows did not necessarily challenge the principles of hierarchy or even of exclusionary citizenship; they were not visibly pursuing citizenship for all Brazilians. Basing their claims on their national service, they did, however, implicitly seek for themselves the rights and protections that citizenship offered. This both made their initiatives radical and ensured that they would fail; veterans' demands were far too threatening to find acceptance among the narrow band of propertied males who enjoyed full citizenship in the empire. In a sense then, what is most significant about the popular claims on citizenship that came out of the Paraguayan War experience is not that they represented the only moment at which Gaúcho plebeians actively attempted to gain a kind of "quotidian exercise of citizenship" before the late 1880s, but that they had to fail.[67] Their failure, after all, suggests how energetically the elite guarded the frontier between citizens and *povo* in the liberal but fundamentally seigniorial political culture of nineteenth-century Brazil.

# 7. Uruguay and the Paraguayan War

## The Military Dimension

The story of the Oriental Division in the Paraguayan War is a tale of the gradual decimation of a handful of bold warriors, veterans of many engagements, who had always fought for their caudillo, Gen. Venancio Flores, and their political faction, the Uruguayan Colorado Party.[1] This division contributed 1,500 soldiers to the allied army, of whom only 150 survived the fighting. From the Uruguayan point of view, the country's involvement in this war was an inevitable and unwanted consequence of the ongoing conflict between its two major political factions, the Colorados and the Blancos. For Uruguayans the Paraguayan War was exclusively a Colorado war. In early 1865, after a two-year campaign, General Flores overthrew the Blanco-supported government. Brazil and Argentina gave Flores significant support to achieve this objective, and he saw no alternative but to join those countries in their war against Paraguay. The Blancos not only opposed the war, many of them fought on the Paraguayan side.

This chapter analyzes the endemic discord between Blancos and Colorados that brought about Uruguayan participation in the Paraguayan War. Second, it examines how Flores's forces shaped a new national army that contributed its finest soldiers to the Paraguayan campaign, from which many never returned. It also considers the role of the Oriental Division in the fighting; after performing noteworthy operations at the initial stages of the campaign, it became an almost insignificant force, assigned to inconsequential tasks, and was largely forgotten by the Uruguayan government.

**Blancos and Colorados**

Nineteenth-century Uruguayans could not escape the fate of becoming either Colorados or Blancos. In fact these designations involved something more than partisan allegiances. They represented different and antagonistic political cultures that oriented the worldviews of every Uruguayan. The Blanco and Colorado factions originated as rural and urban caudillo groups in the 1830s, with clienteles and all the other characteristics of distinct patronage structures. In a country with less than 130,000 inhabitants (by 1835), a very low population density, and a weak state, it is no wonder that people sought protection from caudillos and inevitably became identified with their political factions.[2]

Civil wars between Colorados and Blancos did the rest. The killing of heads of households and their eldest sons, the violence against families, and the confiscation of livestock and lands all created an unyielding and mutual hatred. Allegiance to the causes espoused by the dead seemed altogether natural. It upheld carefully crafted partisan familial traditions and, in the end, two antagonistic cultures. Blancos and Colorados even co-opted European immigrants, who came by hundreds of thousands during the second half of the nineteenth century to practically replace the existing Uruguayan population. Moreover, as both parties had traditional or caudillo sectors as well as conservative and liberal factions, people of different political temperaments could accommodate their ideas and beliefs within each party. This is possibly the reason why Colorados and Blancos still exist today.

Between 1856 and 1865, after a long civil war that associated Blancos with Argentine Federalists and Colorados with Argentine Unitarians (and the Brazilians), some prominent figures in both parties tried to break with the past and implement a "Fusionist" policy that in theory would bring together the two inimical groups. Fusionism attempted to create a national consciousness and to avert the threat that the old transnational connections of both parties posed for Uruguay's future. Many Colorados and Blancos endorsed this movement, and for the first time it was possible to see the two groups working together in legislative chambers, public administration, and the armed forces. In 1858, however, a dogmatic faction of the Colorado Party, the conservatives, supported by the Unitarians of Buenos Aires, revolted against Fusionism. Gabriel Pereira, an erstwhile Colorado and the first Fusionist president, crushed the revolt and ordered the execution of its defeated leaders. These executions, which occurred at Paso de Quinteros along the Negro River, awoke smoldering partisan hatreds, and the Colorados, both conservative and traditional, accused the government of serving "Blanco purposes" and demanded revenge for "the martyrs of Quinteros." Such was the weight of partisan culture.

After the Quinteros episode, President Pereira had to subdue some lesser Colorado revolts and eventually banished from Uruguay many Colorado military men whom he deemed adversaries of Fusionism. Some others deserted from the Uruguayan army and National Guard and, just like the deportees, fled to Entre Ríos to seek help from the principal Colorado caudillo of that time, Gen. Venancio Flores. A former president whom the conservative Colorados had forced to resign in 1855, Flores seemed an implausible avenger.

He had been one of the architects of Fusionism, having joined with the chief of the Blancos, Gen. Manuel Oribe, and some prominent civilian figures of both parties, such as the Colorado Andrés Lamas and the Blanco Bernardo Berro. Flores, moreover, had retired to Entre Ríos in 1856 to work as overseer on one of the many ranches belonging to the Argentine Confederation's president, the Federalist Justo José de Urquiza.

But the arrival of the Uruguayan deportees and deserters, most of them experienced gaucho lancers who had fought many engagements, persuaded Flores to return to Uruguay to reclaim the presidency. This in fact was what the anti-Fusionist Colorados were asking from him. In 1859 Flores turned his back on his protector Urquiza and offered the services of his partisans to the Province of Buenos Aires. At that time Buenos Aires had become virtually independent of the Argentine Confederation and was preparing a military campaign against the rest of Argentina.

After the fashion of a Renaissance *condottiero*, Flores proposed a deal—almost a *condotta* pact—to the war minister of Buenos Aires, Gen. Bartolomé Mitre. He and his men would fight for the Bonaerense cause if Mitre helped him expel the Uruguayan Fusionists. Mitre did not hesitate. Flores commanded cavalry forces accustomed to fighting in the traditional *montonera*, or gaucho, manner, that is, by combining regular cavalry and guerrilla tactics. This brutal and disordered form of warfare witnessed units of mounted lancers clashing in bloody hand-to-hand combat without dismounting (the so-called *entreveros*).[3] But *montonera* war was also efficient in some instances, especially when the enemy employed such tactics, which was the case for Urquiza's horsemen. Hence Mitre accepted Flores's proposal.

Two battles decided the conflict between Buenos Aires and the confederation: Cepeda (23 October 1859) and Pavón (17 September 1861). In the first, which Urquiza won, Flores's men covered the retreat of Mitre's forces. In the second Buenos Aires won a definitive victory, with Flores's lancers fighting in the vanguard of Mitre's army and routing Urquiza's cavalry at several points. Two years later several of Flores's subordinate officers (among them Wenceslao and Mariano Paunero and Ambrosio Sandes) performed a decisive role in subduing the Federalist caudillo Angel Vicente Peñaloza (known as El Chacho) in the Argentine far west. With them were Ignacio Rivas and José Miguel Arredondo, former Colorado military officers whom Flores himself had trained. Mitre, now president of Argentina, granted all of these men high ranks in the Argentine army, but this was not enough. Capitalizing on all the victories that he and his men had achieved, Flores requested that Mitre fulfill his part of their original deal.

From May to June 1863, Argentine ships transported Flores and his men, together with arms, ammunition, and contingents of Argentine volunteers, to the Uruguayan coast. Meanwhile an Argentine naval squadron prevented Uruguayan government ships from interdicting the invaders at the Uruguay River. Flores thus initiated the "Liberating Crusade," as he termed it, to overthrow the second Fusionist president, Bernardo Berro. By this time Flores was accusing the Montevideo government of being Blanco dominated and thus justified his invasion as a new conflict between Colorados and Blancos, resurrecting the Colorado culture and its ancient rancor against the Blancos.[4] Most civilian Colorados in the Uruguayan countryside took up arms and joined him, as did Colorado military officers and soldiers who deserted the constitutional government to join Flores. Even the Brazilian caudillos of Rio Grande do Sul, traditional allies of the Colorados, organized and armed volunteer troops to reinforce Flores's "crusaders."

Yet Flores could not topple President Berro. The Uruguayan National Guard, notwithstanding the departure of numerous Colorados, remained loyal to Fusionism and offered strong resistance to the invaders. Berro completed his term, and a new Fusionist president, Atanasio Aguirre, took over in 1864. But the partisan nature of Flores's revolt in turn awoke old Blanco resentments. Blancos volunteered to form new National Guard battalions, while military officers of Blanco lineage progressively replaced the former officers who had gone over to Flores. Even some Argentine Federalist leaders, such as Urquiza's son Waldino and Juan Saá, came to Uruguay to support a purportedly Blanco cause. In December 1864 Flores executed the Blanco defenders of Paysandú as a Colorado retaliation for the 1858 Quinteros shootings, in the process killing the Fusionist alternative as well. For the time being, until Flores's definitive victory in February 1865, the war once again became a conflict between Colorados and Blancos.

By that time the Brazilian Empire had formally intervened in support of Flores. A Brazilian fleet commanded by the Baron of Tamandaré and Brazilian land forces under Marshal João Patrício Menna Barreto destroyed and occupied the city of Paysandú; Flores's soldiers simply played the role of executioners of the surrendered garrison. The reasons for Brazilian intervention in the Uruguayan conflict were at least four: the empire's fear that Flores's invasion might constitute the first phase of an Argentine plan to annex Uruguay; the previous intervention of Riograndense caudillos to support Flores; the fact that Brazilian ranchers owned most Uruguayan lands north of the Negro River and naturally favored Flores; and the fact that Berro had sought military and diplomatic aid from Paraguay. Brazil and

Paraguay were at that time edging toward war as a result of a territorial dispute.

According to the Brazilian plenipotentiary sent to negotiate Montevideo's capitulation in 1865, the purpose of his country's intervention was to establish a cooperative government in Uruguay in order to have a base of operations against Paraguay. In August 1864 the Asunción government had warned Brazil that it would tolerate no military adventures in Uruguay. In October, however, Brazilian land forces crossed the Uruguayan frontier, and events quickly spun out of control. One month later Paraguay seized the Brazilian steamship *Marquês de Olinda*, broke relations with the empire, and in December invaded the southern reaches of Mato Grosso. In February 1865 a new Uruguayan president, Tomás Villalba, signed the peace treaty that made Flores "provisional governor" of the country. Paraguay then invaded Mitre's Argentina, which it believed was supporting the empire, in April. In May the Brazilian, Argentine, and Uruguayan governments signed the Triple Alliance Treaty against Paraguay.

Flores's victory allowed Brazil to establish the base of operations that it was seeking in Montevideo. Sixteen thousand Brazilian troops and the crews of eighteen warships gathered there and initiated training. Flores meanwhile organized public ceremonies to exalt Colorado virtues and built a monument to the "martyrs of Quinteros." More importantly he ordered the discharge of all remaining Blanco officers and soldiers in the Uruguayan army and fired all public employees suspected of Blanco or Fusionist sympathies.[5] As Colorado newspapers of Montevideo put it, he considered it imperative that public positions be assigned exclusively to members of the Colorado Party.[6]

Once Flores had purged the army, he filled the vacant positions with the Colorado military men who had served under his command in Argentina and in the Liberating Crusade. He also enlisted the numerous volunteers who had joined him during the campaign, including significant numbers of Brazilians from northern Uruguay and Rio Grande do Sul. Flores confirmed the general promotions that he had previously given and also granted new ones.[7] As a result the Uruguayan army became exclusively Colorado, displaying a strong partisan spirit that in some respects has lasted until today.

Uruguayan participation in the alliance, however, was popular among the Colorados only while they feared that a Paraguayan offensive might help the Blancos. At the beginning of the war in early 1865, Paraguay sent two army columns southward along the Uruguay River. These forces, commanded respectively by Maj. Pedro Duarte and Lt. Col. Antonio Estigarribia, were defeated by the allies at Yataí and Uruguaiana (17 August and 18 September

1865). According to Colorado officers who participated in both engagements, the first column was seeking to join forces with Urquiza in conformity
with a secret treaty that linked the Entrerriano caudillo with the Paraguayan
president and Blanco émigrés from Uruguay. Estigarribia certainly intended
to invade Uruguay and reestablish Blanco control; in fact more than thirty
Blanco officers were part of his command.[8] Flores himself argued that the
Paraguayan government had ignored the authority of his Colorado crusade
and that the mere existence of an anti-Colorado regime in Asunción jeop-
ardized Uruguayan security.[9]

But after Uruguaiana fell to the allies in September 1865, Paraguay had
to abandon the areas near the Uruguayan frontier, and the Colorado newspapers began to demand the return of Flores's troops. This later turned into
an open protest against Uruguayan participation in the Paraguayan War once
the complete text of the Triple Alliance Treaty became known. The pact
established that once the war ended, new borders would be drawn between
Paraguay and Argentina and Brazil, to the allied countries' advantage (Article
16); it established as well that Paraguay would reimburse allied war expenses,
in particular those incurred by Uruguay (Article 14).[10] The influential Colorado newspaper *El Siglo* denounced Flores for having joined the alliance
only to repay a debt to Brazil for the empire's help in overthrowing the Blancos. *El Siglo* complained, moreover, that while Argentina and Brazil would
gain Paraguayan territory thanks to the treaty, Uruguay could only hope for
promises of monetary compensation from the defeated nation.

In effect the Colorados had already reached their objectives of seizing political power in Uruguay and making sure that the Blancos could never rise
again—or at least anytime soon; they had no interest in the Paraguayan War.
Now most Colorados saw Uruguayan participation in the alliance as Flores's
personal undertaking and disowned any responsibility for it. Flores himself
abandoned the theater of war in 1866 never to return. All things considered, the Paraguayan War never became a national cause among Uruguayans.
Their participation was nothing but a collateral, and for many an unwanted,
consequence of the perennial struggle between Colorados and Blancos.

**The Oriental Division**

To a great extent the Colorados were right in deeming Uruguay's participation in the Triple Alliance a personal venture of General Flores. A more

precise analysis would have revealed, however, that it was the undertaking of both Flores and his closest subordinates. Most officers in the small Oriental Division were those who had fought under Flores's command at the battles of Cepeda and Pavón and who had accompanied him in his 1863–65 Liberating Crusade.[11] They were in fact a band of professional warriors who, not unlike ancient mercenaries, followed their warlord in a series of adventures.

As a Colorado military historian put it, war was a habit for these men, and they fought recklessly and without mercy, even under the most unfavorable conditions.[12] This was why Mitre made use of Flores and his troops, placing them at the vanguard at Pavón and entrusting them with the campaign against El Chacho. This was also why Brazil wanted them in the Paraguayan War, fighting in the forefront of the allied armies. If Mitre paid for their services by helping them overthrow the Uruguayan Fusionists, Brazil also acknowledged their assistance with a substantial monthly subsidy, paid in gold to the Uruguayan government.[13] Flores in turn never failed to reward his fighters. In Argentina he obtained for them high military ranks; in Uruguay he gave them positions on the general staff of the new army. And during the Paraguayan War they fought for Flores and remained enthusiastic about the allied cause until their caudillo abandoned the effort.

These officers might be called "landlord-warriors," that is, landowners of considerable importance who alternated ranching with soldiering. Such was the case with Flores himself, a great rancher in southwestern Uruguay who had gained fame in earlier civil wars.[14] Similarly Enrique, Gregorio, and Nicomedes Castro were wealthy ranchers from along the Uruguay River who had fled to Entre Ríos after Quinteros. Enrique Castro became Flores's chief of the general staff during the crusade and his successor in command of the Oriental Division in Paraguay. His brother Gregorio was possibly the best example of these landlord-warriors. The Colorado caudillo of Florida (one of the republic's administrative departments), Gregorio Castro had a personal army and took it with him when he crossed over to Entre Ríos. In an agreement between caudillos, the Entrerriano Urquiza made Castro general overseer of his ranches and let him keep his army as both a work and a war force. This army, reinforced with local lancers, later played a central part in Flores's crusade and ultimately became the Florida Battalion of the Oriental Division.[15]

Landlord-warriors also counted among their number the great landowners of the Brazilian border, including José Gregorio "Goyo" Suárez and Fidelis Paes da Silva. Suárez, who ordered the shooting of the defenders of Paysandú, later became cavalry chief in the Oriental Division and Flores's political rival within the Colorado Party. Fidelis Paes, a veteran of the Farroupilha Rebellion (1835–45) in southern Brazil, was instrumental in obtaining support for Flores's crusade from the caudillos of Rio Grande do Sul. He later joined the Oriental Division, bringing with him his battalion of Voluntarios Garibaldinos, a unit largely composed of Brazilian residents in Uruguay. Other landlord-warriors included the cavalry chiefs Nicasio Borges, Wenceslao Regules (organizer of the 24 de Abril Battalion), Máximo Pérez, Simón Martínez, Nicasio Galeano, the Entrerriano Francisco Elías, and the Brazilian Atanasildo Saldanha, who performed noteworthy roles in both Flores's crusade and the Paraguayan War.[16]

The officer corps of the Oriental Division also included some professional military men, such as José Antonio Costa and Spanish-born immigrant León de Palleja. Although ranchers themselves, their principal occupation had always been the military. Costa had served in both the Argentine and Uruguayan armies and became the first chief of the general staff in the Oriental Division. Palleja, a veteran of the Spanish army, provided Flores with decisive military help in overthrowing a Blanco government in 1853 and in becoming president of Uruguay for the first time. During the Paraguayan War Palleja commanded the Florida Battalion and became the principal chronicler of the Oriental Division. Professional officers in the division also included Flores's sons, Fortunato and Eduardo.[17] A special case was that of José Cándido Bustamante, who was neither a landlord-warrior nor a professional soldier. Bustamante, a renowned journalist who created the Colorado cult to the "martyrs of Quinteros," raised a volunteer corps for the Oriental Division, the Voluntarios de la Libertad, which fought bravely at the battle of Yataí.[18]

These were the officers whom Colonel Palleja praised in his journal for their courage, noting that they fought "with the enthusiasm of partisan soldiers" (meaning that they showed strong motivation, just as they did when they fought the Blancos in the Uruguayan civil wars).[19] For them the Paraguayan War was, in effect, an extension of the Colorado crusade of 1863–65, which is to say a Colorado war. Not surprisingly such enthusiasm resulted in many casualties in the officer corps. Eighteen of the ninety-eight Uruguayan chiefs and officers that the Oriental Division had at the beginning of the war fell either dead or wounded at the very first battle (Yataí).[20] Promotions filled vacant positions, but in later engagements, such as Paso de la Patria and Tuyutí, casualties again leveled the leadership ranks.

If audacity decimated the officer corps, desertion, hunger, and disease progressively devastated the troops. In contrast to their enthusiastic officers,

Uruguayan soldiers went to war against their will. Desertion was ultimately their most common response, leading to the almost complete dissolution of the Uruguayan component in the divisional troops by early 1866. Only the forced recruitment of captured Paraguayan soldiers into Uruguayan battalions salvaged the command from extinction. In 1869, when the Oriental Division finally abandoned the war, Gen. Enrique Castro complained to the Montevideo government that it was exclusively Paraguayans who represented the Uruguayan flag in that conflict.[21]

The particular social conditions of rural Uruguay, rather than Blanco or Colorado affiliations, explain Flores's failure to find enthusiastic soldiers for the Paraguayan campaign. The military usually conscripted soldiers in the countryside for either partisan wars or international engagements; separate, locally raised urban corps typically stayed behind to garrison cities and towns. While ranchers and rural workers volunteered for partisan fights, such as Flores's crusade, they had no interest whatsoever in abandoning their families and labors to risk their lives in international conflicts. Even though Flores promoted the Paraguayan campaign as an extension of his crusade, he could not gain volunteers and had to resort to impressment and to the recruitment of prisoners to fill the ranks.

The scarce male population of the Uruguayan countryside consisted of ranchers and their peons (not more than two or three per ranch) and some wandering gauchos. Military authorities could not draft ranchers and peons because this would have caused the collapse of Uruguayan economy, which depended on its livestock reserves. Press gangs therefore had to focus on the gauchos.

Civilian law as well as the then-current military code—the Spanish ordinances of 1768—authorized the armed forces to draft "vagrants and lawbreakers," like the gauchos. In reality gauchos were men who lived from the abundant range cattle, there being no fences or proper demarcations separating ranches nor brands to identify livestock owners. They subsisted by lassoing errant animals and eating from them on the spot. No wonder then that ranchers considered these men lawbreakers, more precisely rustlers. Echoing their complaints, the Colorado journalist Dermidio de María wrote in *El Siglo* that gauchos were "people used to living in rude independence, who refused to acknowledge any authority." For this reason they could never become good soldiers. In fact they were an independent social sector that military authorities sought to control for the first time.[22]

In his chronicle Palleja complains that the soldiers recruited for the Paraguayan campaign were "a disobedient rabble." Certainly the gauchos were unwilling to submit to military discipline, especially since the army could not offer them a salary or a career that might compensate them for their loss of freedom, preferring to discharge troops once campaigns were over. Seizing convicts from prison, as was done twice during the first year of the war, was hardly an answer either. Such conscripts came from the rural jails of Salto and Paysandú, and many were serving time for cattle rustling, others for theft and murder. Accustomed to a life of crime, these men never became trustworthy soldiers.[23] Consequently desertion, squabbles, drunkenness, and theft plagued the Oriental Division, as military reports show. While the division was crossing Corrientes, deserters stole horses and escaped at full gallop before their commanders could react. Thieves sometimes sought refuge in other units under different names. Knife fighting took place constantly, either in campsites, towns, or while on the march. Cases of desertion and insubordination were practically without number.[24]

Flores, who well understood the psychology of his men, frequently re-frained from enforcing military rules. He was unwilling to order summary shootings of apprehended deserters, thieves, and other ne'er-do-wells, though the Spanish ordinances suggested just such measures. Palleja—a Spaniard himself—complained bitterly of this lax attitude.[25] He was probably right. Only two months after the Oriental Division left Uruguay following the victory at Yataí, desertions and casualties had reduced the contingent from fifteen hundred to some seven hundred effectives. But the outcome of this battle offered a solution. From the twelve hundred captured Paraguayans Flores took five hundred to reinforce the Uruguayan troops. Next, after the siege of Uruguaiana, he took an additional fourteen hundred Paraguayan prisoners for the same purpose. Gradually, captured Paraguayans began to replace Uruguayan soldiers.[26]

These replacements, however, failed to stem the dissolution of the Oriental Division. While some Paraguayans resigned themselves to fighting under the orders of Uruguayan officers, others mutinied or deserted back to their own people as soon as they could. In December 1865 Palleja complained that Paraguayans were a "nightmare," fearing that they would turn into enemies within the ranks.[27] They deserted as frequently as gauchos did, and those who remained fell victim to hunger and sickness. According to Palleja, the Paraguayans were so weak and sick that they died by the hour. This led Flores to send six hundred of them to Montevideo, far from the theater of war, to form a new urban battalion and even to give some of them as presents to Correntino ranchers who wanted cheap laborers.[28] Otherwise Flores was not as tolerant of the Paraguayans as he had been of the gauchos. Military reports from late 1865 indicate that the general had decided to shoot deserters and other transgressors by the dozens.[29] In order to prevent further diminution of the division, Flores's successor, General Castro, replaced shootings with lashings: two hundred to three hundred strokes for simple desertion, five hundred for desertion aggravated by theft.[30]

The Oriental Division seemed nonetheless fated to extinction. Lack of food exacerbated the desertion problem and further reduced the division. Shanks of beef were included in soldiers' pay, the monthly salary of four Bolivian pesos being insufficient for their minimal needs. *Raciones de rancho* (portions of beef), however, were only available when expert gauchos could slaughter feral cattle or when Brazilian ranchers from northern Uruguay supplied the livestock. By December 1865 such deliveries ended, and with them also ended the great *carneadas*, during which some thirty gaucho soldiers, led by their standard bearers, butchered cows to feed the entire troops, leaving behind large blazes consuming heads and entrails. When most gauchos left, these tasks fell to Paraguayan soldiers who, perhaps lacking expertise or merely attentive direction, left animal carcasses unburned around the campsites. These soon rotted, spreading diseases. In the last years of the campaign, when the division was almost exclusively Paraguayan, General Castro attempted to feed the soldiers with meat extract produced in the new industries flourishing in Uruguay, then undergoing a boom due to imports of Brazilian gold.[31]

The wet environment of the Entrerriano and Correntino marshlands contributed to spreading diseases among both the officer corps and the ranks. Infantrymen had to cross the wetlands barefoot. Heavy rains flooded camps, and tents sank in the muck. "Each downpour was a defeat," Palleja commented, adding that "marshes turned into seas." Moreover there were no suitable infirmaries (most of them being lean-tos formed from branches) or enough medicines to cure officers and soldiers sick from cold and fever. During the siege of Uruguaiana many men died from cold and hunger. Afterward, during the march toward Paraguay, other soldiers fell dehydrated under the scorching sun. In June 1866 the division surgeon reported that, as a consequence of baths in contaminated ponds, smallpox, dysentery, diarrhea, and blood vomits had begun to decimate the troops. A year later cholera hit the division, and deaths multiplied.[32] Neither reinforcements nor medicines came from Montevideo. Realizing that the government had forgotten them, Palleja grumbled in his journal that the Oriental Division would perish due to the egoism of the ruling Colorados.[33]

## The Campaign

From May to June 1865 General Flores organized the forces that followed him during the Paraguayan War.[34] According to the Triple Alliance Treaty's terms, Flores commanded the Oriental Division and two other small contingents, one Brazilian and one Argentine. The entire force amounted to some nineteen hundred to two thousand effectives, with the Oriental Division itself consisting of fifteen hundred men. Flores arranged this division into five contingents: two infantry battalions, the Florida (commanded by Colonel Palleja) and the 24 de Abril (Colonel Regules); a light artillery regiment, consisting of two squadrons (under the orders of Majs. Bernard Dupuy and Juan B. Yance); and two volunteer corps, Bustamante's Voluntarios de la Libertad, and Fidelis Paes's Voluntarios Garibaldinos.[35] These men, sporting kepis with red bands intended "to evoke the glories of the Colorado Party," left Montevideo amid popular enthusiasm. At that time Colorados believed that the Paraguayan War would be the "three-month military stroll" the Montevideo newspapers predicted.

In July 1865 at Ayuí (Entre Ríos) Flores received Argentine and Brazilian reinforcements. Commanding the Argentine contingent were Gen. Wenceslao Paunero and Cols. Ignacio Rivas and José Miguel Arredondo, Flores's old Uruguayan comrades from his campaigns in Argentina. Here the Oriental Division experienced considerable desertion for the first time, and the first delivery of prisoners came from Uruguay to fill some of the unexpected vacancies. A few days later Flores received reports citing several cases of indiscipline and tumult in the Oriental Division as well as complaints from Entrerriano ranchers that his soldiers were stealing cattle.

Leading the allied forces, Flores defeated Major Duarte's column at Yataí in August 1865. He owed this victory to a large extent to the Uruguayan infantry, commanded by Colonel Palleja. But Palleja's audacious attacks also resulted in the first significant losses for the Oriental Division, 211 casualties.[36] This victory allowed Flores to cross the Uruguay River and join the siege of Estigarribia's larger column at Uruguaiana, which surrendered to the allies in September. There the general organized Paraguayan prisoners, now numbering some seventeen hundred men, into a special battalion. Flores put this infantry unit, designated the Battalion of Independent Volunteers under the command of Major Elías, with Uruguayan sergeants and corporals.[37]

Some Colorado newspapers in Montevideo, particularly *El Siglo*, severely criticized Flores's use of Paraguayan prisoners as soldiers. According to *El Siglo*, it was inhumane to force them to fight against their own brothers. The paper instead supported a solution that Uruguayan salting-factory owners promoted, namely that prisoners of war be sent to Uruguay to work at their *saladeros*. Paraguayans, they argued, might constitute a cheap labor force whose participation would help reduce salaries. Flores and his spokesmen in Montevideo—especially the paper *La Tribuna*—replied that Paraguayans had asked to be incorporated into the Oriental Division (though their high desertion rate immediately afterward would seem to contradict Flores's assertion).

Despite all this criticism the Oriental Division continued its march toward Paraguay accompanied by the new Paraguayan recruits. As the column made its way through Corrientes, the remaining gaucho soldiers deserted. At the same time, Flores learned that Uruguayan ranchers would no longer supply him with cattle and horses. To deal with the lack of livestock he sent Enrique Castro with a small contingent to traverse the province toward Misiones. The purpose of this expedition (which was formally launched to survey the territory) was to seize cattle and horses for the Oriental Division. It was quite successful: Castro returned in December with twenty-two thousand animals. The expedition also gained some military success, clashing with several Paraguayan units scattered across the province after Duarte's defeat and seizing some Paraguayan positions, such as San Carlos and Candelaria (in the disputed zone between Paraguay and Argentina).

At this time the Uruguayan government notified Flores that it was unable to pay his troops. Before Castro returned, the lack of food and pay led to further indiscipline, insubordination, and desertion. Many protests against the soldiers' horse stealing came from Correntino ranchers. Disturbances occurred even within the officer corps, and Flores had to discharge some of his outstanding officers, including Bustamante. General Costa, annoyed by this unruliness, resigned as chief of the general staff. When General Castro returned and found no money to pay his troops, he threatened Flores with abandoning the campaign and taking his entire contingent with him.

Ironically, at the time of this disturbance, the Oriental Division received rifled muskets to replace its old flintlock weapons. Firing squads had the privilege of using the new weapon for the first time against thieves and captured Paraguayan deserters. In December 1865 Colonel Palleja sent an angry letter to Montevideo questioning the government's indifferent attitude: "Is this not a national war?" he demanded.[38] The answer was no. It had been a full-fledged Colorado war until Uruguaiana; now it was an unnecessary adventure.

In January 1866 Flores unexpectedly returned to Uruguay. The Montevideo newspapers speculated that he had come to obtain better support for the campaign. In fact the caudillo's intention was to prevent a clash between Colorados. During his absence conservatives had regained their previous strength and were disputing positions of power with the Floristas. Flores returned to the field four months later just in time to witness the allied victory at Paso de la Patria, which opened the way into Paraguayan territory. In this engagement the Oriental Division suffered heavy bombardment and a great number of casualties. Its next encounter with the enemy was in May at Estero Bellaco, where casualties exceeded even those at Paso de la Patria. At the former, Palleja's Florida Battalion alone lost nineteen officers and one hundred soldiers.

These losses forced Flores to reorganize the division into fewer battalions. He amalgamated the Voluntarios de la Libertad, which had lost most of its personnel, with the Independents (mainly Paraguayans) and also dissolved Colonel Fidelis's battalion of Voluntarios Garibaldinos, which in any case had disbanded after the brave Brazilian colonel had fallen seriously wounded. Not long after, Major Yance, the artillery chief, was killed in action. The deaths of important officers and the evacuation of wounded officers back to Uruguay had destroyed Flores's formerly strong personal army. "These casualties are leaving us in the Paraguayan way," Palleja commented, "with only lieutenants and second lieutenants." But the division still had to face the two bloodiest battles of the war, Tuyutí and Boquerón. In the latter engagement, which went on for three days, Colonel Palleja was killed. In one of the last entries in his journal he notes that unless the Uruguayan government sent reinforcements, "the Oriental Division would be no more," and in another place he reflects sadly, "the government of Montevideo is letting us die."

It probably was the loss of his old comrades that finally spurred Flores's misgivings about the campaign. In a letter to his wife he blamed Mitre's generalship for the high casualties that the Oriental Division had experienced at Estero Bellaco. He criticized both the Argentine and the Brazilian commanders for wasting time in planning instead of attacking. "This is not for me," he wrote, "they do everything by mathematical calculations [and] drawing lines . . . ; they postpone all important actions."[39] During Mitre's meeting with Marshal López at Yataity Corá, a disgruntled Flores walked out, declaring that negotiations were a waste of time. When shortly afterward the allies launched their first attack on Curupayty, Flores refused to cooperate in the operation; a few days later he embarked for Uruguay with the Florida Battalion and his personal escort. Of the old Oriental Division only the very diminished 24 de Abril and Independents Battalions remained in Paraguay under Castro's orders, together with a small artillery unit.

6. Col. León de Palleja's body, 1866 (*Album de la Guerra del Paraguay* [Buenos Aires], 15 September 1893)

Back in Uruguay Flores found that the divide between the Colorado factions had deepened. The caudillo's departure for the battlefield in 1865 had created a power vacuum at the precise moment when his crusade had triumphed and political instability was at its peak. The old rivalry between conservative and traditionalist Colorados (the Floristas) had resurfaced immediately. In order to secure the predominance of his faction, Flores rigged elections in early 1867, ordering the police to arrest conservative voters and herd newly arrived Italian immigrants en masse to the polls. He also closed several conservative newspapers and encouraged his followers to ravage his opponents' printing houses.

The conservatives met violence with violence. In mid-1867 they tried to kill Flores with a bomb smuggled into the government house. The president ordered the arrest of his old comrade General Suárez, who had become the conservatives' caudillo. In February 1868, as a Blanco revolt erupted in Montevideo, a group of cloaked assassins stabbed Flores to death in the streets. Colorados of both affiliations accused the Blancos of the murder, but Flores's wife and sons, as well as the newspapers of Buenos Aires, pointed the finger at General Suárez and the conservatives.

Presidential elections followed in March. Suárez became the candidate of the conservatives, and Gen. Francisco Caraballo represented the Floristas. Caraballo, another landlord–warrior, had been Flores's second in command during the crusade and had remained in Uruguay throughout the Paraguayan campaign as commander in chief of the army.[40]

In the end Congress elected Gen. Lorenzo Batlle, Flores's minister of war, who seemed the perfect man to effect a reconciliation within the Colorado Party. But as a consequence of his takeover, the conservatives viewed him as a Florista, while Floristas considered him a conservative. Batlle had to face insurrections from both quarters while the National Guard declared itself "neutral" between the caudillos and the president. Simultaneously, mutinous army groups and no-less-mutinous departmental police forces devastated the countryside, sacking ranches and towns and killing numerous civilians. Batlle barely completed his term, and as he declared in 1869, his government "could do nothing but resist."[41]

Meanwhile the war in Paraguay had entered an impasse due to the devastating allied defeat at Curupayty. General Castro dedicated his time to disciplining and training his Paraguayan soldiers—for by that time the Oriental Division consisted almost exclusively of enemy nationals. In 1867 the cholera that infested the allied trenches caused still more deaths in the division and general demoralization. Only in August 1867 did the Brazilian fleet manage to suppress Paraguayan resistance at Curupayty. This left the allies ready to march toward the strongest Paraguayan bastion, Humaitá. In December new peace negotiations took place, but the Brazilian and Argentine chiefs left out Castro. In the August 1868 assault on Humaitá, the new Brazilian commander, the Marquis of Caxias, placed the Oriental Division at the vanguard to draw enemy artillery fire. Thereafter the unit became an auxiliary force of the Argentine army, with Gen. Juan Andrés Gelly y Obes employing it in reconnaissance.

By October 1868 all that remained of the Oriental Division was six hundred infantrymen and two hundred cavalrymen. Castro wrote to the new Uruguayan president and to Gen. José Gregorio Suárez (Batlle's war minister) that Caxias was the only chief with "a true army," while he and Gelly "amounted to nothing."[42] By that time hunger and lack of medicine, supplies, and money had become critical. In several letters to Montevideo, Castro reported that his troops were sick and starving, that he had become indebted to private businessmen to obtain horses and supplies, and that he was paying his troops with vouchers. On one occasion, finding that he could not pay for the transportation of the sick and wounded to Uruguay, the general complained that the Montevideo "government's excessive economies make its defenders suffer."[43] When the allies captured Angostura, the Oriental Division took four hundred prisoners, but Castro had to release them because he could not afford to feed more mouths. And another thirty Uruguayan soldiers fell at Angostura. "You can imagine how many true Orientals are left," Castro wrote Suárez.[44]

When the allies entered Asunción in early January 1869, they found the capital abandoned. Along with the Brazilians and Argentines, Castro's forces sacked and occupied the best houses in the city. "I think it better to keep my eyes shut," Castro wrote President Batlle.[45] But the general entered into some shady business himself. That same month he sent to Uruguay several Paraguayan boys and a church bell, destined to General Suárez. The war minister sold the children to Uruguayan ranchers and kept the bell as a souvenir. In February Castro wrote that he had captured "some more Paraguayan boys and girls" so that Suárez could "fulfill agreements with his partners."[46] He also let the Oriental Division plunder warehouses, from which it seized large quantities of cowhides, and sent these hides to Montevideo, expecting to make a significant profit. But the business became publicized, and the government had to embargo the hides. "It is a shame that the first time that we took valuable booty the newspapers had to notice it," Batlle wrote Castro.[47]

The Oriental Division, however, performed one final noteworthy operation in the Paraguayan War. Paradoxically, this was a result of its indiscipline. In April 1869 Maj. Hipólito Coronado had deserted to join a revolt in Corrientes. But the Argentine army apprehended the officer and returned him as a prisoner to General Castro. According to the military ordinances, the latter should have court-martialed Coronado and ordered his execution. But the major volunteered to perform an outstanding mission. If Castro should pardon him, he would seize the Paraguayan foundry and arms factory at Ybycuí. The general acceded but also ordered Coronado not to return alive if he failed. The major rapidly recruited a small contingent and marched toward Ybycuí, which he took in May, securing the foundry and disabling most of its machinery. Furthermore, on the way back, his command seized some of the only livestock left in that area of Paraguay and brought some relief to the hungry division (at the expense of local civilians). Coronado's venture also won the Oriental Division a general promotion from the Uruguayan government for all those ranked sergeant or higher.

Since December 1868 Castro had been requesting the withdrawal of the Oriental Division from Paraguay—"the order to return would never be too premature," he wrote Batlle—but from March 1869 onward he applied increasing pressure on the government.[48] In a letter to General Suárez, Castro stressed that he could "help the government decide to take back the Oriental Division." He offered to give up his Paraguayan soldiers to the Argentines, save for a few that he would take to his ranches. "In this way," he added, "the fictitious Oriental Division would dissolve by itself." Castro also threatened to resign if Montevideo delayed in recalling the division. In the same letter the general wrote that he no longer wished to act as an "errand boy" for the allied chiefs; moreover he threatened to allow his soldiers to run wild and sack as much as they could because they had not received their salaries.[49]

Brazil and Argentina continued to press Uruguay to keep its division in Paraguay, and the government hesitated to disappoint its allies. In November Castro threatened to disband the unit himself and flee to Entre Ríos if the administration failed to withdraw his men immediately.[50] Finally in December the Uruguayan Congress approved the withdrawal. The Oriental Division sailed from Angostura to Montevideo, arriving at the end of the month. There were only 150 Uruguayans—mostly officers—and some one hundred Paraguayans aboard the steamship that brought them back.[51]

### Consequences of the Campaign

The participation of the Oriental Division in the Paraguayan War brought no significant benefits for the Uruguayan military. The country's military scene had already changed with the triumph of Flores's crusade, and in a way that would prove long lasting. This Colorado victory made the Uruguayan army a unified force through the discharge of nearly all Blanco officers and soldiers and their replacement with Colorados.[52] The military thus attained its unity through politicization and within the traditions and ideology of a single political party. (Indeed, the army has remained fundamentally Colorado to the present day.) Military professionalization, which began with the militarist regime of 1876–86, left unaffected the Colorado nature of the armed forces.

The war caused no modifications in the social character of the Uruguayan army. The Oriental Division from the start was a small force of indistinct composition. Uruguayan gaucho soldiers deserted en masse, returning to the "savage" way of life they had always led. And by 1869 the body of the division consisted almost exclusively of Paraguayans. We have no information on their fate. Military service records do not indicate that they made careers in the Uruguayan army; more likely they managed to return to Paraguay or found employment in the civilian sector. Officers in turn were either Flores's landlord-warriors, who had initiated their military careers in the earlier civil wars, or individuals who had joined Flores's Liberating Crusade and won their stripes before the Paraguayan War. Only a few sergeants had gained promotion into the officer corps by the end of the campaign.

Although the Uruguayan political scene had changed radically before the war in consequence of Flores's crusade, the subsequent international conflict had little effect on the country's politics. In 1865 Flores inaugurated a provisional government that his opponents, his followers, foreign papers, and even he himself characterized as dictatorial.[53] The purpose of his authoritarianism was naturally to prevent a reemergence of the Blancos. Yet it was unrealistic to try to restrain the political rights of half of the citizenry. After the Paraguayan War ended, the Blancos launched a powerful counterrevolution (1870–72) that forced the Colorado government to give them exclusive control over a large portion of Uruguayan territory. Blanco revolts continued to erupt periodically until 1904, when the Colorado president José Batlle y Ordóñez ushered in a more modern political system that assured Blanco representation in Congress.

Flores's crusade also brought the country what has been called "the regionalization of caudillismo," in which political power was fragmented among numerous small centers, each one dominated by Colorado political chiefs who became small caudillos themselves. In this sense Montevideo became "the capital of a federation of regions."[54] Both Colorado factions, Floristas and conservatives, relied on these local bosses to contend for political power. The only discernible effect that the Paraguayan War had on Uruguayan political affairs was that it caused Flores's absence from the country when he was most needed to unite the Colorado Party. His absence in 1865–66 exacerbated the struggle between the Colorado factions.

Politics aside, the main consequence that intervention in Paraguay brought to Uruguay was in the economic sphere. The monthly subsidy that Brazil paid in exchange for the services of the Oriental Division during the war caused an artificial economic expansion from 1865 to 1868. The incoming gold allowed Montevideo entrepreneurs to establish new navigation, railroad, telegraph, and building companies as well as new steam factories, new banks, credit brokers, and even mining operations. The city's shipping companies, in particular, made significant profits as middlemen between Brazilian purveyors and the allied armies. Montevideo, meanwhile, experienced one of its beautification campaigns. Gas lighting and paving improved the streets, while streetcars brought better public transportation. The wealthy built palaces in the capital; statues came to glorify their heroes on streets and in plazas; and sea-bathing establishments enhanced the beaches. General Caraballo installed a hippodrome for the amusement of the rich and elegant. And the price of urban property concurrently shot up.

But the overabundance of money fostered inflation. Imports expanded, and with them the price of merchandise. Livestock consumption doubled in 1865–66 because of sales to the allied armies, and the price of cattle and land increased accordingly. This deceptive growth led entrepreneurs to experiment with cold storage for the first time, while meat-extract factories profited by selling their products to the army. In the meantime immigration, especially of Italians, grew exponentially, and ranchers sold farmlands to well-off newcomers at high prices. Other immigrants found reasonably paying jobs in the growing industries. The military in turn demanded better salaries and pensions, which caused the army budget to grow to 70 percent of the total state budget.

Overconfidence led banks to issue currency up to triple of their actual reserves; even credit societies issued currency. This soon made them unable to pay both creditors and depositors, who wanted hard cash. In response the government declared the inconvertibility of paper money in 1866 and again in 1867–68, while more than one caudillo involved in financial businesses, such as Francisco and Manuel Caraballo, José Gregorio Suárez, and Máximo Pérez, rose up in arms to defend either convertibility or inconvertibility.

In 1868, however, Brazilian remittances of gold tapered off. Simultaneously, a drought produced high mortality among livestock, and exports diminished. The cholera epidemic of 1867 caused many deaths among the population of Montevideo, and the consumer market shrunk. And in 1869 most banks and credit societies declared bankruptcy. In other words, as the Paraguayan War drew to a close, the artificial growth that it had fostered in Uruguay also ended.

On the whole the Uruguayan military played a minor role in the Paraguayan War, and its intervention brought no significant changes for the military as an institution. Nor did the conflict foster any enduring changes for the country generally. The ephemeral economic growth had passed by early 1869, well before President-Marshal López's death at Cerro Corá. From the Uruguayan perspective the war was a continuation of Flores's crusade against the Blancos and consequently a partisan conflict directed by and for the

Colorado Party. Furthermore, as the Colorados disowned responsibility for the campaign, the war seemed little more than Flores's personal enterprise. And yet the fighting destroyed what had been his personal army, and after the general was murdered in 1868, the campaign in Paraguay lost all its remaining legitimacy. In later years both Colorados and Blancos preferred to throw a cloak over both the crusade and the Paraguayan venture. Wool exports expanded, Montevideo continued to welcome thousands of immigrants, and eventually the broad prosperity of the few permitted a measure of social justice for the many. Meanwhile, by the end of the nineteenth century, most Uruguayans had forgotten the Paraguayan War.

# 8. Federalism and Opposition to the Paraguayan War in the Argentine Interior

La Rioja, 1865–67

The war against Paraguay encountered strong opposition in the Argentine interior, expressed in numerous ways, from the spread of rumors and the singing of protest songs to draft-dodging and large-scale rebellions. La Rioja, in the far west of the country, was one of the most conflicted provinces during these years. Opposition to the war was part of a larger, dual processes of party struggle and state formation. The conflict between Unitarians and Federalists had dominated Argentine politics since the 1820s but became particularly violent after 1861, when the armies of Gen. Bartolomé Mitre, the Unitarian governor of Buenos Aires, bested those of Justo José de Urquiza at the battle of Pavón. This defeat sealed the fate of the Federalist regime in Argentina. Once in control of the national government, the Unitarians initiated a military campaign in the interior to secure those provinces still under Federalist rule. This new phase in the consolidation of the central government met its strongest resistance in La Rioja, a Federalist redoubt since the 1820s. The Riojano caudillo, Gen. Angel Vicente Peñaloza (El Chacho), twice rose against Mitre's government, first in 1862 and again a year later. While Peñaloza's 1863 assassination did not bring the conflict to an end, the repression unleashed by Mitre's government devastated the province and its population.[1] But the process of state formation affected Riojanos in more insidious ways. New taxation and, after May 1865, impressment also became part of this experience. The Paraguayan War deeply divided Unitarians and Federalists and encouraged the latter to resist the process of state formation as defined by Mitre and Buenos Aires.

### Recruitment and Resistance

The Paraguayan War mainly touched the rural poor, the gauchos, through the recruitment of National Guard contingents for service at the front.[2] Recruiters encountered heavy opposition in the provinces, but this was hardly the first time that the gauchos of the interior had resisted conscription.

Even in peacetime, governments had little success in activating guard units for service.[3] But the conscription for the war with Paraguay, larger in scale than previous drives and politicized as never before, transformed the struggle over the draft into an unprecedented social and political conflict of national importance. From the Litoral to the Andes most provinces under some type of Federalist influence witnessed unrest and resistance. In 1865, mutinies broke out in Santa Fe, contingents of draftees melted away in Entre Ríos, and in Catamarca military authorities could hardly find men for the ranks. Even a province under the rule of loyal Unitarian leaders, such as Santiago del Estero, only reluctantly sent men to the front.[4]

Riojano resistance to recruitment then was hardly exceptional, though it did have some specific traits. Many of the civilian officials and military officers in charge of La Rioja's recruitment, such as Gov. Julio Campos, Col. Ricardo Vera, and Cmdr. José María Linares, were well-known Unitarians. Only a few years earlier all had fought and vanquished the province's Federalist rebels, a fact that undermined conscription's legitimacy.

Equally important, the first modern international war undertaken by the Argentine nation-state demanded numbers of men on an unprecedented scale. Sparsely populated provinces like La Rioja simply could not provide the levies demanded of them. According to instructions from the national government, La Rioja had to supply 1,100 guardsmen for the war effort. Even some Unitarian officers, comparing this number to the provincial population, considered it far too high. According to the 1869 census the province had 8,849 men of military age (sixteen to fifty) out of a total population of 48,746.[5] Such recruitment aggravated the difficulties that many rural families faced in 1865. Many men, whose work supported families, had died in the wars of 1862–63. The new levy thus represented a massive assault on the rural population's domestic economy, and not surprisingly the gauchos resorted to violence in defense of their subsistence.

Conscription rested fundamentally on violence. Military authorities detained gauchos, stripped them, handcuffed them or tied their hands behind their back, and marched them nude to distant assembly points in each province. The men again marched hundreds of miles westward to the city of Rosario, whence they were dispatched upriver to Paraguay. The recruits marched as prisoners, under the watchful eye of armed escorts instructed to shoot resistors. When drafted gauchos managed to escape, commanders issued orders to bring them back "dead or alive."[6] To the rural population wartime recruitment meant the continuation of the 1862–63 wars and the Unitarian repression.

Gauchos resisted in every way that they could. The most direct response was flight. So many men fled to the mountains that it depleted the workforce on Unitarian leaders' haciendas. In November 1865 the wife of a prominent Riojano Unitarian landowner complained: "I cannot find one single peón. Paschi has come by but I can't make him go out and work for anything; he says that you turned him over to the contingent . . . , and he's afraid that they'll call him up again, and nobody wants to hire himself to the house for fear that they'll get taken away."[7] Gauchos also banded together in small groups that wandered the countryside, resorting to robbery in order to survive.[8] In other cases those already inducted incited uprisings among the draftees; when the rebellions failed, the instigators paid with their lives.[9]

Federalist leaders, aware of the magnitude of the problem and of the fact that recruitment targeted their followers (and thus weakened their political base), made conscription part of their discourse. Their appropriation of this issue took several forms, including rumor mongering. Unitarians in San Luis complained that it was difficult to maintain order in that province because of "the infamous works of our enemies, who go to the extreme of inciting the riffraff of both sexes to tell the gauchos and soldiers that they will be soon called to fill the ranks of the army in Paraguay, that they should not comply, that [the Federalist caudillo] Juan Saá and others will be here [from his Chilean exile] within three months. These lies do their work in the countryside and even in the outskirts of the city."[10] These Federalist-inspired rumors framed the resistance within a traditional schema of protection and leadership between caudillos and their followers. But the Federalist articulation of the problem also took on a more modern guise in the form of electoral contests. In the province of Córdoba rural gauchos and the urban lower classes made up the bulk of the electorate and therefore played an important role in the 1866 gubernatorial contest. "In order to foster the candidacy of Luque," one Unitarian explained, "the Rusos [Federalists] led all their country folk and city friends to believe that he would send no one to the slaughterhouse of Paraguay, not one man."[11]

## The Rebellion of Aurelio Zalazar, 1865

La Rioja gauchos also opposed recruitment through participation in acts of collective violence, such as the rebellion led by Aurelio Zalazar in 1865. In late June of that year a few gauchos joined this obscure peon in attacking a train of draftees destined for the Paraguayan front. They liberated the men and formed a *montonera* of some five hundred gauchos. In the lexicon of the day, *montoneros* were men who formed an armed band, or *montonera*, in rebellion against authorities.[12] Zalazar's *montoneros* proclaimed themselves supporters of the Federalist Party and vowed to topple the provincial government. In mid-July, however, national troops defeated the *montonera* on the outskirts of the city of La Rioja, and Zalazar retreated to the Llanos, where he held out until captured in November.

This rebellion marked the beginning of Zalazar's meteoric career in the Federalist ranks. Two years later, during the rebellion of Felipe Varela, he attained the rank of colonel. None of this, however, saved him from capture and execution in 1869. Zalazar's case was hardly exceptional. According to one Riojano Unitarian, this phenomenon had a simple explanation: "In the Argentine provinces one needs neither riches nor talent and education, nor other antecedents save the valor and audacity of the children of the country-side, to move and take control of the destinies of the country. [Many] have begun more or less like Zalazar, apprenticing themselves in the rebellions that they have led with more or less success, but always with audacity and daring."[13] Reporting on Zalazar's rebellion, Lt. Col. Julio Campos, the Unitarian governor of La Rioja and the senior officer responsible for recruitment in the province, noted: "The authors of so scandalous a revolution believed that the disgust which naturally arises among the masses in response to the drafting of military forces would better position them in the opinion of the gauchos, whom they hoped to ensnare by convincing them that this government would offer them up without exception to the Porteños. This circumstance, together with the name of General Urquiza, which they exploited, and the death of el Chacho, for which they claimed revenge, and above all the discontent produced by the contingents on march, gave voice to the revolution."[14] According to Campos, the rebellion intended to depose him and install as provincial governor Manuel Vicente Bustos, a Federalist with a favorable reputation among national officials, whose administration the Mitre government might have eventually tolerated.[15]

In the governor's assessment the rebels had had diverse motives (which he called the "Gauchos' opinion") for launching the revolt. Denunciations of the draft had become an integral part of Federalist discourse, and this was one of the issues upon which *montonera* leaders drew to mobilize their supporters. It is instructive to see how the gauchos articulated this issue. Gen. Wenceslao Paunero reported, "the idea of going to Paraguay is a specter that has these people terrified."[16] This captured the experience of the lower classes, who themselves preferred to use religious language to express their concerns. A couplet sung in praise of Zalazar's rebellion ran:

De dónde salió Zalazar,
Como angelito 'e [*sic*] los cielos
A quitar el contingente
Que traen para los infiernos.

From where Zalazar arose
Like an angel from the heavens
To free the contingent
Being carried off to hell.[17]

A Llanisto who witnessed the enrollment of the contingent by Cmdr. Ricardo Vera (who tortured and killed one of the draftees) later said that "at that time the heresy was big."[18] Such language provided not only a readily comprehensible analysis but in the process also made it legitimate to tether religious imagery to party identification.

*Montonera* leaders also mobilized gauchos by appealing to their perceptions of the national government, which had ordered Paraguayan War conscription, as a *porteño*, Unitarian regime. They regarded the Campos administration in La Rioja as a *porteño* occupation, and given gauchos' experience with the Unitarians in 1862 and 1863, conscription was inherently illegitimate.

According to Governor Campos, the rebels also sought revenge for the death of El Chacho. Pascual Jara, a peon from the Llanos, reported that in the *montonera* "everybody cheered General Peñaloza and Colonel [Felipe] Varela, crying 'death to the government' and especially to Commander [Ricardo] Vera."[19] The memory of the dead caudillo thus entered the Federalist discourse, while one of his lieutenants (at the time in exile in Chile) gained recognition as a leader. Yet the threats against Commander Vera amounted to more than occasional verbal volleys. Vera had captured el Chacho in November 1863 and turned him over to Cmdr. Pablo Irrazábal, who murdered the caudillo. Gauchos identified Vera as one of the Unitarians responsible for Peñaloza's death and made him the target of their bloodiest persecutions.[20] Equally significant (as we have seen), Vera had been one of the commanders in charge of collecting draftees for the Paraguayan campaign.[21]

In his explanation Campos also alluded to the use of General Urquiza's name in mobilizing the gauchos. The invocation of Urquiza was common in the Federalist rebellions in the interior in the 1860s, when the name of the Entrerriano caudillo served to legitimate uprisings. Thus rebel leaders knew that Riojano gauchos acknowledged their membership in a political community of Federalists that reached beyond loyalty to regional caudillos and the rebellions they led. Agustín Barrionuevo, a gaucho from the Llanos, reported that a peon from one of Zalazar's *montoneras* claimed that "the plan [for the rebellion] had come from Entre Ríos, and thus had been ordered by General Urquiza."[22] Juan Carrizo, a cattle rancher from the province of San Juan who had joined the rebellion, declared that Zalazar had told him that "he had orders from General Urquiza to proclaim allegiance to the Federal party and incite an uprising in Los Llanos." Upon hearing this Carrizo "took Zalazar aside and insisted that Zalazar show him the order that he had from Urquiza, to which Zalazar replied that there was no need to show it to Carrizo, that the order was among his papers, and although Carrizo repeated his request to see the order, Zalazar refused to do it."[23] Carrizo's desire to see the written order reveals his conception of the *montonera's* and party's hierarchical structure, according to which the final authority was not Zalazar, but General Urquiza as former head of the confederation. The incident also suggests that a regional leader's manipulation ("exploitation," according to Governor Campos) of the general's name might have its limits. Yet its appearance in Zalazar's rebellion indicates that both the *montonera's* leaders and their gaucho followers tied their actions to a political affiliation that was national in scope.

Finally, according to Campos, Zalazar intended to overthrow his Unitarian provincial government and install in his place Manuel Vicente Bustos. In a province with no more than fifty thousand inhabitants and a minimal state apparatus, political power and authority turned in immediate, personal directions, which made the governor the target of gaucho resentment. Little wonder then that they joined an attempt to oust him from power.

As Campos's statement suggests, gauchos' motives for rebelling had been diverse, an opinion echoed by others. In 1865 Abel Bazán, the senator for La Rioja, also stressed the complexity of the state-formation process and the multiple levels on which the inhabitants of the province lived through it. During El Chacho's uprisings, argued the senator, the war had devastated the Riojano countryside, and "the ground soaked in blood" by "the barbarous executions" carried out by the national troops. Small wonder then that Colonel Campos became the target of the gauchos' "indignation and hatred." In addition Campos's tax collection, which ignored "the Riojanos' poverty" and the fact that "they were not accustomed to paying [taxes] in earlier times," also met with discontent. The governor had imposed a new

sales tax and, more importantly, had tried to enforce the collection of existing taxes. Finally, Bazán said, Riojanos also "saw their companions, friends,
fathers, and brothers, snatched from their homes and sent naked, bound,
and without pay to serve in a war, the importance and necessity of which
was obscure to them. Thus we easily come upon . . . the clear and simple
explanation for that spontaneous commotion that took place in Los Llanos
to liberate the contingents, and for that inclination, later demonstrated, to
overthrow the governor of the province, who was seen as the author of all
these misfortunes."[24] Zalazar's rebellion symbolized the gauchos' resistance
to the changes that the state attempted to impose on the countryside. Not
only recruitment but also repression and taxation were "the misfortunes" that
laid the bases for the rebels' collective violence in 1865 against the national
government and its misbegotten Paraguayan adventure.

## The Rebellion of Felipe Varela, 1866–67

In late 1866 a new and more serious Federalist rebellion shook the Andean
interior of Argentina. Its main leader was Felipe Varela (1819–70), born and
raised in a Federalist family in Catamarca. Like the Riojano caudillo Peñaloza,
he joined the Unitarians against Rosas in 1840, went into exile in Chile, and
returned to Argentina a few years later. He established himself as a grain and
cattle trader in Guandacol in western La Rioja. In the 1850s Varela joined
Urquiza's confederation army and was stationed in the provinces of Córdoba
and Entre Ríos. He fought under Urquiza at Pavón in 1861, and during
Peñaloza's first revolt against Mitre's government in 1862, he became one of
the rebel leader's closest confidants and La Rioja's police chief. In 1863 Varela
again accompanied Peñaloza in rebellion and later fled into exile in Chile.

In November 1866 Varela, together with Juan Saá and Juan de Dios Videla,
caudillos from San Luis and San Juan respectively and also in Chilean exile,
launched a rebellion that initially enjoyed the Chilean government's toler-
ation. The expedition entered Argentina by way of Jachal, in the province
of San Juan. According to the original plans, Saá and Videla were to take
the province of Cuyo, while Varela would secure La Rioja and Catamarca
to gain control of the rest of the north. With luck they might then march
toward the coastal provinces to oust Mitre and the national government. As
with Peñaloza in 1862 and 1863, Varela and his allies tried but failed to gain
Urquiza's support.

The Federalists of Mendoza also rebelled in November, joining what was called the Revolution of the Colorados (from the red color of the Federalist Party). In short order they controlled the province, which briefly facilitated Saá and Videla's campaign in Cuyo. But on 1 April 1867 national troops defeated the two caudillos at the battle of San Ignacio (San Luis) and forced them to retreat in disorder toward Chile. Meanwhile by early March Varela had managed to recruit more than three thousand men in one of the largest mobilizations ever seen in the interior. Nine days later, however, Manuel Taboada, a Unitarian from Santiago del Estero, decisively defeated Varela at the battle of Pozo de Vargas (outside the city of La Rioja). Federalist resistance continued in the rural departments, and in May Varela's underlings returned to seize the city, only to be expelled two months later. Without a firm base in La Rioja, Varela had to retreat northward in an attempt to reach safety in Bolivia. During this retreat, which lasted three months, he captured the city of Salta, with the sole purpose of supplying his troops. Finally defeated after a year of campaigning, Varela arrived at the Bolivian border in November 1867. Still in that country a year later, he organized a new rebellion that failed even to reach Argentine territory. Finding himself again in Chilean exile, Varela died in 1870.

Varela justified and explained his uprising in a printed proclamation distributed during his campaign and in a manifesto published in Bolivia after his defeat. These documents identified his struggle as being equally against Buenos Aires, the Unitarian Party, and the Paraguayan War. Varela called on Argentines to defend the "Democratic, Republican, and Federal" Constitution of 1853, which had guided the government of the confederation until Pavón. Varela also denounced the "odious centralism" of Buenos Aires, whose government had, among other things, monopolized the port's customs receipts, leaving the provincial governments impoverished. As part of this struggle, Varela denounced "the war that Mitre has carried out [against] Paraguay, in order to weaken [the provinces and the Federalists], to disarm us, to ruin us." Instead Varela demanded "peace and friendship with Paraguay."[25]

The rebel's identification with Paraguay formed part of Federalist political traditions. Unitarians from the interior had feared association between Paraguay and Federalism as early as May 1865. When Argentina joined the Triple Alliance, Unitarians doubted the Federalists' loyalty to Mitre's government and worried that they might ally with the enemy.[26] Francisco Solano López in fact counted on winning such allies in Argentina.[27] In La Rioja the identification of Federalism with Paraguay went so deep that, even before

Argentina joined the war, wags dubbed the Federalist Party the "Paraguayan Club."[28]

How many of these ideas formed part of popular political culture and the extent to which the lower classes of the interior perceived Paraguay as a traditional political ally of Federalism is difficult to assess. It is possible, of course, that Federalist leaders spread this idea among their followers. According to Paunero, when Chacho prepared to avenge Urquiza's later 1861 defeat at Pavón, he believed that the caudillo had "20,000 Paraguayans and many thousands of Orientales [Uruguayans] ready to march on Buenos Aires."[29] And (as we have seen) in the proclamations widely distributed in some areas of the interior during the rebellion, Varela publicly proposed "peace and friendship with Paraguay." The rank and file among his followers felt the same, at least judging by the testimony of one of his Chilean followers, the miner Toribio Urrutia.[30]

Resistance against conscription reappeared in Varela's rebellion as part of a broader Federalist popular discourse that effectively reached gauchos and persisted for decades in collective memory. Thus one of the stanzas of a song composed during the rebellion (but only collected in 1921) notes:

Esta patria que ha reinado
No nos era conveniente,
Al que más bien se ha portado
Lo han marchado al contingente.
Nada vale ser prudente
Ni amistoso en la ocasión,
Al pobre con más razón,
Porque ni razones tiene.
Hoy Varela nos conviene
Por ser un jefe de honor.

This reigning patria
Does us no good
He who has done no wrong
Is ferried off to the contingent.
Nothing is gained by prudence
Or cordiality on this occasion,
Above all for the poor,
Who have no rights at all.
Now Varela is good for us
Because he is a man of honor.[31]

The song denounced the Unitarian government (the "reigning patria") for denying gauchos a voice and reserving for them the obligation of going to war (being "ferried off to the contingent") in Paraguay.

Conscription was also at the heart of the violent revenge exacted by the gauchos who joined the *montonera*. During the rebellion several gauchos from the departments of Vinchina and Guandacol captured Camilo Castellanos, a well-connected hacienda owner from Vinchina, who together with the Unitarian commander Linares had recruited gauchos in 1865.[32] Castellanos's role also left its mark in collective memory. In 1921 an old foreman recalled that, while he and his twelve peons were driving oxen in 1865, Castellanos took them by surprise, made them "prisoners," and forcibly inducted them into the army. Some of the draftees later rebelled but were quickly put down by Castellanos and other recruiters. The next day, according to this old gaucho, Castellanos executed the two ringleaders.[33]

When Castellanos himself fell into the rebels' hands, he was tried by a drumhead court-martial (a normal practice in these rebellions) and sentenced to death. As he was led on horseback to his execution, Castellanos tried to escape, but an illiterate peasant (*labrador*) toppled him from his mount with a blow from his sword, shouting, "this is how the contingent is drafted!" Another rebel, a native of the nearby village of Jaguel, slit the *hacendado*'s throat. The man later bragged of having "killed a savage [Unitarian]." Agustín Molina, another peasant from Guandacol who witnessed the killing, later declared that "the [rebels] fought for the Federalist Party" and offered this explanation: "The reason that they had to assassinate him was that they believed, according to what he had heard [from one of his confederates], that Castellanos was a spy for Lieutenant-Colonel Linares, since he was an officer of the troops of said Colonel, and the man from Jaguel who killed him did so because it was Castellanos who had conscripted the contingent for the army in Paraguay."[34] Opposition to forced recruitment ran deep in the interior, and when they could gauchos fought back against those who sought to impress them, but Varela sought to channel this discontent into a larger political project.

## Republican Unity and the International Dimensions of Varela's Revolt

Felipe Varela's opposition to the war had other, broader dimensions that linked his rebellion to a defense of continental republican traditions. The Spanish American republics faced assaults from European monarchies throughout the

1860s. The French invasion of Mexico, followed by Paris's sponsorship of Emperor Maximilian (1862–67); the Spanish reoccupation of Santo Domingo; and the war of Spain against Peru over the guano-rich Chincha Islands, which Chile and eventually Bolivia and Ecuador joined as Peru's allies (1864–66), aroused concern among Spanish American leaders about the weakness of republicanism on the continent as threatened by this dangerous new wave of colonial projects.[35] They saw the war between Paraguay and Brazil in the same light. Brazil, the only surviving monarchy on the continent and the only independent state that still sanctioned slavery, seemed equally reactionary.[36]

With this perceived monarchical offensive against Spanish American republics in mind, the nations along the Pacific Ocean asked Argentina to enter an alliance against Spain in 1865. Mitre's government, however, was already engaged against Paraguay and rejected participation in this new conflict, declaring itself neutral. Moreover Mitre had already negotiated an important treaty of friendship and commerce with Spain in 1863, which was ratified in 1864.[37] The Argentine government even allowed the Spanish navy to purchase supplies in Buenos Aires before sailing on to raid the Pacific coast. Chile in particular saw Argentina's neutrality as thinly veiled support for Spain; Chilean liberals viewed the alliance of the Argentine government with Brazil as an ominous sign.[38]

Concerns over Mitre's international policies caused Chile to tolerate, if not actually encourage, the campaigns of Varela, Saá, and Videla. The rebel forces in fact included not only exiled Argentine Federalists but also privately recruited miners from Copiapó who went by the name of the Chilean Vanguard.[39]

While in exile, Varela contacted an international republican association, the Unión Americana (American Union), that had offices in Chile (including one in Copiapó), Bolivia, and Argentina as well as in other countries. The association sought to influence public opinion and the policies of the Spanish American governments to fight against any threat to republicanism. Although it is not clear whether he became a member, Varela adhered publicly to the organization's principles. He called for "the alliance of the [American] Republics to repel the monarchical ambitions of Europe," particularly those of Spain. He invoked the wars of independence, styling himself "a soldier of liberty," and accused Mitre of having committed "a crime of treason against American unity [*lesa Unión Americana*]" by refusing to join the struggle against Spain in the Pacific. Instead the Argentine leader had embroiled himself in a war with Paraguay, which went "against the holy principles of the American Union, whose fundamental basis is the preservation of each Republic's sovereignty."That Argentina signed an alliance with Brazil, a slavocrat monarchy, aggravated the crime. Not coincidentally,Varela referred to Mitre and his followers as *"negreros"* (slave dealers) and recalled the exploits of Gen. Carlos María de Alvear, the national hero who had led Argentine forces during the Cisplatine War against Brazil (1826–28).[40]

The rebels' anti-Brazilian discourse met with some success. A Riojano Unitarian remembered that Varela and his rebels "exploited . . . among those rustic peoples the idea of freedom from slavery to which they [the gauchos] would be subjected by the authorities, disseminating the idea that the men were taken [by the recruiters] to be sold, and many other lies and tricks like this. . . . Thus the riff-raff joined [Varela]."[41]

Varela's republican and antimonarchical discourse seems to have worked more effectively against the Spanish presence in the Pacific. Analysis of this aspect of the rebellion allows a more complete understanding of the origins and extent of the popular republicanism that sustained the Federalist opposition to Mitre's international engagements, including his involvement in Paraguay. According to one historian, Chilean mineworkers enlisted in the rebel army because they had been led to believe that "Argentina had made a pact with Spain, which was to attack Chile through Argentine territory; [Spanish troops] had already disembarked in Buenos Aires and [the Chileans] had come to block them and liberate the Argentines just as the Argentines had liberated Chileans before."[42] Like Varela's manifesto, these rumors and manipulations appealed to the still-vibrant revolutionary and anti-Spanish tradition. A Federalist and Urquiza operative in the interior also observed that the Chilean government considered the Argentines *"Anti-Americans"* because of our good relations with Spain" and added, "the worst of all is that their conduct is applauded and that the [Argentine] masses sing to Chile, calling her the Liberator, and follow her men and her flag, fully conscious of what they are doing."[43]

Varela used this same anti-Spanish sentiment to propose an alliance with Chile. The last stanza of the rebel song transcribed in 1921 also calls for such a pact:

La pretensión de un Varela
Que ha venido hoy en el día
A borrar esta anarquía
Levantando su bandera.
Unirla con la chilena
Esa era su pretensión,

Para la constitución
Dos repúblicas hermanas,
De donde bien nos dimana.
*¡Viva la Federación!*

The ambition of one Varela
Who comes before us today
Is to wipe out this anarchy
Raising his banner high.
To unite with the Chilean flag
That was his ambition,
For the constitution of
Two sister republics,
Source of all our hope.
*Long live the Federation!*[44]

Such an alliance between Argentina and Chile would benefit both nations, an idea echoed in the printed proclamations that had been "distributed with profusion" in western Rioja.[45] Varela's proclamation proposed "union with the other American republics" (not excluding Paraguay). Toribio Urrutia, the Chilean miner, knew what he was fighting for and told his interrogators that he envisioned "a fraternal alliance" between the two countries.[46] Thus the anti-Spanish and pro-Chilean discourse suggests the depth of the republicanism that fed the Federalist opposition to Mitre's international commitments, including the war against Paraguay in alliance with the Brazilian Empire.

The Paraguayan War elicited strong opposition from the Federalists of the Argentine interior, particularly those in La Rioja. This resistance should be seen as part of the larger processes of party struggle and state and nation formation that affected the gauchos in several ways. Federalists reacted against the draft that specifically targeted their followers and undermined their political base, but rebels also rose against the Unitarian repression unleashed against the Federalists of previous years and against new taxation. Insurgents also opposed Mitre's international policies more generally because they seemed to threaten republicanism in Spanish America.

Opposition to the war did have other broader, long-term consequences as part of the resistance to state formation. Contrary to what has often been argued, the evidence presented here shows that the formation of the state generated resistance among the lower classes, especially in the interior provinces where the majority was still affiliated with Federalism. This in turn helps explain why the Federal constitution survived despite the strong process of political centralization that took place between 1862 and 1880.[47]

The study of Federalist popular resistance to the war also allows for a dialogue with recent Latin American historiography that has focused on politics from the bottom up, particularly on *caudillismo* and the participation of peasants in the larger historical processes of state and nation formation. Ties between leaders and followers reflected not just patron-client relationships but also meaningful political demands on the part of the followers.[48] The exploration of these issues underscores the capacity of the largely illiterate lower classes to understand both national and international political developments, thus giving them agency and bringing them back into the historical process.[49] Finally, these questions call once again for the consideration of international processes as fundamental forces in the development of nationalism among the illiterate rural lower classes—a consideration that applies just as aptly, and just as tragically, to the doomed soldiers of López's Paraguay or the Brazilian recruits sent to fight thousands of miles from home.[50]

# 9. Images of War

## Photographers and Sketch Artists of the Triple Alliance Conflict

The Triple Alliance, or Paraguayan, War pitted the armies of Paraguay, led by Francisco Solano López, against the combined forces of Argentina, Brazil, and Uruguay in the longest and bloodiest military confrontation in South American history. It was in many ways a modern war, for the combatants tested new weapons and military innovations imported from abroad. It also saw the introduction to wartime use of a rather recent invention: the camera. This was the first South American conflict to be recorded by photographers, but they have rarely been given their due in the historiography of the war. Photographers not only produced dramatic and sometimes even shocking images of combat's aftermath but also created works (along with sketch artists) that formed the basis for many of the lithographs that appeared in the illustrated press of Buenos Aires, Rio de Janeiro, and European capitals.[1] Furthermore, their photographs were key sources for the historical paintings depicting battles and other aspects of the conflict that proliferated in the last decades of the nineteenth century.

Photography advanced unevenly in South America during the 1850s and 1860s, from the early use of the daguerreotype to the rapid expansion of photography after the introduction of the wet-collodion process that made possible the popular *cartes de visite*, or calling cards. But the war provided numerous new opportunities for photographers, and an enterprising team from the Montevideo gallery of Bate & Co. set out to photograph the allied armies in 1866, hoping to sell the images to a Platine public hungry for news from the front. Sketch artists too were present at the front by this time, as were painters. These men's works were widely reproduced (though often uncredited) in illustrated newspapers. Tracing the connections among these different art forms reveals the processes by which these "soldiers in the service of memory" shaped the images of the war held by contemporaries and by modern historians.

### Secure the Shadow: Photography in the 1850s and 1860s

Although twenty years had elapsed since the introduction of the daguerreo-type to South America, photography was still an uncertain enterprise in the region during the 1860s. A French clergyman, Louis Compte, gave the first demonstrations of the daguerreotype in Buenos Aires, just five months after the process was presented to the Academy of Science in Paris in 1839.[2] Compte's exposition was little more than a scientific curiosity, though it earned him great publicity in the newspapers of that time. Instead the definitive introduction of Daguerre's invention to the continent fell to a handful of itinerant North American and French daguerreotypists who came to Latin America in search of new markets. They traveled from town to town, setting up temporary galleries and advertising their services in local newspapers.

At the height of the daguerreotype period in the 1850s, photography was an expensive and solemn ritual usually restricted to the studio. Formal studio portraits made up more than 95 percent of the images produced during that time and were thus the photographer's main source of income. Outdoor views were exceedingly rare, and most of those were static views of streets or unpeopled landscapes. The daguerreotype process had its disadvantages: it was costly, and each picture constituted a unique, nonreproducible image. Only members of the bourgeoisie could afford it. Politicians, merchants, military officers, members of the clergy, and rich ranchers and their families composed the photographers' clientele, but few others found their way into the studios.

During this era technological limitations made it impossible to capture action. Few photographers ventured to record current events or newsworthy scenes. The daguerreotypes of the U.S.–Mexico War (1846–48) or the siege of Rome (1849), however, are pioneering examples of documentary photography. These and other instances proved photography's utility as a documentary tool, and the public came to view the camera as a faithful witness.

Frederick S. Archer developed the wet-collodion process in 1851, thereby overcoming the limitations of earlier photographic methods.[3] It was a positive-negative process that permitted the multiple duplication of photographs, printed on salt- or albumen-treated paper. Despite the complex manipulations involved, the collodion negative could record fine detail and subtle tones, and it was much more light sensitive, making it possible to record events as they occurred. In 1855 Roger Fenton and James Robertson showed the world the potential uses of this photographic technology with their scenes from the Crimean War (1855–56). Subsequently Mathew Brady and his assistants, notably Alexander Gardner, made a comprehensive photographic record of the U.S. Civil War (1861–65) and the personalities involved in it. Brady and Gardner produced a remarkably complete visual record of that conflict for future generations, and their work had a great influence in the development of documentary photography and photojournalism.

During the Paraguayan War the Uruguayan firm of George Thomas Bate pioneered photojournalism in the Plata. Bate, an Irishman, and his brother arrived in Buenos Aires in 1859 from the United States. At that time the profession still offered only a limited chance for profit. Most photographers were itinerants, and Bate was no exception. During 1859 and 1860 he traveled several times between Buenos Aires and Montevideo, advertising his services in the newspapers of both cities. In 1861 he finally settled in the latter city, announcing the opening of his gallery in impressive terms: "The new photographic studio of Bate & Co. is being opened to the public today at its new and comfortable premises located at 369, 25 de Mayo St., Mariani's upper floor. Portraits from one *patacón* will always be available."[4] The Bate brothers announced themselves as "American portrait artists well-known in Buenos Aires." The reverse of their business cards bore an elaborate design of a female figure holding a shield with the Stars and Stripes pattern and their logo emblazoned with the inscription "American photographers."[5] In 1862 Belgian chemist Juan Vander Weyde joined the Bates as a partner.

At this time portraits were photographers' bread and butter. As French historian Giselle Freund points out, the invention of photography proved a decisive stage in the democratization of art. Portrait painting was the first branch of art directly affected by the invention of the daguerreotype.[6] But given the cost of daguerreotypes and the fact that they produced only a single image, their use for portraits was limited. The wet-collodion process, which dealt a death blow to the daguerreotype, made possible the proliferation of portraits through the *carte de visite*. This calling-card-sized photograph was made with a multilens camera that could take several images on a single negative. The albumen prints made from this negative were mounted on 4-by-2.5-inch cards that usually bore the photographer's name and address. Adolphe Disderi patented this new format in Paris in 1854, and French photographer Federico Artigue introduced it in Buenos Aires two years later. The *carte de visite* promoted the social diffusion of portraits, and with its introduction photography in South America became both a business and a profession. These images were cheaper by far than daguerreotypes, and almost every family of means soon owned an album filled not only with their own pictures but also those of relatives and friends. The popularity of *cartes de visite* reached its climax during the war years.

By providing a steady source of income for photographers, *cartes de visite* also stimulated a significant expansion in the number of studios throughout the region. Rio de Janeiro, then the largest city in South America with a population of some 250,000 people, site of the imperial court, and Brazil's

7. George Thomas Bate (Vandyke, *carte de visite*, circa 1865, Collection of Miguel and Mirta Cuarterolo)

most cosmopolitan and sophisticated center, had three photographic studios in 1847. Ten years later that figure had jumped to eleven, and by 1864 it had reached thirty, according to the city's almanac. Photographic galleries could also be found in all of the empire's major cities as well as in smaller centers such as São Paulo and Porto Alegre.[7]

Likewise the rapidly growing capital of Argentina, Buenos Aires, whose population doubled to 186,000 between 1855 and 1869 (mostly due to European immigration), boasted numerous photographic studios, twenty-four in 1866, the most popular being those of Bartolomé Loudet, Luigi Bartoli, Meeks & Kelsey, Emilio Lahore, Juan Portal, and Federico Artigue. There were also permanent studios in Rosario and even in Corrientes, where Frenchman Pierre Bernardet settled in 1862; his brother opened a branch of the business in Asunción.[8] Itinerant photographers were also very common, as was the case with Emilio Bertin, who traveled among the troops, selling portraits to the soldiers. From January to May 1866 Bertin ran a studio in Rosario.[9] Montevideo too had several photographic galleries in addition to the one founded by the Bate brothers in 1861. As in Rio de Janeiro and Buenos Aires, most were run by foreigners, such as the Frenchmen Desiderio Jouant, Alfred Vigoroux, and Anselm Freurquin; the Italian Juan Varonne; the Swiss Enrique Schikendantz; and the Irish Bate brothers. The presence of foreign photographers was so common that Martinez & Bidart, owners of the La Paz gallery, felt obliged to point out that they were the "only Oriental [Uruguayan] photographers!"[10]

Even Paraguay, despite its relative isolation, had been exposed to photography. Soon after the introduction of the daguerreotype to South America, several itinerant photographers, such as the Italian Aristides Stephani and the Americans Walter Bradley and Charles de Forest Fredricks, surprised the local elites with the marvelous invention. When the war broke out, the most active galleries in Asunción were those of the French-born Bernardet brothers and the Italian Agostino Forni; the Brazilian government later contracted both firms to document the city's occupation.[11]

Soldiers on both sides showed great interest in photographers. During the first months of the fighting, studios did brisk business as officers (and even some enlisted men) rushed to the galleries in their new uniforms to pose for photographs to send home to loved ones. In April 1865 a Buenos Aires gallery advertised "Portraits at 50 pesos a dozen for our soldiers going to war."[12] To exchange likenesses with relatives and friends became fashionable. In August Argentine physician Benjamín Canard detailed how he had given away six photographs: "One for home, another for a girl of this town, the rest were practically grabbed by my colleagues. As I was intending not to give them away, I had ordered only half a dozen. Since my wish is to please you, I promise to have more pictures taken as soon as we get to Corrientes or to any other town where there is a photographer."[13] In another letter Capt. Domingo "Dominguito" Fidel Sarmiento, son of the future president of Argentina, asked his mother to send him "any pictures of girls and friends that you can get."[14]

During the war the galleries made large profits selling photographs of politicians and military officers. In Rosario George Alfeld produced a *carte de visite* with the portraits of all the officers of that city's First Battalion. A year later Emilio Bertin published a series of photographs of both allied and Paraguayan officers, including Bartolomé Mitre, Leandro Gómez, Antonio Estigarribia, and Vicente Barrios, which he sold for four reales each.[15] These pictures were frequently reproduced by other photographers who had little regard for copyright considerations and were marketed to take advantage of the news coming from the front. On the very day that Paraguayan forces under Estigarribia surrendered at Uruguaiana, *El Siglo* advertised "*cartes de visite* of the Paraguayan officer on sale only at Lastiria and Maricot's bookstore, Bousquet's store, and Bate's gallery."[16]

## Wartime Opportunities: Photographers at the Front

Photographing newly outfitted officers and selling portraits of local patriots or enemy commanders, however, was no different from the work that the studios had been doing for years. Taking pictures of battles and soldiers at the front was another matter entirely, and in this area George Bate and his company played the leading role. In early 1864 he had traveled to New York City, where he visited the famous galleries of photographers Jeremy Gurney and Abraham Bogardus. There he saw for himself how lucrative war photography could be; he almost certainly saw the work of Mathew Brady and his team and became well aware of its commercial possibilities. Moreover he must have seen the many engravings based on these photographs and published in the press to illustrate war correspondents' articles.

Likely influenced by Brady's coverage of the U.S. Civil War, Bate decided to risk sending a team of photographers, probably led by Esteban García, to record the aftermath of the siege of Paysandú, in which Colorado forces led by Gen. Venancio Flores and supported by the Brazilian navy invested and then overwhelmed the Blanco defenders of this little port along the Uruguay River.[17] On 2 January 1865, after twenty-eight days of siege, the devastated town fell to Flores and his Brazilian allies. During the next few days French photographer Emilio Lahore and the Uruguayan staff of Bate & Co. took the first images of the destruction. Bate's photographers arrived on 9 January and captured staggering views of the aftermath of battle. From the negatives taken by his men, Bate published a series of ten views that later sold in Montevideo for one real each. Lahore, who ran photographic galleries in both Buenos Aires and Montevideo, arrived at Paysandú one day after the Colorados had taken the city. He was evidently the first photographer to reach the scene of battle, for none of the chroniclers of its defense mention the presence of any photographer during the siege. Lahore made at least fifteen striking images, including the haunting photograph of a corpse in the town's square, ignored by the men standing around a cannon.[18]

Five months after the fall of that city, Argentina, Brazil, and Uruguay formally entered into an alliance against López's Paraguay. By that time George Bate had already sold his share of the company to his partner, Juan Vander Weyde, and had returned to England by way of the United States. In July Vander Weyde announced that although Bate had departed, he would continue running the studio under the same trade name, Bate & Co., to which he added a "W." But his operations did not include returning to the battlefields, and for the rest of 1865 no photographers traversed the theater of conflict. In November 1865 Uruguayan colonel León de Palleja wondered why none of the many photographers in Buenos Aires and Montevideo had followed the allied armies into the field.[19] Dionísio Cerqueira, then a junior officer in the Brazilian forces, later recalled that not a single camera was present in the allied camps to record the scenes that he felt unable to describe.[20]

On 5 May 1866 Bate & Co. W. took up the challenge and applied for a pass from the Uruguayan command to send a team of photographers, led by Javier López, to the front. In his application Vander Weyde explained:

> Bate & Co. W., photographers, declare that, in accordance with repeated requests of allied correspondents and with the patriotic suggestions of several people in this capital, we have decided to send at our expense a qualified artist to follow the troops in order to record the views of all the towns, battles, rivers, and people who may deserve our utmost attention. The circulation of these views in this city and their reproduction in European illustrated newspapers will contribute to bringing into prominence before the civilized world the actions of the greatest force ever recruited in Spanish-speaking America. Our photographs, which will be sold at reasonable prices, will provide the families of our brave soldiers with a memento of their task and of their glories, and the world with vivid views of the imposing appearance of the towns and cities of that country. In order to accomplish this task, we will have to support the heavy cost of this undertaking, and assume the risk of having no compensation in case that our views are copied and distributed by others, as has already happened. Therefore, in order to carry this enterprise into practice, we request that Your Excellency protect the property rights of all our works and provide

8. Death in Paysandú (Emilio Lahore, albumen print, 11 x 18 cm, 1865, Collection of Fernando Schulkin)

free transportation for our artist to the theater of the war. We offer in return two collections of all the views taken to be preserved in archives. We also request that Your Excellency allow no one, for at least six months after the conclusion of the war, to sell copies of our views without our authorization, and to make all the necessary arrangements for the transportation of our artist.[21]

On 22 May the war minister granted the request, ordering that "the necessary steps to be taken to transport them to the theater of the war, on our account, guaranteeing them, as they demand, the property rights to the views taken by them, and granting them exclusive rights to sell copies of their pictures for a six-month term after the conclusion of the war."[22] The next day *El Siglo* enthusiastically reported, "Messrs. Bate & Co. W. will be the first in this country to apply their photographic art to the recording of military operations. . . . [S]uch an enterprise, worthy of the Yankee genius, deserves our support and it is our wish that it be carried out without the pacific machine being struck by the bullets of any enemy of the photographic process."[23]

Bate & Co. W. apparently undertook the task of documenting the siege of Paysandú and then the greater war because they saw the possibility of profit in the sale of such photographs, which justified the effort that such an enterprise demanded and made the dangers worthwhile. The application for a pass suggests that the company enjoyed no connection to the Uruguayan authorities; the photographers were acting as private entrepreneurs. They sought a pass and free transportation to the front not only to cover part of the heavy costs but also to facilitate the movement of their photographers through the Paraguayan swamps and forests. Moreover the request also expresses concern for copyright protection against piratical reproduction of the resulting pictures. At that time copyright existed only in France, where it had been established in 1862; Uruguay would not institute such protections until 1937.[24]

The Bate photographers arrived at Corrientes in early June 1866, too late to record the allied crossing into Paraguay (April) and their victory at the battle of Tuyutí (24 May), but they were on hand to record the next bloody engagement, Boquerón (16–18 July), in which the allied advance was temporarily halted. Javier López and his team, meanwhile, established their base of operation at the allied camp, that "immense city of white tents" so well described by Cerqueira. All kinds of services could be found there: restaurants, saloons, billiard parlors, and even "barbers and photographers."[25] López and his assistants stayed at the front for almost two months. Unlike the photographers of the Crimean and Civil Wars, who utilized wagons fitted as both darkroom and residence, Bate's men worked in tents, which were easier to transport through the Paraguayan swamps. They camped close to the Uruguayan forces, which held the center of the allied line, flanked by the Argentines and the Brazilians. Their tents bore the inscription "Bate & Co. W. Photographers" on both sides. Still, it was no easy task to take photographs under these conditions. They had to coat the extremely fragile collodion glass plates in the darkroom, run to the camera, insert the plateholder into it, make the exposure (anywhere from three to twenty seconds), and then rush back to the darkroom to process the negative before the emulsion dried. The whole operation had to be completed in no more than twenty minutes. Even then, extreme temperatures and dust could ruin the plates. The process of making a photograph was thus arduous and sometimes even hazardous, for the darkroom tent could never be far from the frontline.

Nonetheless Javier López and his team produced some remarkable images. At the end of July he returned very ill from Paraguay, a casualty of the

9. The darkroom tent and an observation tower (Bate & Co. W., albumen print, 11 x 18 cm, 1866, Fundación Centro de Documentación de Arquitectura Latinoamericana, Buenos Aires)

epidemics that broke out due to the great number of dead animals and half-buried Paraguayan corpses lying about Itapirú and beyond. "This intrepid artist," as *El Siglo* described him, brought back from the front a series of negatives, some of them taken very close to the firing line.[26] He immediately published his photographs and advertised them widely in Montevideo and Buenos Aires, attracting considerable attention. "Photographic views of the war against Paraguay are available," announced *El Siglo* of Montevideo, while *The Standard* of Buenos Aires announced under the headline "Pictures of the War" that Bate & Co. W. had sent a set of nine war views.[27] At least thirteen images from this first trip to Paraguay have survived. They include scenes of troops in the trenches at Tuyutí and cannon ready for battle, views of camp life and military hospitals, and a photograph of Uruguayan commander Col. León de Palleja's corpse, later published as a photogravure by Francisco Fortuny (see figure 6). These views were published under the titles "The War against Paraguay" and "The Illustrated War."[28]

Six weeks in Montevideo were evidently enough to restore Javier López's health, and on 12 September, the same day on which Paraguayan and allied commanders held inconclusive peace talks, the photographer announced his return to the front to continue his "successful undertaking." He took two assistants and a new camera imported from the Unites States, promising to

10. The 24 de Abril Battalion in the trenches at Tuyutí (Bate & Co. W., albumen print, 11 x 18 cm, 1866, Fundación Centro de Documentación de Arquitectura Latinoamericana, Buenos Aires)

bring back a visual record of the events to come, "which will soon be presented to the attention of the public."[29] The Bate team arrived in Paraguay just in time to document the aftermath of the devastating allied defeat at Curupayty (22 September), where they suffered some nine thousand casualties in an ill-conceived attempt to storm the Paraguayan earthworks.

At the end of October the team returned to Montevideo, and on 4 November Bate and Co. W. issued a series of photographs under the title "The War against Paraguay." Most were new pictures taken during September and October 1866, but some of the views offered in this second series, including the three shocking shots of stacked Paraguayan corpses after the battle of Boquerón, were among the negatives taken during the first trip but not published in August. Twenty-two of these images are extant, including one showing the photographers' tent close to an observation tower (see figure 9). Several feature senior commanders and their staffs, but the photographers also took time to document the presence of Indians at the allied camps.[30]

The reception of the Bate photographs was mixed. Montevideo's *El Siglo*

11. Paraguayan corpses after the battle of Boquerón, July 1866 (Bate & Co. W., albumen print, 11 x 18 cm, 1866, Museo Mitre, Buenos Aires)

hailed the photographers' work as "an undertaking without equal in South America, considering the hardships that they have to face, and of the utmost importance because they faithfully document . . . scenes of this bloody war whose end is yet impossible to foresee." The new views "taken by the intrepid Bate team constitute a visual story comprehensible to everyone, full of action and variety, with its sordid pages—the ones that depict the killing fields— and the pictures that record camp life, the soldiers at leisure time, gathered around the bonfire, remembering their families, their home, and the friends whom they perhaps will never see again."[31] For three weeks, according to the newspaper, "the photographic views taken by the skillful operator of Messrs. Bate & Co. had managed to keep public curiosity alive. In fact it is much more comfortable to be a spectator at this drama, which has drawn the attention of the most important European powers, than to play any role within the reach of enemy bullets."[32]

In Buenos Aires, though, public interest in war photographs waned almost immediately after the battle of Curupayty. Thousands of young *porteños* died in front of the Paraguayan guns that day, and the photographs that showed the war's effects with brutal reality must have shocked the public. Residents marched in the streets to demonstrate against the conflict, and the press severely questioned Argentine participation in the war.[33] Nonetheless, the photographs went on sale in Buenos Aires; by the middle of the month, ten war views were on display at Loedel's Librería Inglesa, their price being 225 pesos.[34] Both the albumen prints sold in Montevideo and those offered in Buenos Aires measured eight by five inches and were mounted on eleven-by-nine cards. Each bore an identical title in gilded letters, "La Guerra contra el Paraguay [The War against Paraguay]," and a descriptive caption. They also bore the photographer's credit, Bate & Co. W., in the lower left corner and the word "Montevideo" in the lower right.

Despite the interest sparked by Bate & Co. W.'s war photographs, the company went bankrupt in early 1867, and Vander Weyde was obliged to sell his equipment and thousands of plates, including the wartime scenes, to a business rival. Javier López, the man who, according to newspaper accounts, deserves the credit for photographing events at the battlefields, disappears from the newspaper record after November 1866, when he returned from his second trip to the front. Esteban García, who covered the Paysandú siege and probably served as López's assistant in Paraguay, lived until the 1930s, periodically suffering from malaria likely contracted in the Paraguayan swamps.[35]

Bate & Co. W's pioneering battlefield photography was unique in the war against Paraguay, and few other photographers recorded the conflict's military dimensions. Those who did so worked in an official capacity. In 1867 the Brazilian government sent Carlos César to document the assault on Humaitá, the Paraguayan bastion whose siege lasted until 1868. Some of the best photographs taken during the Humaitá campaign were included in his album *Recordações da Guerra do Paraguai* (Recollections of the Paraguayan War); one shows the massive church in the fortress after its destruction by a Brazilian naval bombardment. Dedicated to the Marquis of Rio Branco, this album was a striking visual record of the last stages of the conflict.[36] Among these images were two poignant shots of prisoners of war. One of the men, Antonio Gómez, photographed in Porto Alegre on 27 April 1867, was captured at Uruguaiana at the beginning of the fighting and was said to be twenty-one years old.[37] The other prisoner, unidentified by name, was captured a year and a half later at Lomas Valentinas when he was but ten years of age. By then Marshal López had recruited every man and child still on his feet in a desperate effort to save Asunción—all to no avail.

No photographers, unfortunately, documented the Paraguayan side of the conflict, but like members of the elite in the allied countries, President López regularly sat for photographs. The last was taken near the Aquidabán River in early 1870, when the remnants of his government and army had

12. The church at Humaitá, destroyed by Brazilian artillery (Carlos César, albumen print, 13 x 18 cm, 1868, Collection of Miguel and Mirta Cuarterolo)

effectively been destroyed. Shortly thereafter he and his remaining defenders were overwhelmed by the Brazilians; the marshal, his son Pancho, and a score of other high-ranking Paraguayans died in the final engagement. Col. George Thompson, who served as an engineer in the Paraguayan army until December 1868, noted that the marshal's last photograph was the work of Domingo Parodi. This Italian chemist and botanist had come to Paraguay to research the curative properties of certain plants in 1858 and had found himself stranded by the war.[38] Sketch artist Francisco Fortuny used this photograph as a model for his portrait of López in the *Album de la Guerra del Paraguay* (1893–94), a Buenos Aires magazine written by and for veterans of the conflict.[39] Fortuny had no such model, however, to sketch the marshal's death, for when Brazilian troops crushed López's last defenders on 1 March 1870, no photographers accompanied them to record this last action of the Paraguayan War.

### Drawn from Life: Painters and Sketch Artists at the Front

Photographers were not the only artists to leave a visual record of the Paraguayan War, which was the most thoroughly recorded event in South

American history up to that time. For the first time, war correspondents, sketch artists, newspaper publishers, lithographers, and photographers chronicled a military struggle, satisfying the public's desire for firsthand information. Many of the artists who left a graphic record of the war were members of the military forces engaged in the conflict. A few were regular or amateur reporters, but most had been eyewitnesses of the events they would later depict.

Swiss-born painter Adolf Methfessel (1836–1909), who arrived in Buenos Aires in 1860, accompanied the allied troops to the theater of the war and stayed with them for four years. In 1869 *La Tribuna* of Buenos Aires reported, "this young artist is the only one to follow the allied army, making drawings of all the places conquered by our forces, [and] maps and sketches of the battles."[40] His works were lithographed and published in the Buenos Aires and foreign illustrated press (see below). Years later Methfessel returned to the sites of the battles with Argentine writer Estanislao Zeballos, who was planning to write a monumental illustrated work on the war. The book never appeared. Nonetheless the painter had access to all the materials on the conflict that the author had assembled, a huge collection of photographs, maps, and documents. Methfessel also produced a series of oils and watercolors, works of great historic value as eyewitness accounts (and because of the author's thorough documentation). His painting *El Paraguay después de la Guerra* (Paraguay after the War) is based on a *carte de visite* of a starving boy taken by an unknown photographer. Methfessel portrayed him in the uniform of López's Guard, thus paying homage to the heroic boys pressed into service. The artist also illustrated Alberto Amerlán's *Bosquejos de la Guerra del Paraguay* (Sketches of the Paraguayan War).[41]

When the war broke out, Cándido López (1840–1902) had been making his living for a number of years as a painter and photographer, having received his training from Italian painters Cayetano Descalzi and Baltazar Verazi. In the early 1860s he entered into partnership with daguerreotypist Juan Soula, and both toured the province of Buenos Aires, making photographic portraits. He enlisted in the Argentine army as a volunteer and rose to the rank of second lieutenant. When he went to the front, he began to make sketches and take notes. General Mitre subsequently learned about his work through Gen. Wenceslao Paunero and requested to see the sketches. "Keep them properly," he then told artist. "One day they will depict history."[42] On 20 September 1866 Cándido López drew his last sketch with his right hand. Two days later he had his right arm amputated as a result of wounds received at Curupayty. Amazingly he retrained himself to paint with his left hand. Twenty years later

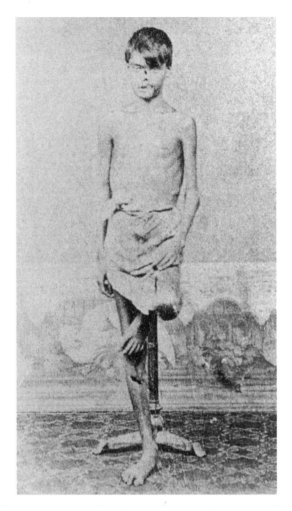

13. A young Paraguayan prisoner of war (unknown photographer, *carte de visite*, 1868, Museo Histórico Nacional, Buenos Aires)

he managed to produce some fifty-eight panoramic views of the war based on his earlier sketches and notes. His obsession with rendering these scenes with the highest degree of veracity led him to contact the aging Mitre to certify their accuracy. The commander of the allied forces wrote back that the "paintings are historically valuable documents, outstanding for their accuracy, which will become glorious mementos of the events that they depict."[43]

The most important Argentine chronicler of the Paraguayan War was José

14. *The Battle of Yataí*, Corrientes, 17 August 1865 (Cándido López, oil on canvas, 40 x 104 cm, 1876–85, Museo Histórico Nacional, Buenos Aires [detail])

Ignacio Garmendia (1842–1925). He had served as a captain (and later general) in the Argentine army, and in addition was a prolific writer and painter. Garmendia worked as correspondent for *La Tribuna* of Buenos Aires and later wrote several books that included sketches of battles and other scenes of the conflict, most notably his memoirs of the war.[44] He painted 149 watercolors, some based on the sketches that he had made on the spot, others on the photographs by Bate & Co. W. Like many artists, he chose to rely upon photographs as visual resources for his paintings because he recognized the truthfulness implied in the photographic image and understood that the medium had already gained public approval. His works illustrated the *Album de la Guerra del Paraguay*; some of these prints bear the legend "from a photograph" (not a common practice at that time).

Argentine-born Nicolás Granada (1840–1915) earned his living as journalist and teacher; he had been a pupil of the famous Argentine painter Prilidiano Pueyrredón.[45] At the outbreak of the war, Granada's close friend General Mitre appointed him aide-de-camp, with the rank of colonel. This advantageous position gave Granada extraordinary access to events in Paraguay. His gifts as an etcher and writer served him well in making vivid graphic and written depictions of the battles and scenes of camp life. Like Garmendia,

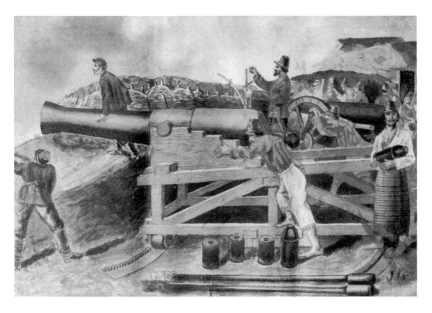

15. *Paraguayan Battery* (José Ignacio Garmendia, watercolor, 20.6 x 30 cm, circa 1870, Museo Saavedra, Buenos Aires)

he contributed articles and sketches to the Buenos Aires and Montevideo newspapers; like Fortuny's works, his drawings also graced the *Album de la Guerra del Paraguay*.

In 1866 Brazilian painter Vitor Meireles de Lima (1832–1903) complained of the thoughtlessness of imperial authorities in "not having sent a photographer to document the war against Paraguay and the national victories."[46] Meireles had studied painting in Rio de Janeiro and later in Europe, returning to Brazil in 1862 to accept appointment as professor at the Academia de Belas Artes. In late 1865 the government commissioned him to document the naval battle of the Riachuelo, which had occurred in June. From the deck of a warship, he witnessed the fleet fire daily barrages into Humaitá and prepared for the two canvases that would make him famous upon his return to Rio de Janeiro: *Batalha Naval do Riachuelo* (Naval Battle of the Riachuelo) and *Passagem de Humaitá* (The Passage by Humaitá). The former ultimately went on to the 1876 international exhibition in Philadelphia, but it was lost at sea on its return; Meireles then painted a second and equally grand version of the painting, which now hangs in Rio de Janeiro's Museu Histórico Nacional along with *Passagem de Humaitá*.[47]

16. Argentine camp at Ensenada, Corrientes (Nicolás Granada, lithographed by Henry Meyer, *Correo del Domingo* [Buenos Aires], 25 February 1866)

In 1865 Uruguayan general Venancio Flores commissioned Juan Manuel Blanes, his country's first successful professional painter, to commemorate the sicge of Paysandú.[48] Flores intended to give the painting as a present to Admiral Tamandaré, who had directed naval operations during the siege. According to Blanes, accurate documentation was necessary before preparing his canvas. Thus he avidly gathered information, collecting engravings, portraits, lithographs, eyewitness accounts, and photos. As he began the preparatory work for *Ataque General a Paysandú* (General Attack on Paysandú), the artist traveled to Concepción del Uruguay, then crossed the river to Paysandú. He arrived mere days after it fell to Flores's army and took up lodging with Colonel Murature aboard his ship.[49] Blanes must have continued to collect photographs of the siege, for the surviving reproductions of his panoramic painting (now lost) have points in common with one of them: A group of figures in the foreground stand opposite the city on an island that served as a refuge for women and children, an image copied from a photograph in Murature's album.[50]

During the final decades of the nineteenth century the Platine countries experienced rapid population growth due to a great influx of European immigrants. The traditional colonial society changed rapidly, and governments and educators felt it necessary to stress their country's historical achievements to incorporate the new arrivals into the nation. The creation of a patriotic iconography served that purpose. Spanish-born Francisco Fortuny (1865–1942), a painter who settled in Argentina, helped give form to the Argentine image.[51] Unlike the artists discussed up to this point, he had not witnessed the wartime events that he portrayed. Nevertheless he collected written and graphic materials held in archives and museums and photographic portraits and views kept in family albums. His portrayal of the 12 September 1866 meeting between General Mitre and Marshal López thus scrupulously followed George Thompson's account of the inconclusive parlay at Yataity Corá.[52] Armed with this material, he not only depicted scenes of the conflict but also produced for the *Album de la Guerra del Paraguay* a "Gallery of Notable Warriors" whose faces he copied from *cartes de visite* kept in family albums. In 1904 some of his images were included in the handsomely illustrated Argentine edition of Thompson's *The War in Paraguay*.[53]

In Uruguay painter and lithographer Diógenes Hequet painted several large-scale oils depicting scenes of the Paraguayan War in 1887. His father, owner of a lithographic firm, had sent him to Europe in the early 1880s to perfect his knowledge of the art. He also studied drawing and eventually specialized in historical themes. Hequet was born in Montevideo in 1866, during the war, and thus witnessed none of its battles. Like Fortuny, he gathered visual and written information: books, newspaper articles, lithographs, and photographs, among them Bate's images. His paintings of the battles of Boquerón, Estero Bellaco, and Tuyutí (today held by the Museo Histórico Nacional in Montevideo) were later mass reproduced as woodburytypes.[54]

**The War on Paper**

An enormous debt is owed to sketch artists and photographers for the legacy of their visual record of the war. But lithographic publishers and newspaper editors also deserve credit for meeting the public's demand for firsthand information about the fighting. They made possible the wider distribution

17. The meeting between Bartolomé Mitre and Francisco Solano López, Yataytí Corá, 12 September 1866 (Francisco Fortuny, *Album de la Guerra del Paraguay* [Buenos Aires], 15 March 1893)

of photographers' and sketch artists' work. The 1850s witnessed a revolution in the newspaper industry as innovations in printmaking technology made it possible to use lithography, which in turn launched mass-circulation illustrated newspapers in Britain, France, and the United States.[55]

On the eve of the war numerous newspapers were published in the Plata; the four largest in Buenos Aires had a combined circulation of 14,700. There were also two lithographic firms in the Argentine capital, one run by the German Rodolf Kratzenstein and the other by the Frenchman Jules Pelvilain. In Montevideo French-born José Adolfo Hequet (Diógenes' father), a painter, drawer, and lithographer, opened his own lithographic operation in 1860. Despite the presence of these facilities, Argentine and Uruguayan newspapers had neither the technology nor the financial means to satisfy the public's desire for illustrations and rarely published them. But in August 1865 *La Tribuna* included a sketch map of the battlefields credited to military engineer Roberto Chodasiewicz and dedicated to "the Argentine people."[56]

The only Buenos Aires newspaper that regularly included journalistic illustrations was *El Correo del Domingo* (1864–68), published by José María Cantilo, which had French sketch-artist and lithographer Henry Meyer and lithographer Pelvilain as contributors. Meyer usually based his works on sketches sent to him from the front (see, for example, figure 16), on photographs available in the market, and on verbal or written accounts from eyewitnesses. *El Correo* published its first illustration of the conflict in late January 1865, showing the church of Paysandú destroyed by artillery. Drawn by Meyer and lithographed by Pelvilain, the image was clearly based on a photograph, though no credit was assigned, as was then typical in the region.[57] The public's appetite for fresh news of the war grew appreciably as the armies mobilized and marched to the front. After López met Mitre and Flores on 12 September 1866, the paper ran an illustration by Meyer probably drawn from written or oral sources. It inaccurately featured all three commanders on horseback (according to Thompson, Mitre and López began their conference at a hastily prepared table, while Flores took no part in the conversation, as in figure 17).[58]

*El Correo* frequently published lithograph portraits of military leaders, but the necessary pictorial authentication of public figures was only assured by the camera. Even so the photographer never received credit. Once in 1865 *El Correo* regretted being unable to publish some portraits because, upon reflection, they did not resemble the "personages well known to the public."[59] Obviously these lithographs had not been based on photographs. In October 1866, as the *porteños* recovered from the shocking news of the allied defeat at Curupayty, *El Correo* published a double-spread page that included obituaries with portraits of Capt. Francisco Paz, son of Vice President Marcos Paz, and Capt. Dominguito Sarmiento.[60] The following year the paper illustrated the return of Mitre and his troops to Buenos Aires with a double-page lithograph by Pelvilain.[61] Not surprisingly public interest in the war had ebbed somewhat, and it was not until August that the paper published a likeness of the Marquis of Caxias, the new commander in chief of allied forces. This portrait accompanied a long article explaining Mitre's reasons for returning from the front.[62]

Several foreign newspapers circulated in the Plata, though their illustrations did not always achieve high standards of accuracy. The Spanish-language *Correo de Ultramar*, published in Paris by the Catalan Xavier de Lasalle y Melan, featured illustrations by French or Spanish artists who had never set foot in South America. They based their scenic portrayals on sketches or photographs sent by correspondents. If this material failed to arrive in time to meet deadlines, they fell back on written eyewitness accounts, and in such cases the prints generally turned out to be topographically inaccurate. Like many other papers, the *Correo de Ultramar* never assigned proper credit to the photographers, though Methfessel's drawings found a place in its pages. A number of French newspapers, including *L'Illustration Universelle* and *Le Monde Illustre*, published illustrated articles on the South American conflict. The latter published a double-spread page with five lithographs and an allegorical sketch by several artists on the aftermath of the siege of Paysandú.[63] The illustrations were based on photographs credited to Bate & Co. W. (unlike their Platine counterparts, French newspapers meticulously assigned credit to photographers for the images that provided the basis for their lithographs). Newspapers published on both sides of the Río de la Plata were important sources for the illustrations that appeared in European newspapers. When the Bate team departed for the front, *El Siglo* commented: "when their views get to Europe, we will no longer see the [erroneous] daubs that usually illustrate their [commentary on the war. Thanks to their efforts,] Brazil will not be the only country known through such illustrations, as has been the case thus far only because not a single sketch artist had been recruited to our army and no photographer had dared face the risks of this enterprise."[64]

As *El Siglo* suggested, the Brazilian press had achieved high standards in printing illustrations. The most important illustrated newspapers, which circulated both in São Paulo and Rio de Janeiro, were *Semana Ilustrada* (1860–82), *Cabrião* (1866–67), *O Arlequim* (1867–68), and *A Vida Fluminense* (1868–79). These journals, especially *Semana Ilustrada* and *A Vida Fluminense*, often included maps, portraits of officers and commanders, and sketches of the battles and life at the front—all based on photographs, drawings, or eyewitness reports (for example, see figure 3). Photographers were not usually credited. Well-known artists such as Henrique Fleiuss, Ângelo Agostini, Américo de Campos, and Antônio Manoel dos Reis contributed to these publications, which in turn had great influence on the development of political caricature.[65]

The Paraguayan government operated an impressive patriotic and nationalistic press. *El Centinela*, the first illustrated newspaper in the country, came out on 25 April 1867, two years after the war began.[66] Its articles and illustrations stressed the heroism and triumphs of Paraguayan arms and ridiculed the allies. Italian-born architect Alejandro Ravizza was its most outstanding artist, and Manuel Colunga and Juan José Benitez, two soldiers who had been withdrawn from the front, acted as designers. The woodcuts that illustrate its pages have distinct styles. Those intended to stress Paraguayan sacrifices and achievements feature a neoclassic or romantic style (for example, see

18. *The Secret Treaty*. This cartoon shows Emperor Pedro II (center) insisting that the other allied leaders (Bartolomé Mitre and Venancio Flores) abide by the terms of the Triple Alliance Treaty's secret protocol instead of accepting a peace offer proposed by the United States. (*Cabichuí* [Paso Pucú], 1 July 1867)

figure 1). Those meant to ridicule the enemy adopt instead the style of political caricature. This weekly, printed in Asunción with text in both Guaraní and Spanish, was smuggled into the allies' camps. The most significant and innovative Paraguayan publication of the period, however, was the fiercely patriotic *Cabichui*, whose first issue appeared in April 1867. This fortnightly newspaper was printed at Paso Pucú, just behind the front. Most of its illustrations, especially those that referred to the allies, were caricatures. Except for Saturío Ríos, none of the artists who contributed to it had received any formal training. Their woodcuts were noteworthy for their vivid and dynamic strokes, though they did not conform to the realistic style then in vogue in other illustrated newspapers of the world. The latter papers published images as lifelike as possible in order to meet the demands of a public that had learned to trust and appreciate photography.

## Conclusion

While in the United States the photographs of the Civil War have always been considered reliable glimpses into different aspects of the conflict, in South America these first wartime images only received their due as historical documents in the 1980s. Historians have often preferred to illustrate books on the Paraguayan War with lithographs, many of which had their origins in photographs—most of the photographs that illustrate this chapter remained hidden during the last 130 years in old family albums or in long-forgotten cupboards in archives or museums. Yet the labors of those pioneering photographers laid the basis for documentary photography in South America, while the works of sketch artists made reliable news available to a hungry public. The images recorded by these "soldiers in the service of memory," who risked their lives accompanying the troops to the battlefields, mark a milestone in the history of South American photography and journalism. Together they shaped contemporary perceptions of the war and provided historians with a remarkable record of the conflict and the evolution of its memory.

# 10. The Paraguayan War

## A Catalyst for Nationalism in South America

Commentators in Brazil and the Platine states tend to focus today on the regional economy, asking whether the MERCOSUR (MERCOSUL in Portuguese) free-trade model can serve as an adequate instrument in meeting people's aspirations for a better life. Such questions are altogether appropriate for our troubled times. Yet the current spirit of cooperation contrasts greatly with the period of the Paraguayan War. All four countries that today make up MERCOSUR suffered during that conflict, though some more than others. The war was crucial in fomenting a broad nationalism in the region. This in turn provided the building blocks of an innovative politics, wherein the idea of MERCOSUR eventually became palatable. The conflict, to put it concretely, proved the great catalyst in pushing Argentina, Brazil, Paraguay, and Uruguay into the modern age.

The war had striking political ramifications that went far beyond words and ideologies. It helped turn Argentina into a united nation-state. It cast the military into a position of importance in Brazilian politics, a trend that ulti-mately weakened the monarchy. It opened a new chapter in the internecine conflict between the Blanco and Colorado Parties in Uruguay. And it utterly wrecked Paraguay, ruining the nation's economy and causing its population of 450,000 to fall by over 60 percent.[1] As the chapters in this volume indicate, the Paraguayan War was as broadly significant for the people of the MERCOSUR countries as anything they have ever experienced.

The war's origins and effects reflect the political contradictions of the 1800s. That different approaches to nation building should arise in South America during the nineteenth century followed as a natural consequence of independence. Elite figures steeped in the political discourse of Europe anxiously sought to build new nation-states on the rubble of the colonial order. Yet they faced many challenges. They had to contend with popular apathy and with the selfish ambitions of caudillos. And like European na-tionalists of the same generation, they often disagreed among themselves on how to construct a new regime.

The elites only rarely found sympathy or understanding for their ideas among their prospective fellow citizens. In simplest form a nation is a com-munity of people composed of one or more nationalities with its own terri-tory and government.[2] Nineteenth-century South America could boast few such polities. The turmoil of the independence wars and the consequent flight or suppression of many talented, responsible people impeded the transition to a new political order. The common inhabitants of the southern continent, moreover, faced a plethora of daily problems. They thus paid little attention to a "nation" that was as nebulous as it was distant. They had minimal regard for "citizenship," for how could that help them harvest their crops? If other "citizens" had different customs, a different language, and a different *weltanschauung*, then how could they belong to the same nation?

To convince the average South American to join a community greater than the *republiqueta* was no easy matter. Still, as the quest for expanded power was a constant feature of politics, the ruling elite in every newly independent South American country attempted to construct a "nation" around itself. These leaders included some brilliant promoters who, like Giuseppe Mazzini of Italy and Lajos Kossuth of Hungary, had lucid ideas of how to proceed toward a national ideal. Yet their continual debate never produced a consensus or a common set of ideals to unite a nation.

## Paraguay: The Community Writ Large

By the 1860s, Paraguay could claim to be the only "near nation" in the Plata. It had a virtually homogeneous population that shared narrow traditions of patrimonialism and community solidarity. This social environment provided Paraguayans with their own language, Guaraní, and with an identity that seemed broadly "national" even under colonial rule.[3] Neither Argentina nor Brazil nor Uruguay could claim anything like it.

The social and political cohesion that characterized Paraguay owed a great deal to Dr. José Gaspar de Francia, who ruled the inland republic from 1814 to 1840. More like a seasoned Bourbon governor than a bloody-handed caudillo, the Supreme Dictator kept political power tightly in his grip. He insulated his country from the outside, effectively closing its borders prior to 1820. Although Paraguay experienced some periodic confrontations with neighboring powers (as well as the Indians, with whom Paraguayans often shared language but not culture), in general this closed-door policy saved the country from the political trauma that engulfed Argentina and the Banda Oriental for decades after independence.[4]

Yet Paraguay paid dearly for internal stability and peace. In many ways society stagnated under an autarkical reign. This permitted many earlier

Hispano-Guaraní cultural traits—the paternalism, the mistrust of outsiders, the narrow focus on the local community—to reassert themselves. The economy reverted to the self-sufficiency, barter, and reciprocity (*jopói*) of an earlier day. Meaningful political changes, once so inviting, withered into insignificance.

The Paraguayan government was a republic in name only. Francia's officers translated his wishes into policy at the local level. In general the country people acquiesced in this arrangement. They saw their government as having a strong but just hand, as being legitimate because it fit their concept of how a responsible paternal regime should act. Dr. Francia's government did not clash with their traditions, it embraced them. This brought a sense of identity among the Paraguayans, a broad acceptance of their status as a separate people full of quiet pride if not power. As one Paraguayan commentator explained some decades later: "[Our] state or nation is a reunion of a great family that has come together to guarantee itself against the advances of other societies . . . , and in guiding its common interests, it has submitted to a person chosen by society, and to the laws dictated by that submission. . . . The politics [of the chosen government] have forged the key that opens the door to happiness or unhappiness depending on how it is used."[5]

Dr. Francia upheld this view of the proper role of politics. When he died in 1840, however, his place was taken by an ambitious country lawyer, Carlos Antonio López, who rejected some of the older interpretations on governance and statecraft, though not their essential spirit. López began a detailed revamping of Paraguayan administration. He self-consciously created a new state apparatus to replace the colonial structures that had been the mainstay of the Francia regime. His innovations included modern ministerial positions, a reorganized treasury, and an officer corps for the military. He filled these posts with individuals of talent. López was willing to experiment, to learn from past mistakes. If his basic impulses proved as authoritarian as those of Francia, he balanced them with a "liberal" flexibility. Such was definitely the case when López authored a new constitution for Paraguay in 1844 that featured minor borrowings from the French and Spanish legal treatises he had studied as a youth but that had little in it of representative democracy.

Why did López feel constrained to draft such a document? His predecessor had ruled for decades by fiat, and in practice little had changed in Paraguay. Carlos Antonio López, however, considered himself a modern, "civilized" man. Every European state, he observed, had established a legal structure appropriate to its needs and to the times, and Paraguay ought to be no different. The nation deserved to take the "road to modernity," to gain a sunny place among the other new nations of the world. López also had less abstract goals: he wanted Paraguay open to outside trade, and before foreigners arrived en masse, he wanted them to understand who ruled the country.[6]

Notably absent from these considerations was any reference to Paraguay's Hispano-Guaraní character. López never thought of the "nation" in Indian terms, nor did he need to. Since colonial times the state and the community were parallel entities that intersected only rarely. One was Spanish-oriented and scripted, the other Guaraní and directed inward as part of Paraguay's oral culture. The modernization that López proposed had little to do with the latter, and in truth Guaraní had no words to express many critically important political concepts.[7] But then the new president had no reason to consult those Paraguayans who spoke no Spanish. An autocrat could afford to take such people for granted—his idea of nationhood did not depend on them or their language.[8] Thus the people had no role in the organization of the Paraguayan state, which to López was altogether natural and proper.[9] To maintain and expand his power, however, he needed a legal framework for his country that outsiders could respect. And the chief message that he, as founding father, sought to convey in the constitution was that the president was all-powerful and Paraguay belonged to him.

Not all outsiders supported this interpretation. The various governments in Buenos Aires frequently regarded Paraguay as a breakaway province that someday would reunite with the Argentine motherland. Brazil for its part harbored no such formal claims on Paraguay, though the empire's relationship with Asunción was always laced with suspicion and by a general recognition that the border between the two countries had never been negotiated, nor had the status of navigation on the rivers that they held in common. And these were not the only possible enemies with which Paraguay had to contend. During the course of the 1840s and 1850s the López government faced diplomatic crises with France, Great Britain, and the United States; it was not improbable that the wrath of such enemies would make itself felt at some future date—a fact already recognized in Asunción.[10]

Paraguayans still pay homage to Carlos Antonio López, and he richly merits their praise. During his twenty-year rule he oversaw the construction of a shipyard, a foundry and industrial smithy, a national theater, an arsenal, a legislative palace, several presidential residences and ministerial buildings, and various military facilities.[11] He introduced the railroad to Paraguay, the first such innovation in the Plata.[12]

These projects not only demonstrated López's enthusiasm for steam and iron but also revealed a neurotic concern that the Paraguayan state be universally acclaimed. The new state edifices had this effect, for they stood out like leviathans among the adobe and thatch of Asunción. Yet such projects required considerable labor. In this López made extensive use of convict workers. He also enacted a broad-based conscription law—nearly universal for young men—and set the soldiers to work at state projects. The cultivation of foodstuffs for private consumption was left to women, who had done much of the agricultural labor previously and now stepped in to do the rest. While many of these labor practices had colonial antecedents, López made more extensive use of them than either Dr. Francia or his Bourbon predecessors. And he gave them a clearer sense of direction. Such widespread mobilization had clear social and political repercussions. López managed to popularize the various state projects as being the business not just of his government but also of Paraguay as a community. His was ultimately an appeal to a national sentiment.

Whereas the prudence of Carlos Antonio López won him the plaudits of those who had lived as adults under Dr. Francia, for the younger generation of Paraguayans he seemed overly cautious, perhaps too willing to relinquish their rights in exchange for a nebulous peace. These younger eyes turned instead to Francisco Solano López, the president's son, who far more than his father regarded modernity and national greatness as one and the same. When the thirty-seven-year-old Solano López succeeded to the presidency in 1862, he inherited his father's ambitions for the country but little of his patience. The younger López had spent the previous decade as war minister, the man charged with modernizing the military. Thanks to his obsessive efforts, the Paraguayan armed forces could boast some strikingly modern features: a flotilla of steamers, several new artillery pieces, Congreve rockets, an ample supply and medical corps, and a world-class fortress at Humaitá, along the Paraguay River, that European observers likened to Sebastopol. Solano López also hired British engineers and specialists to train his troops, which now numbered in the tens of thousands.[13]

This militarization helped solidify the nationalism of the average Paraguayans, who now saw their earlier xenophobia receive official sanction.[14] Patriotic festivals, celebrations of the president's birthday, and anti-Argentine and anti-Brazilian diatribes in the state newspapers (some of which were written in Guaraní) helped reinforce national pride even as they conveyed the dangerous idea that Paraguay had to defend itself or be overwhelmed: *¡Viva la república del Paraguay! ¡Independencia o muerte!*

## Brazil: The Politics of Enormity

Brazil's situation contrasted greatly with that of Paraguay. It was a huge country of complex social character and little homogeneity. The far north and northeast could not have been more different from cities like Rio de Janeiro and Recife, and in turn the cities had nothing in common with the broad plains of Rio Grande do Sul. True, the Portuguese language and certain Old World traditions knitted Brazil together in a sense. Individual regions drew far more upon these traditions than others, however, and one important social group—the African slaves—were, on account of their subordinated status, outside the standard cultural milieu (and created their own in consequence).[15] Above all, the provinces of the new empire suffered from an unavoidable isolation—a defect made very obvious during the Cisplatine War (1825–28), when an equally weak Argentina fought the empire to a standstill in the Banda Oriental.

Of course what Brazil lacked in social cohesion, it partly made up by the tenacity of its ruling elites and their dedication to the institutions of slavery and the Bragança monarchy. The Brazilian "nation," such as it was, broadly reflected their interests. The elites were great merchants, bureaucrats, ranchers, and planters—well-placed persons who married among themselves. Many had earned legal or medical degrees at Coimbra in Portugal and, by the late 1820s, law degrees in Olinda and São Paulo in Brazil itself.[16] They took coffee and madeira together and dressed alike in frock coats and boiled collars despite the tropical heat.

Not surprisingly, given their aristocratic birth, these elites considered power their exclusive preserve and politics the means to its preservation. They held the government in their hands while pursuing their own narrow interests. Despite various squabbles, they found ways to fit together like mutually reinforcing pieces on a chessboard, at the center of which was Pedro II, who began his personal reign in 1840 after a turbulent nine-year regency. The elites awarded him an exalted position in relation to the greater society. They acknowledged his patronage, his sovereign right to protect them, just as they protected their retainers and their slaves.

The Brazil that the elites wished to create explicitly linked the role of monarch and nation, the better to defend their traditional privileges while promoting a more modern economy. The monarch, they argued, prevented the breakdown of society, while the nominal republicanism of their Spanish American neighbors yielded only strife. The emperor could sustain a modern political system, they believed, for he symbolized all that was noble, all that was civilized, and all that the country should aspire to. Whether such assumptions encouraged the development of national sentiment in Brazil was quite beside the point.

Looked at retrospectively, Brazil's monarchist project still has its impressive side. Pedro became the focus of loyalty in widely separated areas of the realm. Backlanders and Bahians could consider themselves his subjects, though otherwise they recognized few links with the people of Santa Catarina, São Paulo, or the Amazon. The emperor was an indispensable figure, and in 1840 parliament recognized his early majority, transferring to him the full responsibility of power. The symbolic value of this move was conspicuous in a country tired of the sterile politicking of the regency period. The new monarch was youthful, Brazilian born, and unsullied by political infighting— in sum, just the person the "nation" required to foment positive change while preserving the established social hierarchy. The emperor's subjects showered him with a love and respect that continued to grow. His portrait appeared in government buildings and private homes throughout the country. The ancient Portuguese ceremony of public hand-kissing (*beija-mão*), in which imperial officials made a ritual show of obedience and servility, was revived to general approval. People hung on every word as the emperor delivered his annual throne speech. And his birthday celebration became one of the most important civic ceremonies.[17]

The display of sympathy and regard for Pedro had little in it of an unadulterated nationalism, yet it was more mature as a political sentiment than anything that had come before. Brazilians liked Pedro, though they felt less certain about monarchical institutions. The more-astute politicians hoped that admiration for the one would translate into support for the other, but no one could be certain.

National consciousness developed unevenly in the country. A literary *indigenismo* sought Brazil's origins and identity in an idealized and safely remote Indian past, while sometimes violent anti-Portuguese nativism, especially strong in the port cities, helped define "Brazilian-ness" for the native-born free poor.[18] But the former was too esoteric and the latter too radical (for those in power) to constitute a national identity. Local loyalties and attachments to the home province remained strong. Whenever local or provincial interests clashed with those of the "nation," no one could say which would prevail, as the Farroupilha Rebellion (1835–45) in Rio Grande do Sul so clearly demonstrated. The "ragamuffin" cattle ranchers of that southern province opted to create their own republic when the planter-dominated central government refused to change its tariff policies, which had favored the importation of Argentine dried beef (as slave rations) at the expense of the Riograndense product.[19]

The imperial government could never permit any openly secessionist movement to succeed, for such an agenda gave primacy to the parts over the whole and thus subverted the accepted concept of nationhood. If other provinces followed Rio Grande's lead, then Brazil could have fallen apart. To forestall this fate the government eventually offered economic and political concessions to the rebels and incorporated erstwhile rebel leaders into the armed forces in Rio Grande do Sul.[20] But in upholding certain Riograndense claims in Uruguay, the empire set the stage for the even more tragic conflict with Paraguay.

After four decades of independent life, Brazil had witnessed few real changes in its basic political and social structures. The empire still looked like an aggregation of regional economies, all oriented outward to Europe rather than to each other. The introduction of printing presses and steamships had improved communications, but isolation still remained the dominant feature in most provinces. Although the Riograndenses declared a renewed fealty to the imperial system after the Farroupilha's defeat, they nonetheless maintained their distinctiveness.

Pedro actively promoted the idea of a Brazilian nation, yet it was difficult for him or anyone else to inspire a widely felt nationalism in the country. However much they might admire the emperor, the poor of Brazil understood that his reign upheld elite interests over their own. They could afford to acquiesce in the established order, but nothing more.

For the Brazilian elites, who saw nationhood in terms of European models, the resignation of the populace seemed altogether natural. It had its advantages, for apathetic subjects rarely threaten traditional privileges. Yet the same elites believed that Brazil was on the verge of a great material expansion in which all would share, if only all would contribute. This sort of modernization was contingent, they thought, on the projection of Brazilian power, for only great nations like Britain and France earned the unalloyed support of their people.[21] For the empire to follow suit it had to stand firmly against external opponents like the Argentine dictator Rosas and ultimately Paraguay.

## Argentina and Uruguay: The Partisan Quagmire

No consideration of Platine politics would be complete without extensive reference to Buenos Aires. As the main port for the region, the chief entrepôt for European ideas as well as foreign goods, the city had a distinctly modern ambience. Even before independence in 1810, the people of Buenos Aires were more literate and more in touch with Old World civilization. They saw themselves as the Plata's great reason for optimism. Not only did they think the whole region rightfully belonged to them through inheritance from Spain but also their financing of the failed campaigns to liberate Paraguay (1811) and Upper Peru (1813) and their strong support of San Martín's successful expedition to Chile (1817) indicated their clear commitment to the future. It also reinforced the idea that only they deserved the leadership role.

Such an assumption failed to convince the understandably skeptical provinces of the Litoral and Interior. The country people had as many biases as their city cousins and certainly displayed little grasp of the vagaries of politics. And yet these vagaries proved all important. Bernardino Rivadavia, the head of the Unitarian faction in the 1820s, was impeccably "liberal," impeccably anglophilic, and assuredly naive. So were the few individuals who endorsed his arguments. But others favored a decentralized political order—one that would better guarantee their traditional privileges. These men resented Rivadavia's alliances with provincial leaders outside of Buenos Aires. And as the Cisplatine conflict with Brazil dragged on, they also came to resent their funding of the greatest share of that struggle.

Revolts in the Interior started the unraveling of Rivadavia's tentative new order, but his opponents—the Federalists—finished the job. When Rivadavia resigned in 1827, his successor, Manuel Dorrego, nullified the centralist constitution, reaffirmed the principal of provincial autonomy, and made himself governor of Buenos Aires. These acts cost him his life, for the Unitarians swiftly rebelled and had him executed. His death set off a chain of events that brought yet another uprising by Federalist landowners and a new government led by Juan Manuel de Rosas (1793–1877).[22]

Rosas succeeded where other caudillos failed in part because he controlled the customs revenues for the port of Buenos Aires. He could arm his troops more lavishly than his opponents. But he was also remarkably shrewd. Rosas understood that in the absence of a coherent nation-state, his best chance for survival lay in mobilizing the local gauchos in a partisan rather than national struggle. In this he was equal to none. He knew both city and Pampa. Rosas could ride as hard and as long as any gaucho and could fight the Indians exactly as they fought each other. Yet he could entertain European visitors in near-regal style and took pride in speaking the language of whomever he was with, high or low. Unlike his predecessors Rosas knew that partisan antagonisms in Buenos Aires had gone so far as to be irreversible and that political stability depended on the complete victory of one party over the other.[23]

The caudillo governed his province for over twenty years and, by the rough standards of his era, was remarkably successful. Although a titular Federalist, Rosas spent much of his time promoting local cattle interests—a favor to his home province that made him seem more Unitarian than the Unitarians and earned him the animosity of many Interior ranchers. Yet he always seemed one step ahead of his enemies.[24] He offered his rivals concessions and threats. In the city he demanded and received dictatorial powers. Any educated man who henceforth risked voicing a dissident opinion might end up knifed by agents of his political police, the Mazorca.

Rosas tamed much of his country through a blend of diplomacy and coercion. The client caudillos whom he supported in the Interior and Litoral recognized his authority and gave him scant trouble. With time he believed that he could effect the same hegemony over the Banda Oriental, but such an effort required a delicate hand. The region had already seen a rival federalism during the campaign of José Gervasio Artigas, the Oriental chieftain who opposed both *porteños* and the Portuguese until his flight into Paraguay in 1820. Not wishing to revisit this circumstance, Rosas decided to take no chances. He sponsored a puppet, Manuel Oribe, who attempted to rule Uruguay through the Blanco Party, while in fact he did Rosas's bidding. As Juan Manuel Casal points out in chapter 7, Rosas took advantage of a longstanding pattern in which Uruguayan political factions ignored a national orientation and explicitly affiliated with patrons in the Argentine provinces, in Buenos Aires, or in southern Brazil.

Given this fact, it was little surprise that Rosas's domestic enemies found support in Montevideo, which rejected the Blanco cause in favor of Uruguay's Colorado Party. Argentina's so-called Generation of 1837 was very much at home in the Uruguayan capital (and in Chile). As a group it included such important figures as Juan Bautista Alberdi, Domingo Faustino Sarmiento, and Bartolomé Mitre—all men in their late twenties and early thirties. Despite their differences in temperament, outlook, and place of birth, all were committed revolutionaries and wished to see Argentina transformed from a geographic concept into a modern nation.

Although they owed much to the early Unitarians, the Men of 1837 argued that Rivadavia and his associates had not gone far enough in some respects and had gone too far in others. As Alberdi noted: "Rivadavia left only scaffolding. His localist creations in Buenos Aires, in isolation from the nation, were intended to prepare the land for the building of national government.

[Those who glorify him] take lodging in the scaffolding, covering it with tarps. Now they call this sort of country tent a definitive building."[25]

By contrast these new statesmen-in-waiting promised a comprehensive reordering of society that would eliminate *caudillismo* and all the "barbarism" of the colonial past and replace them with viable liberal institutions. Although they themselves avidly championed Jeremy Bentham, John Locke, and the Count de Saint-Simon, they thought their predecessors foolhardy in trying to impose foreign political fashions. Argentina was an American country that required a liberal American regime.[26]

Not surprisingly Rosas rejected these silly musings as the work of delinquents. Oribe and the Blancos (and most of the Litoral caudillos) thought likewise. And yet for all of their windiness, the Men of 1837 were making a dangerous suggestion. The young revolutionaries demanded the right to address broad concerns in a "national" fashion. And they had some clear answers for Argentina's problems.

These leaders sought a broad restructuring of politics so as to encourage European immigration and bring education and culture to the countryside. Such a program spurned the Argentina of the Pampas; it demanded a national identity that bypassed *caudillismo* in favor of an elitist, urbane democracy. Those social groups whom the Men of 1837 deemed incapable of assimilation could ultimately be driven like so many cattle onto the Patagonian frontier, where, like the protagonist of *Martín Fierro*, they could live out their last brutish days.

Of course such an interpretation of "democracy" had more in it of *porteño* hegemony than of popular sentiment, yet its proponents carefully disguised their intentions. Such deception was justified, for as the revolutionaries saw it their nation building was equivalent to fostering human progress. To see the plan succeed they would barter with the devil or leave thousands of their fellow citizens outside their idealized future. In this they resembled the elites of Brazil, though, significantly, not those of Paraguay.

The men exiled in Montevideo were under no illusions about the challenges they faced. They knew that the provinces had their own interests and would pursue them no matter what. As Esteban Echeverría mockingly noted: "The patria for the Correntino is Corrientes, for the Cordobés Córdoba, for the Tucumano Tucumán, for the Porteño Buenos Aires, for the gaucho the dirt upon which he was born. The life and common interests that make up the rational sentiment of homeland is an incomprehensible abstraction for them, and they cannot bear to see the unity of the Republic symbolized in a [single] name."[27]

The Men of 1837 thus promised to bring the "civilization" that Europe always praised and that Argentina deserved. But why should their program have any more success than that of Rivadavia? For one thing the revolutionaries were not romantic idealists so much as practiced dealmakers. They gained their maturity under Rosas, knew his strengths and weaknesses (and those of the country), and put their efforts into winnable causes. They rejected the rigid factionalism that Rosas had emphasized and claimed instead the mantle of a future that eschewed partisan divisions. They even showed a willingness to talk with moderate Federalists—especially in the Litoral—and possibly coax then away from Rosas.

In the end this strategy worked. Rosas had stretched himself thin in the 1840s. He launched campaigns in the northeastern provinces to contain his internal enemies, continued to fund Oribe's fight against the Colorados in the Banda Oriental, played cat-and-mouse games with British and French warships in the Río de la Plata, and tried to weaken the Brazilians by intriguing with Farrapo insurgents in Rio Grande do Sul. Eventually all of these enemies were bound to unite against him.

The dam burst in 1851, when Rosas's oldest ally in the Litoral, Justo José de Urquiza, turned against him and sparked the very rebellion that Mitre and the other revolutionaries had long desired. The Brazilians sent more than four thousand men to join Urquiza's army of twenty-four thousand Entrerrianos, Correntinos, and Orientals. Carlos Antonio López sent words of support but no troops. It scarcely mattered; in a matter of months the old order collapsed, forcing Rosas to flee to the protection of a British warship and a long exile. The man who for so long had kept the passions of the body politic in check ended his days as a poor country squire outside of Southampton.

Meanwhile his successors got to work building a new regime dedicated to their notion of civic virtue. Their belief in nation building seemed naive to Urquiza and others from the provinces, who preferred a loose confederation. Mitre and his colleagues were nonetheless single minded. Like many of their European contemporaries, they defined "progress" in "national" terms so that creating a "progressive order" also meant creating a "nation." And the means to that end, paradoxically, was violence—first against Rosas, seven years later against Urquiza, in 1863–65 against the Uruguayan Blancos, and ultimately against Francisco Solano López and the Paraguayans. Each of these groups in turn assumed the role of barbarians for Mitre and his associates. And each had to be destroyed.

By now war, not on a miniscule, hit-and-run scale, but as a grand, full-fledged showdown between the old and the new, had become the key ingredient in South America's transition to a more modern politics. In breaking their enemies the Men of 1837—now mature (and even somewhat jaded) statesmen—did not merely wish to replace them; they wanted to change politics fundamentally, transforming an ill-fitting set of weak provinces into a unified nation and projecting that nation's influence throughout the continent. The Brazilian elites had a similar goal, though in their case the campaign to destroy Rosas, Oribe, and ultimately López was less a matter of constructing a nation than of preserving a threatened political order.

As for Paraguay, there the process of nation building turned on the whims of one all-powerful man, his wife, sons, and daughters. In joining the crusade against *caudillismo*, the regime of the elder López signaled its commitment to a "modern" vision of the country (and especially of its military). At the same time, however, such a commitment necessarily intermingled with traditional political assumptions, especially the idea that Paraguay's neighbors wished to swallow that country whole. Building the Paraguayan nation, then, was not so much a matter of preserving social privileges, defining borders, or recasting political institutions—it was a matter of survival. And the younger López recognized this from the outset.

### The War Destroys, the War Transforms

The great war of 1864–70 profoundly shaped South American politics. When the struggle began the Paraguayan population was already highly mobilized. No one in the country openly challenged Paraguay's right to a major role in Platine affairs, especially in restoring the balance of power that had supposedly characterized regional politics up to that point.[28] Yet the memoirs left by eyewitnesses suggest little real enthusiasm for the war in its first few months. Although it fared well in the Mato Grosso campaign, the Paraguayan military fought poorly and in very disorganized fashion in Argentina and Rio Grande do Sul. Officers and men alike failed to focus on an overall objective because they had little understanding of what that goal might be.

This failure not only reflected a lack of military sense on the part of Francisco Solano López but also revealed a basic historical pattern: when called upon to defend the homeland, Paraguayans "circled the wagons" to await the enemy assault. They did not move outside their own territory to carry the attack to the enemy. This long-established defensive posture reasserted itself during the siege at Humaitá. There the allies discovered the stubbornness of the average Paraguayan soldier. "It would not unfrequently occur," a U.S.

diplomat wrote, "that one Paraguayan would be surrounded by a dozen of the enemy, all calling on him to surrender, . . . [instead, he would fight on until] killed; or, if by chance he was disarmed during the unequal contest and forcibly made a prisoner, he would take the first opportunity when his hands were free to seize a musket or bludgeon . . . and kill as many as possible, until he was himself knocked senseless."[29]

Why did the Paraguayans fight with such determination? Certainly not because of López's despotism; a tyrant can command obedience but not courage and self-sacrifice. Rather the explanation hinges on the Paraguayans' belief that their community, their wives, their children, and everything they held dear faced imminent destruction at allied hands. Their extermination as a people seemed a real possibility, and they therefore resisted until the bitter end.

The entire Paraguayan society wrapped itself around this quest for national survival. As Barbara Potthast and Jerry Cooney point out, the people on the home front added an enormous measure to the resistance. They supplied Humaitá with dwindling quantities of munitions, provisions, and medicine, an effort that took food out of their own mouths without promising anything better than a protracted death. Compulsion was clearly a part of this picture, yet so was a deep patriotic feeling. Such loyalty ultimately produced an army of skeletal boys who wore false beards at Acosta Ñu (16 August 1869) to fool the allied soldiers into thinking them grown men still capable of fighting. And at Cerro Corá, when Marshal López exclaimed, "Muero con mi patria [I die with my country]!" he spoke the truth, for more than 60 percent of the Paraguayans had died.

In Brazil the situation was completely different. Initially Brazilians could claim no comparable dedication to the national cause, though this did not mean that they reacted with indifference. When news of the occupation of Corumbá became generally known in January 1865, Brazilians felt a sense of outrage, aggravated by government propaganda that portrayed the Paraguayans as murderers. In sharp contrast to the indifference displayed forty years earlier during the Cisplatine War, a wave of volunteerism swept through the empire's cities. Hendrik Kraay shows that much of this was openhanded. Seamstresses offered to sew shirts for the army and navy at no charge while black artisans signed up to serve in the Zuavo companies. The general display of patriotism, however, was less convincing, for a majority of the contributors were members of the small (but growing) middle class. Such individuals wished to establish their own bona fides as coequal citizens in an elite-oriented nation. As such they did what Frenchmen or Germans were expected to do in like circumstances. A good many supporters also had some connection with the government or stood to benefit from their patriotic offers. The director of a private *gymnasium* in Salvador, for instance, reserved five free places at his school for twelve-year-old boys, the sons of officers sent to Paraguay. His offer could be seen as either patriotism or good advertising.[30]

The greatest show of volunteerism came in the form of men anxious to fight. From all over Brazil they donned uniforms to show their zeal for this new conflict as well as their interest in the monetary awards allotted such recruits. Nonetheless a great many "volunteers" were not really joining of their own free will but were instead seized on the streets by press gangs, especially as the war wore on.[31] Not surprisingly they made poor soldiers, and like their fellows in the National Guard, they made little headway against the obdurate Paraguayans.

The war turned to the empire's favor only when a more professional class of officers came to dominate the scene. This started in 1866 under the command of the Marquis of Caxias and continued under his successor, the Count of Eu. The new officers, mostly of humble or obscure background, entered the fray with a heightened esprit de corps and with a more comprehensive sense of mission that manifested itself in a desire to modernize Brazil. Under Caxias the Brazilian army worked with great autonomy from Rio de Janeiro for the first time since independence.[32] It was ironic, though perhaps not too surprising, that Eu (who was son-in-law of an emperor who presided over the largest slaveholding society in the world) should press the provisional government in Asunción to formally abolish slavery.[33]

Such a forward-thinking policy found no immediate parallel in Brazil proper. To be sure, Pedro II had raised the issue of abolition in his 1867 speech from the throne, but the question was tabled for the remainder of the war. In 1871 parliament passed a free-womb law, a measure that some have seen as a consequence of the Paraguayan conflict. Perhaps so, but all knew that the end of the slave trade in the 1850s had already sealed the institution's fate. The slaves, moreover, were becoming more restive, especially in São Paulo. This encouraged planters to put together a new system of labor relations. Slavery itself endured until 1888, and in its aftermath the planter class forged new mechanisms of social control that effectively preserved its power.[34]

The war's effect on Brazilian nationalism is more difficult to assess. During and after the campaign, streets and neighborhoods were renamed in honor of the country's war heroes and battlefield victories: Salvador and Rio de Janeiro have boroughs called Humaitá and Aquidabã and streets named Voluntários da Pátria and Uruguaiana. In other ways, however, Brazilians failed to commemorate their victory as much as one might expect. Strenuous efforts to construct a war monument in Rio de Janeiro came to naught in the 1870s (though residents of Salvador did erect an obelisk to celebrate the battle of the Riachuelo).[35] The Paraguayan war monuments that today dominate so many squares in Rio de Janeiro were built under later republican regimes and the Estado Novo dictatorship of 1937–45.[36]

Young army officer veterans over time constructed a new Brazilian nationalism based on their common sacrifices in Paraguay, on a positivist interpretation of Brazil's future, and finally in the 1880s on republicanism. As Renato Lemos shows, Benjamin Constant's disillusionment with the war contributed to his rejection of the imperial regime. Under his influence cadets and junior officers eventually threw their support to a coup that unseated Pedro II and established the United States of Brazil on the ashes of his empire. Positivist ideologues thus sought to impose their own republican model on the Brazilian nation. This effort enjoyed only ephemeral success, and the old aristocratic elites managed to reassert themselves by the end of the 1890s.[37]

As Roger Kittleson shows in chapter 6, the war politicized rank-and-file veterans who demanded citizenship on the basis of wartime service. Like the black officers and men of the Bahian Zuavo companies, soldiers from Porto Alegre were bitterly disappointed at war's end. Few received the material benefits (and the implicit citizenship) promised the Voluntários da Pátria with such fanfare in January 1865. In 1881 an electoral "reform" put that citizenship further out of reach by making literacy a requirement for voting, which in effect reduced the franchise by some 90 percent. The new republic retained this law.[38]

The postwar political views of ordinary Brazilians remain nebulous. Dom Obá II, the sometime Zuavo officer and self-styled leader of Rio de Janeiro's Afro-Brazilian community, expressed a strong devotion to the monarchy. The perceived centrality of the royal family in the final abolition of slavery helped cement this loyalty.[39] In 1888 and 1889 the so-called Guarda Negra (Black Guard) routinely beat up republicans. In Salvador popular anti-republican violence erupted on 15–16 November 1889 before the city government acquiesced to the regime change and quelled the protest one day later.[40] While this politicization did not derive solely from the rank and file's wartime experience, it underscored the wide gulf that still divided Brazilian society— a chasm that wartime enthusiasm for the lower classes' patriotism could only paper over.

In Argentina the war brought considerable earnings to the merchants and cattlemen of Buenos Aires and the Litoral who provided the allied armies with foodstuffs and other supplies. Their prosperity fostered the growing influence of the state, which took advantage of Brazil's preoccupation with Paraguay to consolidate its hold over the Litoral and Interior provinces. The *provincianos* allowed themselves a few last gasps in defense of their old Federalist ideals. As Ariel de la Fuente points out, the Felipe Varela rebellion of the late 1860s and the Ricardo López Jordan uprising a few years later purportedly were launched in favor of a López-style "Americanism," though in fact both stressed provincial autonomy as the key objective. Both failed.

Mitre yielded to his elected successor, Sarmiento, in 1868, and Sarmiento to Nicolás Avellaneda in 1874. Although these various "oligarchs" continued to bicker among themselves (and there was one serious episode in 1874 in which former president Mitre attempted to overthrow Avellaneda), the political pattern in Argentina was now set for a generation. An elite of liberal-conservative landowners based in Buenos Aires held the reins of power. These men sponsored policies that expanded the economy, built railroads, and attracted European immigrants without ever calling into question their own right to rule.[41]

The government also enacted the educational reforms so dear to Sarmiento's heart, establishing public schools even in the most isolated locales. Each had primers and textbooks, published in the capital, that drew in truncated form on Mitre's *Historia de San Martín* and *Historia de Belgrano*.[42] These works sought to instill a sense of civic pride by lionizing the early patriots as the founders of Argentina and the oligarchs as the proper custodians of common national interests. Children, as they learned their ABCs, also learned this Whiggish interpretation of their nation's past, which was given visual form by the late-nineteenth-century painters discussed by Miguel Angel Cuarterolo. And they broadly came to accept it. To their young eyes Facundo Quiroga, José Gervasio Artigas, and Rosas himself looked like regrettable aberrations in an otherwise glorious history. As for the Paraguayan War, it served as proof that the Argentine people could stand up as a single, unbeatable force (much like their contemporaries in Germany). The popularity of this image, flawed and ahistorical though it was, simply underlined the fact that Buenos Aires had won its struggle with the countryside.[43]

The coalescence of a Buenos Aires–based Argentine nationalism found no parallel across the river in Uruguay. As Casal demonstrates in great detail, the Paraguayan War failed to engender the political changes in the Banda Oriental that might promote a clear-cut Uruguayan nationalism. On the contrary most Uruguayans viewed the war as Venancio Flores's personal business. Even other Colorados came to regard the conflict as a nuisance that kept politics at home in limbo. Everyone talked in terms of party; no one talked in terms of nation.

It was not until the military dictatorships of Lorenzo Latorre (1876–80) and Máximo Santos (1882–86) that constructing a national identity became a government priority. The national flag and coat of arms were now more commonly displayed than the banners of the Blanco and Colorado Parties. Furthermore, the cult of Artigas as national hero was inculcated in the press, in public meetings, and in every classroom. And even when the dictatorship fell, the cult remained as the central component of Uruguayan nationalism.[44] During the 1920s, when the Uruguayan national soccer team held the world title, local athletes briefly eclipsed Artigas as a focus of pride. But the old chieftain—who spent his last thirty years in exile in Paraguay—never abdicated his central role as national icon. The two parties endured, but so did the symbol of Artigas, the selfless Uruguayan patriot. The Paraguayan War, by contrast, disappeared from the popular imagination. Aside from the nostalgic musings of a few old veterans, it was as if the war had never happened.

In Paraguay itself one could not so easily ignore the effects of the conflict. The nation was stricken demographically, economically, and politically and needed "time for its thousands of orphan boys to attain the strength of manhood."[45] Meanwhile the thousands of sutlers and carpetbaggers who accompanied the allied army into Paraguay cared only for making quick profits from what was left of the prostrate country. Precious little remained. "Is there a thinking Paraguayan left in the land?" wondered one observer. "If there is, let him come forward and tell the world his country's future—explain the crimes of his native land that demanded such awful expiation. . . . I can compare Paraguay to nothing save a tree withered, scorched, blighted by a flash of lightning. . . . I fear for the unutterable woes of these unfortunate people; the land is cursed, and its future is a blank."[46]

If Paraguay was indeed a blank slate, then its political character and its national identity could be completely reconstructed so as to repudiate its authoritarian past.[47] This at least was the task that the provisional government set for itself. Yet as Potthast makes clear, many of the changes that the new government contemplated seemed wildly out of place. Why should Paraguay adopt the Argentine national holiday (25 May) as its own? Why should the national interest require the suppression of the Guaraní language? The answers seem obvious enough now: the members of the provisional government had their political upbringing as exiles in Buenos Aires, and it was a *porteño*-style modernity, not a Paraguayan one, that they wished to foster.

In any case such plans for the future ran aground on the political realities of late-nineteenth-century Paraguay. The country was wrecked, the population dispersed, and the occupying armies mistrustful of the provisional government and of each other.[48] Returning diplomats of the old López regime added their own, supposedly more authentic Paraguayan voice to the cacophony of political opinion. Not surprisingly a long spate of factional rivalry followed. Political groups split apart, reunited with new membership, split apart again, and reunited again. The Brazilian and Argentine occupiers spent time and money trying to prop up various surrogates, only to be disappointed with the results.

Out of this mire two political parties came into existence in the 1880s, the Liberals and the Colorados. Their mutual antagonism—which plagued the country for decades thereafter—was in many ways reminiscent of the Uruguayan experience. And yet both parties were composed of an unwieldy mix of Lopiztas and Anti-Lopiztas, "modernists" and "traditionalists." An outsider would have been hard pressed to tell them apart.

But some political differences in Paraguay were nonetheless crucial. Concomitant with the establishment of the two parties, a new debate erupted. The controversy concerned not so much how the country should shape its future but how it should understand its recent past. One side held that Marshal López had fought a righteous war to uphold the nation against foreign domination. The other side instead portrayed him as an irredeemable tyrant who deserved his fate, and those who had opposed him were heroes, not traitors.[49] The intemperate language that proponents of these two positions reserved for each other tends to shock the eye today. Yet in Paraguay of the late 1800s virtually all political vitality turned in one way or another on this Lopizta–Anti-Lopizta dynamic, and both sides saw the debate in terms that admitted no compromise.

That the marshal's reputation could rebound at all during the postwar period was a powerful testimony to the war's hold on the popular imagination. Neither the work of the provisional government nor that of the Brazilian and Argentine occupiers changed any minds. Young children who had heard their grandparents bemoan the lost cause began to think of it as their own without understanding any of its historical context. Their impudent show of pride on this point annoyed many old liberals who had suffered under the marshal's dictatorship. In 1898, for instance, the head of the state teacher's college issued an angry report that censured parents for speaking favorably of López and permitting their children to use notebooks that featured his image.[50]

This was only the beginning. Within a few years the mounting dispute with Bolivia over the Gran Chaco territory fueled a general revalidation of the marshal and his war. Now, in the skilled hands of polemicists Manuel Domínguez and Juan E. O'Leary, López became a "maximum hero" and the war an "*epopeya* [epic]."[51] In future generations Paraguayans accepted it as only natural that their identity as a people was defined by their forefathers' actions in the 1864–70 struggle.

What then can we say about how the Paraguayan War affected the development of nationalism in South America? It engendered the doom—or at least the radical decimation—of one nation, Paraguay, while it also made possible the modern expression of another, Brazil. Argentina, or rather Buenos Aires, also benefited, for it used the war first to consolidate and then to legitimize its hegemony. Only Uruguay saw its fractious politics emerge unaffected from the fighting—an ironic comment on the contradictions of nation building.

All four of the countries involved in the Paraguayan War saw their status as nations confirmed and in different ways transformed. The changes wrought by the conflict proved calamitous for certain people but full of promise for others. Yet as a whole the nations emerged better positioned to face the challenges of the modern age and ultimately better able to deal with each other in terms more amicable than violent. In this sense the war—for all of its tragedy—set the region on the path toward a broad integration, the final and most profound expression of which can be found in today's MERCOSUR.

# Notes

## Abbreviations

| | |
|---|---|
| AEME | Archivo del Estado Mayor del Ejército, Montevideo |
| AFZ/CTD | Archivo Familia Zamora, La Rioja, Correspondencia de Tristán Dávila |
| AHAA | Archivo Histórico de la Armada Argentina |
| AHEX/RQ | Arquivo Histórico do Exército, Requerimentos |
| AHRGS | Arquivo Histórico do Rio Grande do Sul |
| AHLR/CNB | Archivo Histórico de La Rioja, Correspondencia de Nicolás Barros |
| AJFLR | Archivo de la Justicia Federal, La Rioja |
| AFSB/CRGNO | Archivo Ferreira de Sánchez Bretón, Córdoba, Correspondencia de Ramón Gil Navarro Ocampo |
| ANA/CRB | Archivo Nacional, Asunción, Colección Rio Branco |
| ANA/SH | Archivo Nacional, Asunción, Sección Histórica |
| ANA/SNE | Archivo Nacional, Asunción, Sección Nueva Encuadernación |
| ANRJ/FGP | Arquivo Nacional, Rio de Janeiro, Fichário da Guerra do Paraguai |
| ANRJ/SPE | Arquivo Nacional, Rio de Janeiro, Seção do Poder Executivo |
| APEBa/SACP | Arquivo Público do Estado da Bahia, Seção de Arquivo Colonial e Provincial |
| APEBa/SJ | Arquivo Público do Estado da Bahia, Seção Judicária |
| APERGS | Arquivo Público do Estado do Rio Grande do Sul |
| *BHEME* | *Boletin Histórico del Estado Mayor del Ejército* |
| BNRJ/SM | Biblioteca Nacional, Rio de Janeiro, Seção de Manuscritos |
| CFED | Colección de Folklore de la Encuesta Docente, Instituto Nacional de Antropologia y Pensamiento Latinoamericano, Buenos Aires |
| CM&MC | Colección Miguel and Mirta Cuarterolo |
| MCBC/ABC | Museu Casa Benjamin Constant, Arquivo Benjamin Constant |
| MHN | Museo Histórico Nacional, Montevideo |
| MM/AIM | Museo Mitre, Archivo Inédito del General Mitre |
| MM/AP | Museo Mitre, Archivo del General Wenceslao Paunero |
| *Semanario* | *El Semanario de Avisos y Conocimientos Utiles*, Asunción |

## 1. Introduction

1. Leslie Bethell, "A Guerra do Paraguai: História e historiografia," in *Guerra do Paraguai: 130 anos depois*, ed. Maria Eduarda Castro Magalhães Marques (Rio de Janeiro: Relume-Dumará, 1995), 22; Miguel Angel Centeno, *Blood and Debt: War and the Nation-State in Latin America* (University Park: Pennsylvania State University Press, 2002), 35–47. Of course civil wars accounted for more casualties than interstate conflicts.

2. Ricardo Salles, *Guerra do Paraguai: Escravidão e cidadania na formação do exército* (Rio de Janeiro: Paz e Terra, 1990), 8; Vera Blinn Reber, "A Case of Total War: Paraguay, 1865–1870," *Journal of Iberian and Latin American Studies* 5, no. 1 (July 1999): 15–40; Francisco Doratioto, *Maldita guerra: Nova história da Guerra do Paraguai* (São Paulo: Companhia das Letras, 2002), 195, 477.

3. Thomas L. Whigham and Barbara Potthast, "The Paraguayan Rosetta Stone: New Insights into the Demographics of the Paraguayan War, 1864–1870," *Latin American Research Review* 34, no. 1 (1999): 174–86.

4. "Crônica," *A Semana* (Rio de Janeiro), 25 Mar. 1894, in Joaquim Maria Machado de Assis, *Obra completa*, 3 vols., ed. Afrânio Coutinho (Rio de Janeiro: Editora José Aguilar, 1962), 3:604.

5. Jay Winter, "Paris, London, Berlin, 1914–1919: Capital Cities at War," in *Capital Cities at War: Paris, London, Berlin, 1914–1919*, ed. Jay Winter and Jean-Louis Robert (New York: Cambridge University Press, 1997), 3–4.

6. On the colonial struggles between Spanish and Portuguese, see Dauril Alden, *Royal Government in Colonial Brazil, with Special Reference to the Administration of the Marquis of Lavradio, Viceroy, 1769–1779* (Berkeley: University of California Press, 1968), chaps. 3–10; and [Luiz Alberto] Moniz Bandeira, *O expansionismo brasileiro e a formação dos estados na Bacia do Prata: Da colonização à Guerra da Tríplice Aliança* (Brasília: Editora da UNB; São Paulo: Ensaio, 1995), chaps. 1–3.

7. The literature on postindependence politics and international relations in the region is extensive. Standard works include Efraím Cardozo, *El imperio del Brasil y el Río de la Plata* (Buenos Aires: Librería del Plata, 1961); Cardozo, *Vísperas de la Guerra del Paraguay* (Buenos Aires: Ateneo, 1954); Ron Seckinger, *The Brazilian Monarchy and the South American Republics, 1822–1831: Diplomacy and State Building* (Baton Rouge: Louisiana State University Press, 1984); Bandeira, *Expansionismo*; Thomas L. Whigham, *The Paraguayan War: Volume 1, Causes and Early Conduct* (Lincoln: University of Nebraska Press, 2002), chaps. 1–6; Pelham Horton Box, *The Origins of the Paraguayan War*, 2 vols. (Urbana: University of Illinois, 1929); John Lynch, "The River Plate Republics," in *Spanish America after Independence, c. 1820–c. 1870*, ed. Leslie Bethell (Cambridge: Cambridge University Press, 1987), 314–75; Lynch, *Argentine Dictator: Juan Manuel de Rosas, 1829–1852* (Oxford: Clarendon, 1981); Ariel de la Fuente, *Children of Facundo: Caudillo and Gaucho Insurgency during the Argentine State-Formation Process (La Rioja, 1853–1870)* (Durham NC: Duke University Press, 2000); John Hoyt

Williams, *The Rise and Fall of the Paraguayan Republic, 1800–1870* (Austin: Institute for Latin American Studies, University of Texas at Austin, 1979); Roderick J. Barman, *Brazil: The Forging of a Nation, 1798–1852* (Stanford CA: Stanford University Press, 1988); Doratioto, *Maldita guerra*, chap. 1; and Fernando López Alves, *State Formation and Democracy in Latin America, 1810–1900* (Durham NC: Duke University Press, 2000).

8. For a convenient summary of the four countries' relative strengths, see Diego Abente, "The War of the Triple Alliance: Three Explanatory Models," *Latin American Research Review* 22, no. 2 (1987): 52–56.

9. The following survey of the war's course is based on the extensive historiography of the conflict analyzed below.

10. Harris G. Warren, *Paraguay and the Triple Alliance: The Postwar Decade, 1869–1878* (Austin: University of Texas Press, 1978); Harris G. Warren and Katherine F. Warren, *Rebirth of the Paraguayan Republic: The First Colorado Era, 1878–1904* (Pittsburgh: University of Pittsburgh Press, 1985); Doratioto, *Maldita guerra*, 419–37, 463–70. Postwar Paraguay deserves more scholarly attention. In addition to the works cited above, see Hector Francisco Decord's classic, *Sobre los escombros de la guerra: Una década de vida nacional, 1869–1880* (Asunción: Talleres Nacionales de H. Kraus, 1925). The social history of the era is best treated in Barbara Potthast-Jutkeit, *"Paradies Mohammeds" oder "Land der Frauen"? Zur Rolle von Frau und Familie in Paraguay im 19. Jahrhundert* (Cologne: Bohlau Verlag, 1994), esp. 331–88; and more tangentially in Juan Carlos Herken Krauer, *Ferrocarriles, conspiraciones y negocios en el Paraguay, 1910–1914* (Asunción: Arte Nuevo, 1984).

11. Letters of João Manoel da Silva to his brother, in Daví Carneiro, *O Paraná na Guerra do Paraguai* (Rio de Janeiro: Americana, [1940]), 211, 215; Francisco Borges Ribeiro to Agostinha Maria de Jezus, Humaitá, 16 Apr. 1869, AHEX/RQ JJ-259-6322. On the Paraguayan side see Juan Manuel and José María Aquino to Raymundo and Ramona Aquino, Humaitá, 25 Oct. 1865, ANA/SNE 2412; Benjamín Candia to Félix Candia, Humaitá, 8 Jan. 1868, ANA/SNE 2491; and the miscellaneous correspondence in the Estanislao Zeballos Collection, Museo Histórico Militar (Asunción).

12. Dionísio Cerqueira, *Reminiscências da campanha do Paraguai*, Edição Especial (Rio de Janeiro: Biblioteca do Exército, 1980); Francisco Seeber, *Cartas sobre la Guerra del Paraguay, 1865–66* (Buenos Aires: L. J. Rossio, 1907). See also chapter 5.

13. "Campanha do Paraguai: Diários do Exército em Operações sob o commando em chefe do Exmo. Sr. Marechal do Exército Marquez de Caxias," *Revista do Instituto Histórico e Geográfico Brasileiro* 91, no. 145 (1922): 71, 104, 134, 158, 183. The medical history of the Paraguayan War is relatively extensive. The chief apothecary of the Paraguayan army was an Englishman, George Frederick Masterman, whose *Seven Eventful Years in Paraguay* (London: Samson, Low, Son, and Marston, 1869) makes extensive references to all questions medical; on the Argentine side see the memoirs of three army surgeons, Benjamín Canard, Joaquín Cascallar, and Miguel Gallegos, *Cartas sobre la Guerra del Paraguay* (Buenos Aires: Academia Nacional de la Historia, 1999).

14. Cristiano Pletz, "Memória de um Voluntário da Pátria"; João Manoel da Silva to his brother, Tuyutí, 8 Sept. 1866; and n.p., 15 July 1868, in Carneiro, *Paraná*, 91, 211, 214.

15. Cerqueira, *Reminiscências*, 329; Benjamin Constant Botelho de Magalhães to Maria Joaquina de Magalhães, on board *Cuevas*, 7 July 1867, in *Cartas da guerra: Benjamin Constant na campanha do Paraguai*, ed. Renato Lemos (Rio de Janeiro: IPHAN and Museu Casa de Benjamin Constant, 1999), 192; José Luiz Rodrigues da Silva, *Recordações da campanha do Paraguay* (São Paulo: Melhoramentos, 1924), 42. On the massacres see Doratioto, *Maldita guerra*, 409–11, 417–18, 438.

16. See, for example, "El sapo imperial fecundado," *Cabichuí* (Paso Pucú), 6 Feb. 1868. Even level-headed officers in the Paraguayan service who should have known better wrote contemptuously of the allied army, if they discussed their enemies in human form at all. See, for example, Francisco Isidoro Resquín, *Datos históricos de la guerra del Paraguay con la Triple Alianza* (Buenos Aires: Billetes de Banco, 1896). One exception to this general trend was Juan Crisóstomo Centurión, a colonel who always regarded the Brazilians with a wary respect. See his *Memorias o reminiscencias históricas sobre la Guerra del Paraguay*, 4 vols. (Asunción: El Lector, 1987).

17. Peter M. Beattie, *The Tribute of Blood: Army, Honor, Race, and Nation in Brazil, 1864–1945* (Durham NC: Duke University Press, 2001), chap. 2; Hendrik Kraay, "Reconsidering Recruitment in Imperial Brazil," *The Americas* 55, no. 1 (July 1998): 20–23; Vitor Izecksohn, "Resistência ao recrutamento para o Exército durante as guerras Civil e do Paraguai: Brasil e Estados Unidos na década de 1860," *Estudos Históricos* (Rio de Janeiro) 27 (2001): 87–95.

18. Whigham, *Paraguayan War*, 384–85.

19. Cerqueira, *Reminiscências*, 91–94; Silva, *Recordações*, 106.

20. Doratioto, *Maldita guerra*, 274–74, 366–67.

21. Alfredo d'Escragnolle Taunay, *A retirada da Laguna: Episódio da Guerra do Paraguai*, 11th ed. (São Paulo: Melhoramentos, n.d.).

22. Cerqueira, *Reminiscências*, 45; Silva, *Recordações*, 7.

23. Carlos Guido y Spano, *Ráfagas*, 2 vols. (Buenos Aires: Igon Hnos., 1879), 1:323–38.

24. Juan Bautista Alberdi, *Obras completas*, 8 vols. (Buenos Aires: La Tribuna Nacional, 1886), 7:29.

25. George Thompson, *The War in Paraguay: With a Historical Sketch of the Country and Notes upon the Military Engineering of the War* (London: Longmans, Green, 1869). In particular see Antônio de Sena Madureira, *Guerra do Paraguai: Resposta ao Senhor Jorge Thompson, auctor da "Guerra del Paraguay"* (Rio de Janeiro: Instituto Artístico, 1870).

26. *La Nación* (Buenos Aires), 2–3 Dec. 1903; *Jornal do Commercio* (Rio de Janeiro), 22 Dec. 1903. See also Doratioto, *Maldita Guerra*, 299–300.

27. See, for example, Augusto Tasso Fragoso, *História da guerra entre a Tríplice Aliança e o Paraguai*, 5 vols. (Rio de Janeiro: Imprensa do Estado Maior do Exército, 1934); Ramón José Cárcano, *Guerra del Paraguay: Orígenes y causas* (Buenos Aires: Viau, 1939);

and José Ignacio Garmendia, *Campaña de Corrientes y de Rio Grande* (Buenos Aires: Peuser, 1904). English-language works based largely on these early-twentieth-century studies include Charles J. Kolinski, *Independence or Death! The Story of the Paraguayan War* (Gainesville: University Press of Florida, 1965); Gilbert Phelps, *The Tragedy of Paraguay* (London: C. Knight, 1975); Chris Leuchars, *To the Bitter End: Paraguay and the War of the Triple Alliance* (Westport CT: Greenwood, 2002); Robert L. Scheina, "The War of the Triple Alliance, 1864–70," in *Latin America's Wars*, vol. 1, *The Age of the Caudillo, 1791–1899* (Washington DC: Brassey's, 2003), 313–32.

28. The nationalist interpretation is best exemplified in the many works of Juan E. O'Leary, whose statue still graces one of Asuncion's main plazas. See in particular his *El mariscal Lopez* (Asuncion: Tall. Graf. "La Prensa," 1920); and *El heroe del Paraguay en el LX aniversario de su gloriosa muerte* (Montevideo: Prometeo, 1930).

29. León Pomer, *La Guerra del Paraguay: Gran negocio!* (Buenos Aires: Ediciones Calden, 1968); Eduardo H. Galeano, *Open Veins of Latin America: Five Centuries of the Pillage of a Continent*, trans. Cedric Belfrage (New York: Monthly Review, 1973), 206–16; E. Bradford Burns, *The Poverty of Progress: Latin America in the Nineteenth Century* (Berkeley: University of California Press, 1980), 128–31. On Paraguay see also Richard Alan White, *Paraguay's Autonomous Revolution, 1810–1840* (Albuquerque: University of New Mexico Press, 1978).

30. Juan Carlos Herken Krauer and María Giménez de Herken, *Gran Bretaña y la guerra de la Triple Alianza* (Asunción: Editorial Arte Nuevo, 1982). See also Leslie Bethell, "O imperialismo britânico e a Guerra do Paraguay," in Marques, *Guerra do Paraguai*, 131–50.

31. José Luiz Werneck da Silva, *As duas faces da moeda: A política externa do Brasil monárquico (1831–1876)* (Rio de Janeiro: Universidade Aberta, 1990), 72; Bandeira, *Expansionismo*, 157–58.

32. Francisco Otaviano [de Almeida Rosa] to José Antônio Saraiva, Buenos Aires, 12 Jan. 1866, in Francisco Otaviano [de Almeida Rosa], *Cartas de Francisco Otaviano*, ed. Wanderley Pinho (Rio de Janeiro: Civilização Brasileira, 1977), 145.

33. Bandeira, *Expansionismo*; Whigham, *Paraguayan War*; Doratioto, *Maldita guerra*. Early hints of this interpretation are found in F. J. McLynn, "The Causes of the War of the Triple Alliance: An Interpretation," *Inter-American Economic Affairs* 33 (autumn 1979): 21–43.

34. León Pomer, "A Guerra do Paraguai e a formação do Estado na Argentina"; Bethell, "Imperialismo britânico"; Alberto da Costa e Silva, "Da guerra ao Mercosur: Evolução das relações diplomáticas Brasil-Paraguai," in Marques, *Guerra do Paraguai*, 118–19, 147, 171.

35. Joaquim Nabuco, *Um estadista do império*, 3d ed. ([1898–99]; Rio de Janeiro: Aguilar, 1975), 439–40; Nabuco, *O Abolicionismo* ([1883]; reprint, Recife: Fundação Joaquim Nabuco and Massangana, 1988), 62.

36. The most recent works in this vein are John Schulz, *O Exército na política: Origens da intervenção militar, 1850–1894* (São Paulo: Editora da Universidade de São

Paulo, 1994); Wilma Peres Costa, *A espada de Dâmocles: O exército, a guerra do Paraguai e a crise do império* (São Paulo: Hucitec and Editora da UNICAMP, 1996); and Vitor Izecksohn, *O cerne da discórdia: A Guerra do Paraguai e o núcleo profissional do exército* (Rio de Janeiro: E-papers, 2002).

37. Júlio José Chiavenato, *Os Voluntários da Pátria (e outros mitos)* (São Paulo: Global, 1983), 27; Chiavenato, *O negro no Brasil da senzala à Guerra do Paraguai* (São Paulo: Brasiliense, 1980), 194–201; Chiavenato, *Genocídio americano: A Guerra do Paraguai* (São Paulo: Brasiliense, 1979), 115–17.

38. Chiavenato, *Genocídio*, 139; *Jornal do Brasil* (Rio de Janeiro), 21 Oct., 11, 25 Nov. 2001.

39. *Jornal do Brasil* (Rio de Janeiro), 12 May 1988.

40. Hendrik Kraay, "Slavery, Citizenship, and Military Service in Brazil's Mobilization for the Paraguayan War," *Slavery and Abolition* 18, no. 3 (Dec. 1997): 228–56. Jorge Prata de Sousa's work, despite the author's argument, tends to confirm the small number of slaves recruited. *Escravidão ou morte: Os escravos brasileiros na Guerra do Paraguai* (Rio de Janeiro: Mauad and ADESA, 1996).

41. Marco Antonio Cunha, *A chama da nacionalidade: Ecos da Guerra do Paraguai* (Rio de Janeiro: Biblioteca do Exército, 2000); Anatólio Alves de Assis, *Pequena história da Guerra do Paraguai* (Belo Horizonte: Imprensa Oficial de Minas Gerais, 1984); Assis, *Genocídio na Guerra do Paraguai* (Belo Horizonte: Imprensa Oficial de Minas Gerais, 1986). On the creation of Caxias as the Brazilian army's patron, see Celso Castro, *A invenção do Exército brasileiro* (Rio de Janeiro: Jorge Zahar, 2002).

42. In addition to the works on slaves cited above, see Eduardo Silva, *Prince of the People: The Life and Times of a Brazilian Free Man of Colour*, trans. Moyra Ashford (London: Verso, 1993); and chapter 4.

43. John Hemming, *Amazon Frontier: The Defeat of the Brazilian Indians* (Cambridge: Harvard University Press, 1987), 264, 301; president to minister of war, Salvador, 30 Oct. 1865, Arquivo do Instituto Histórico e Geográfico Brasileiro, lata 272, pasta 30, doc. 6; James Schofield Saeger, "Warfare, Reorganization, and Readaptation at the Margins of Spanish Rule—the Chaco and Paraguay (1573–1882)," in *The Cambridge History of the Native Peoples of the Americas*, vol. 3, *South America*, ed. Frank Salomon and Stuart B. Schwartz (Cambridge: Cambridge University Press, 1999), pt. 2, pp. 263–64; Saeger, *The Chaco Mission Frontier: The Guaycuruan Experience* (Tucson: University of Arizona Press, 2000), 174.

44. Hemming, *Amazon Frontier*, 439–41; Doratioto, *Maldita guerra*, 104–6, 126–28; Robin M. Wright with Manuela Carneiro da Cunha, "Destruction, Resistance, and Transformation—Southern, Coastal, and Northern Brazil (1580–1890)," in *Cambridge History of Native Peoples*, vol. 3, *South America*, ed. Salomon and Schwartz, pt. 2, pp. 327–38; Saeger, *Chaco Mission Frontier*, 169, 178; Silvia M. Schmuziger, "Chaco: Encruzilhada de povos e 'melting pot' cultural, suas relações com a bacia do Paraná e o Sul Mato-grossense," in *História dos índios no Brasil*, 2d ed., ed. Manuela Carneiro da Cunha (São Paulo: Companhia das Letras, 1998), 468, 470 (photograph).

45. Vera Blinn Reber, "The Demographics of Paraguay: A Reinterpretation of the Great War, 1864–1870," *Hispanic American Historical Review* 68, no. 2 (May 1988): 289–319; Thomas L. Whigham and Barbara Potthast, "Some Strong Reservations: A Critique of Vera Blinn Reber's 'The Demographics of Paraguay: A Reinterpretation of the Great War,'" *Hispanic American Historical Review* 70, no. 4 (Nov. 1990): 667–76.

46. Whigham and Potthast, "Paraguayan Rosetta Stone."

47. Vera Blinn Reber, "Comment on 'The Paraguayan Rosetta Stone,'" *Latin American Research Review* 37, no. 3 (2002): 129–36; Jan M. G. Kleinpenning, "Strong Reservations about 'New Insights into the Demographics of the Paraguayan War,'" *Latin American Research Review* 37, no. 3 (2002): 137–42; Thomas L. Whigham and Barbara Potthast, "Refining the Numbers: A Response to Reber and Kleinpenning," *Latin American Research Review* 37, no. 3 (2002): 143–48; Doratioto, *Maldita guerra*, 457–58.

## 2. Economy and Manpower

This chapter is an expansion of a paper read before the Society for Military History meeting, Calgary, Alberta, May 2001. The author wishes to thank Thomas L. Whigham and Hendrik Kraay for their advice and encouragement in the preparation of this study.

1. Whigham, *Paraguayan War*. Dated but still useful is Box, *Origins of the Paraguayan War*.

2. While military studies of Paraguay's effort abound, there has been no serious in-depth investigation of the nation's war economy. A recent article that does address certain of the country's mobilization problems is Reber, "Case of Total War," 15–40. This article offers useful comments upon the financial mobilization of wartime Paraguay and foreigners' roles therein, though the "total war" thesis that Reber presents is less than convincing. Her analysis of population loss is flawed, as is her treatment of "contraband" traffic in and out of wartime Paraguay.

3. For the state of the Paraguayan treasury on the eve of war, see Juan Bautista Rivarola Paoli, *Historia monetaria del Paraguay: Moneda, bancos, crédito público* (Asunción: Published by the author, 1982), 110–11. Paraguay had no foreign debt in 1864.

4. Rivarola Paoli, *Historia monetaria del Paraguay*, 116–20.

5. Decree of President Francisco Solano López, Asunción, 25 Mar. 1865, ANA/SH 343.

6. Decree of Solano López, Asunción, 10 Apr. 1865, *Semanario*, 15 Apr. 1865.

7. French Consul Émile Laurent-Cochelet to French minister of foreign affairs Édouard Drouyn de L'Huys, Asunción, 21 Aug. 1864; and Laurent-Cochelet to Drouyn de L'Huys, Asunción, 6 Feb. 1865, in Milda Rivarola, *La polémica francesa sobre la Guerra Grande: Eliseo Reclus, La Guerra del Paraguay; Laurent-Cochelet, correspondencia consular* (Asunción: Editorial Histórico, 1988), 152, 154.

8. Laurent-Cochelet to Drouyn de L'Huys, Asunción, 31 July 1865, in Rivarola, *Polémica*, 155.

9. Nicasio Martínez Díaz, *La moneda y la política monetaria en el Paraguay* (Asunción: La Colmena, 1952), 67–70. With Paraguay's defeat in 1870, the currency emitted during the two López regimes became essentially worthless, and those holding paper pesos were ruined. Rivarola Paoli, *Historia monetaria del Paraguay*, 138–39.

10. Rivarola Paoli, *Historia monetaria del Paraguay*, 121–24; *Semanario*, 12 Jan., 2 Mar. 1867; Thompson, *War in Paraguay*, 200–201.

11. Julio César Chavez, *El Presidente López: Vida y gobierno de don Carlos*, 2d ed. (Buenos Aires: Ediciones Depalma, 1968); Juan F. Pérez Acosta, *Carlos Antonio López, obrero máximo: Labor administrativa y constructiva* (Asunción: Editorial Guaranía, 1948). A good overview of the international problems facing Carlos Antonio López in the 1850s is found in Williams, *Rise and Fall of the Paraguayan Republic*, 157–76.

12. Thompson, *War in Paraguay*, 54.

13. Cardozo, *Imperio del Brasil*, 524–30.

14. Thompson, *War in Paraguay*, 97.

15. Efraím Cardozo, *Hace cien años: Crónicas de la guerra de 1864–1870 publicadas en "La Tribuna" de Asunción en el centenario de la epopeya nacional*, 11 vols. (Asunción, EMASA, 1967–80), 4:179.

16. Thompson, *War in Paraguay*, 39. See also "Razón numérica de los cañones de bronce y municiones traídos de la fuerte de Coimbra por el vapor Salto Guayrá," Cuartel del Primer Batallón, Asunción [?], 5 Jan. 1865, ANA/SH 343.

17. Cardozo, *Imperio del Brasil*, 524.

18. Juan B. Otaño, *Orígen, desarrollo y fin de la marina desaparecida en la guerra de 1864–1870* (Asunción: La Colmena, 1942), 3–12.

19. Cardozo, *Hace cien años*, 4:77.

20. Otaño, *Origen*, 13–14.

21. For a brief but good analysis of the decline of international trade and its effect upon Asunción merchants, see Rivarola, *Polémica*, 151–55.

22. An extensive list of the medicines needed may be found in Cardozo, *Hace cien años*, 5:240.

23. Cardozo, *Hace cien años*, 5:238–39.

24. Barbara Potthast-Jutkeit, *"Paraíso de Mahoma" o "País de la mujeres"? El rol de la familia en la sociedad paraguaya del siglo XIX*, trans. Carmen Livieres de Maynzhausen (Asunción: Instituto Cultural Paraguayo-Alemán, 1996), 251–52.

25. "Sobre existencia de azufre y salitre en esa jurisdicción," Francisco Bareiro to militia commander and justice of the peace of Caaguazú, Asunción, 24 Jan. 1867, ANA/SH 352.

26. Thompson, *War in Paraguay*, 208–9.

27. Thomas L. Whigham, "Paraguay and the World Cotton Market: The 'Crisis' of the 1860s," *Agricultural History* 68, no. 3 (summer 1994): 1–15.

28. Potthast-Jutkeit, *"Paraíso,"* 248.

29. Decree of López, Paso Pucú, 12 Feb. 1867, *Semanario*, 16 Feb. 1867.

30. Centurión, *Memorias*, 2:249.

31. Vice President Domingo Francisco Sánchez to militia commanders and justices of the peace, Asunción, 12 Mar. 1866 (circular), ANA/SH 347.

32. Cardozo, *Hace cien años*, 6:108.

33. Cardozo, *Hace cien años*, 6:79.

34. Sánchez to comandantes, militia commanders, and justices of the peace, Asunción, 7 July 1867, ANA/SH 352.

35. Pérez Acosta, *Carlos Antonio López*, 12–15.

36. John Hoyt Williams, "Paraguay's Nineteenth-Century *Estancias de la República*," *Agricultural History* 47, no. 3 (July 1973): 215.

37. For the work and contributions of these foreign technicians, see Josefina Pla, *The British in Paraguay, 1850–1870* (Richmond, Eng.: Richmond, 1976); and John Hoyt Williams, "Foreign *Técnicos* and the Modernization of Paraguay, 1840–1870," *Journal of Inter-American Affairs and World Affairs* 19, no. 2 (May 1977): 233–57. Pérez Acosta, *Carlos Antonio López*, is also quite useful, particularly for the Paraguayan technicians working in these foreign-directed establishments.

38. Harris G. Warren, "The Paraguay Central Railway, 1856–1869," *Inter-American Economic Affairs* 20, no. 4 (spring 1967): 3–22.

39. Thomas L. Whigham, "The Iron Works of Ybicuí: Paraguayan Industrial Development in the Mid–Nineteenth Century," *The Americas* 35, no. 2 (Oct. 1978): 211–17.

40. Cardozo, *Hace cien años*, 6:335.

41. Treasurer Saturnino Bedoya to militia commander and justice of the peace of Caaguazú, Asunción, 4 Jan. 1867, ANA/SH 352.

42. Whigham and Potthast, "Paraguayan Rosetta Stone," 174–86. I have also inspected the 1870 census held by the Archivo del Ministerio de Defensa Nacional and concur with Whigham and Potthast that it presents convincing evidence of the traditional view of a great population disaster as a result of the war.

43. Laurent-Cochelet to Drouyn de L'Huys, Asunción, 12 Dec. 1864, in Rivarola, *Polémica*, 129.

44. Laurent-Cochelet to Drouyn de L'Huys, Asunción, 21 Aug. 1864, in Rivarola, *Polémica*, 152.

45. Rivarola, *Polémica*, 151–52.

46. Williams, *Rise and Fall of the Paraguayan Republic*, 217–18.

47. Cardozo, *Hace cien años*, 4:126.

48. This may well be a conservative estimate of the losses in the early stages of the war. Thompson estimates that from the beginning of recruitment in early 1864 to the withdrawal across the Paraná River in 1865, Paraguay had lost forty thousand dead and ten thousand wounded. *War in Paraguay*, 100.

49. Decree of López, Asunción, 23 Feb. 1866, ANA/SH 347.

50. Circular of Sánchez, Asunción, 30 May 1866, ANA/SH 347. For the repetition of general-mobilization orders in the first six months of 1866, see Potthast-Jutkeit, "*Paraíso*," 247 n.

51. Cardozo, *Hace cien años*, 4:27.

52. Juan Bautista Ortíz to justices of the peace and militia commanders, Asunción, 10 May 1866 (circular), ANA/SH 350.

53. Ironworks Director Julián Ynsfrán to López, Ybicuí, 30 Sept. 1868, ANA/CRB, I-30, 14, 162, nos. 1–3. This establishment was very labor intensive, for fully one-half of the workmen were engaged in making charcoal.

54. Thompson, *War in Paraguay*, 201–2.

55. Cardozo, *Hace cien años*, 3:68–69.

56. Cardozo, *Hace cien años*, 5:238.

57. Masterman, *Seven Eventful Years*, 128. Masterman strangely does not mention dysentery in his list of diseases, though this was a common killer of soldiers.

58. Thompson, *War in Paraguay*, 202.

59. A Prussian General Staff officer within the Paraguayan lines in 1867 considered the medical service to be wretched. Max von Versen, *História da Guerra do Paraguai*, trans. Manuel Tomás Alves Nogueira (São Paulo: Editora da Universidade de São Paulo, 1976), 102–3.

60. Sánchez to Militia Commanders and Justices of the Peace, Asunción, 6 and 9 Sept. 1866, ANA/CRB, I-30, 6, 75.

61. Cardozo, *Hace cien años*, 4:57–58. A brief but excellent analysis of the military manpower crisis in which Paraguay found itself in early 1867 is Williams, *Rise and Fall of the Paraguayan Republic*, 214–16.

62. *Semanario*, 6 Apr. 1867, quoted in Cardozo, *Hace cien años*, 6:91.

63. Circular of Sánchez, Asunción, 19 May 1867, ANA/SH 352.

64. Examples of military requisitions and payments to suppliers are found in Olinda Massare de Kostianovsky, *El Vice Presidente Domingo Francisco Sánchez* (Asunción: Escuela Tecnica Salesiana, 1972), 171–96.

65. See, for instance, "Circular sobre compra y remisión de maíz y vestuarios para el Ejército," Bedoya to militia commanders and justices of the peace of Caaguazú, Asunción, 18 Mar. 1867, ANA/SH 352.

66. Charles Ames Washburn, *The History of Paraguay, with Notes of Personal Observations, and Reminiscences of Diplomacy under Difficulties*, 2 vols. (Boston: Lee & Shepard, 1871), 2:170.

67. Cardozo, *Hace cien años*, 6:260. Large numbers of cattle existed in the far north until 1869.

68. Barbara J. Ganson, "Following Their Children into Battle: Women at War in Paraguay, 1864–1870," *The Americas* 46, no. 3 (Jan. 1990): 335–71. See also Potthast-Jutkeit, "*Paraíso*," 247–56.

69. "Circular sobre trabajos de agricultura," Sánchez to militia commanders and justices of the peace, Asunción, 18 July 1866, ANA/SH 351.

70. Cardozo, *Hace cien años*, 6:132. See also *Semanario*, 19 Oct. 1867, quoted in Massare de Kostianovsky, *Sánchez*, 92–93.

71. Cardozo, *Hace cien años*, 5:140.

72. *Semanario*, 19 Oct. 1867, quoted in Massare de Kostianovsky, *Sánchez*, 92–93. John Hoyt Williams reports a significant decline in land under cultivation from 1866 through 1867. *Rise and Fall of the Paraguayan Republic*, 218–19. The data from Cardozo and Massare de Kostianovsky do not bear this out.

73. Williams defines a *liño* as 1.85 acres. *Rise and Fall of the Paraguayan Republic*, 218. Ganson states that it equals 0.4 acre. "Following Their Children into Battle," 349. Reber defines a *liño* as .015 acre. "Case of Total War," 17.

74. Thompson, *War in Paraguay*, 208.

75. Centurión, *Memorias*, 2:257.

76. Thompson, *War in Paraguay*, 97. There was a continual need for fresh horses for the Paraguayan cavalry in this region. Sánchez to militia commanders and justices of the peace, Asunción, 28 May 1866 (circular), ANA/SH 347.

77. A good account of the hazards of overland travel in southwestern Paraguay and the coastal road north to Asunción, particularly during the winter, is found in John Parish and William Parish Robertson, *Letters on Paraguay: Comprising an Account of a Four Years' Residence in that Republic under the Government of the Dictator Francia*, 3 vols. (London: John Murray, 1838), 2:246–63. The journey described in this work occurred in 1813, but conditions did not change appreciably for travelers over the next half century.

78. López to commander and justice of the peace of Villarrica, Asunción, 12 Oct. 1865, ANA/SH 345; Reber, "Case of Total War," 21.

79. A good description of the camp life of these women is Ganson, "Following Their Children into Battle," 356–58. See also Potthast-Jutkeit, "*Paraíso*," 253–56.

80. Thompson, *War in Paraguay*, 149. On the same theme see Gustavo Barroso, *A guerra do Lopez, contos e episodios da campanha do Paraguai*, 3d ed. (São Paulo: Companhia Editora Nacional, 1929), 106.

81. Bedoya to militia commanders and justices of the peace, Asunción, 12 June 1867 (circular), ANA/SH 352.

82. Versen, *História*, 102.

83. Bedoya to militia commanders and justices of the peace, Asunción, 12 June 1867 (circular); and "Circular sobre compra y remisión de maíz y vestuarios para el Ejercito," Bedoya to militia commanders and justices of the peace of Caaguazú, Asunción, 18 Mar. 1867, ANA/SH 352.

84. Alfred Marbais du Graty, *La République du Paraguay* (Brussels: C. Muquardt, 1862), 166–271; Laurent-Cochelt to Drouyn de L'Huys, Asunción, 26 Feb. 1865, in Rivarola, *Polémica*, 120.

85. Secretary of the British Legation in Buenos Aires and Charge d'Affaires in Paraguay G. Z. Gould to British Minister to Argentina Buckley Mathew, Head-Quarters, Paraguayan Army, Paso Pucú, 10 Sept. 1867, ANA/SH 352. In this commu-

nication Gould massively exaggerated the size of the Paraguayan population as well as the mortality of the troops. But his *eyewitness* account of Paraguayan troops at Humaitá can be trusted.

86. Sánchez to militia commanders and justices of the peace, Piribebuí, 18 May 1869 (circular), ANA/SH 356.

87. Sánchez to militia commanders, Piribebuí, 14 Feb., 5, 22 Apr., 18, and 26 May 1869 (circulars), ANA/SH 356.

88. Cerqueira, *Reminiscências*, 329.

89. A good concise summary of the revolutionary consequences of the Industrial Revolution upon warfare in the mid–nineteenth century is found in Michael Howard, *The Franco-Prussian War: The German Invasion of France, 1870–1871* (New York: Macmillan, 1962), 1–8.

### 3. Protagonists, Victims, and Heroes

I would like to thank the editors for their comments and stylistic improvements to this chapter. Unless otherwise indicated, all newspapers cited in this chapter were published in Asunción.

1. "Crónica del acto en que las aregueñas solicitan su admisión en el ejército," 15 Dec. 1867, quoted in Cardozo, *Hace cien años*, 7:384.

2. *La Regeneración*, 2 Dec. 1869.

3. On Mexican *soldaderas* see Elizabeth Salas, *Soldaderas in the Mexican Military: Myth and History* (Austin: University of Texas Press, 1990).

4. Olinda Massare de Kostianovsky, *La mujer paraguaya: Su participación en la Guerra Grande* (Asunción: n.p., 1970), 15.

5. Potthast-Jutkeit, "Paradies," 115–16. For a discussion of the colonial and Guaraní roots of this division of labor, see Barbara Potthast-Jutkeit, "The Creation of the 'Mestizo Family Model': The Example of Paraguay," *The History of the Family* 2, no. 2 (1997): 123–39.

6. Michael G. Mulhall, *The Cotton Fields of Paraguay and Corrientes: Being an Account of a Tour through these Countries, Preceeded by Annals of Cotton-Planting in the River-Plate Territories from 1862 to 1864* (Buenos Aires: M. G. and E. T. Mulhall, 1864), 90, 104; Washburn, *History of Paraguay*, 2:267.

7. Potthast-Jutkeit, "Paradies," 276–78; Ganson, "Following Their Children into Battle," 335–71, esp. 350; Williams, "Paraguay's Nineteenth-Century *Estancias de la República*," 206–16.

8. Potthast-Jutkeit, "Paradies," 130–31.

9. See the lists in *Semanario* for 1866 and 1867.

10. Émile Laurent-Cochelet to Édouard Drouyn de L'Huys, Asunción, 26 Feb. 1865, in Rivarola, *Polémica*, 141.

11. George Thompson, *La guerra del Paraguay*, 2d ed., trans. Diego Lewis and Angel Estrada (Buenos Aires: L. H. Rosso, 1910), 76, 87, 143; Cardozo, *Hace cien años*, 3:15, 4:76. See also ANA/CRB 4334, 4354, 4876.

12. See Barbara Potthast-Jutkeit, "The Ass of the Mare and Other Scandals: Marriage and Extramarital Relations in Nineteenth-Century Paraguay," *Journal of Family History* 16, no. 3 (1991): 215–39; Potthast-Jutkeit, "La moral pública en Paraguay: Iglesia, Estado y relaciones ilícitas en el siglo XIX," in *Familia y vida privada en la historia de Iberoamérica*, ed. Pilar Gonzalbo Aizpuru and Cecilia Rabell Romero (México: El Colégio de México, 1996), 133–59; and Potthast-Jutkeit, "*Paradies*," 132–35.

13. Vice president to militia commander of Ybytymí, Asunción, 3 July 1867, ANA/ SH 352.

14. Potthast-Jutkeit, "*Paradies*," 271–73.

15. It is not clear whether butchering was a new occupation for women. Washburn asserts that it was, and his assessment has been accepted by at least one historian. *History of Paraguay*, 2:177; Ganson, "Following Their Children into Battle," 370. I found that about 15 percent of butcher shops were run by women before the war. "*Paradies*," 124–25, table 21. That women ran these businesses does not necessarily mean that they also processed the meat. During the colonial period women were allowed to run butcher shops but not slaughter animals and dress meat themselves.

16. Decree of 14 Feb. 1866, ANA/SH 347. For details and similar later decrees see Potthast-Jutkeit, "*Paradies*," 271–72; and Ganson, "Following Their Children into Battle," 352.

17. Max von Versen, *Reisen in Südamerika und der Südamerikanische Krieg* (Breslau: M. Mälzer, 1872), 183; Arthur H. Davis, ed., *Martin T. McMahon: Diplomático en el estridor de las armas* (Asunción: Editora Litocolor, 1985), 392; Laurent-Cochelet to Drouyn de L'Huys, Asunción, 5 July 1866, in Rivarola, *Polémica*, 124; paylist of the military hospital, Cerro León, July–Oct. 1866, ANA/SNE 2836; George Frederick Masterman, *Siete años de aventuras en el Paraguay*, trans. David Lewis (Buenos Aires: Imprenta Americana, 1870), 110, 120–21, 154. Masterman, a British pharmacist, was sceptical about the efficacy of traditional Paraguayan medicines.

18. Vivid descriptions are given in Versen, *Reisen*, 135, 153–55, 198; Thompson, *Guerra del Paraguay*, 207–8; Masterman, *Siete años*, 224; and Centurión, *Memorias*, 2:268. See also an article about the *sargenta* known as Ña Severa in *El Orden*, 5 Mar. 1927; as well as Ganson, "Following Their Children into Battle," 356–57.

19. Cardozo, *Hace cien años*, 3:222.

20. *El Centinela*, 9 May 1867. See also the case of Carolina Valenzuela of Itacurubí del Rosario, who was accused of lacking patriotism because she had refused to dance with soldiers who were marching through town. She saved herself by convincing the judge that she had done so only because the men were too dirty. ANA/CRB 4695.

21. These patriotic assemblies are described extensively in Kostianovsky, *Mujer paraguaya*, 16–42; Idalia Flores de Zarza, *La mujer paraguaya, protagonista de la historia*,

*1537–1870* (Asunción: El Lector, 1987), 135–231, 265–89; and Cardozo, *Hace cien años*, passim, in which *Semanario's* reports are reproduced.

22. Standard Paraguayan historiography interprets these acts as a true reflection of the women's unconditional support and voluntary adherence to "the national cause." Kostianovsky, *Mujer paraguaya*; Flores de Zarza, *Mujer paraguaya*. Somewhat more critical but still in this line of argument is Ganson, "Following Their Children into Battle." I disagree with Ganson when she takes the speeches of theses women as genuine manifestations of their thoughts and sentiments. I will show below that this is not the case. Moreover we do not know the complete speeches but only the (long) extracts in the newspaper reports.

23. Carlota Arévalo de Gill to Escolástica Barrios de Gill, Villetta, 19 Jan. 1867, ANA/SNE 757. For more datails see Potthast-Jutkeit, "*Paradies*," 285–88.

24. Quoted in *Residentas, destinadas y traidoras*, ed. Guido Rodríguez Alcalá (Asunción: RP–Ediciones Criterio, 1991), 93.

25. Justice of the peace to vice president, Villeta, 29 July 1865, ANA/SH 418.

26. Potthast-Jutkeit, "*Paradies*," 289–90.

27. *Baltimore American and Commercial Adviser*, 26 June 1868. See also Herken Krauer and Giménez de Herken, *Gran Bretaña y la Guerra de la Triple Alianza*, 118–19; Versen, *Reisen*, 149, 184–85; and Ulrich Lopacher and Alfred Tobler, *Un suizo en la Guerra del Paraguay* (Asunción: Editorial del Centenario, 1969), 29–30. Reports about women in combat appear in Centurión, *Memorias*, 3:131–32; Rivarola, *Polémica*, 89; and Cardozo, *Hace cien años*, 9:195–97. Ganson presents these reports and songs as illustrations of "women's partriotic, propagandistic, sentimental, and racial feelings." "Following Their Children into Battle," 362.

28. *Cabichuí* (Paso Pucú), 22 June 1868. See also Potthast-Jutkeit, "*Paradies*," 293; and Barbara Potthast, "Residentas, Destinadas y otras heroínas: El nacionalismo paraguayo y el rol de las mujeres en la guerra de la Triple Alianza," in *Las mujeres y las naciones: Problemas de inclusión y exclusión*, ed. Barbara Potthast and Eugenia Scarzanella (Frankfurt and Madrid: Vervurt and Iberoamericana, 2001), 77–92.

29. *Semanario*, 2 Jan. 1867; *El Centinela*, 18 July 1867. See also *Semanario*, 12 Jan., 26 Feb., 8 Sept., and 29 Aug. 1867.

30. Francesca Miller, *Latin American Women and the Search for Social Justice* (Hanover NH: University Press of New England, 1991), 114.

31. For the tensions between elite women and Elisa Lynch before the war, see Potthast-Jutkeit, "*Paradies*," 240–50; for the postwar memoirs see the *destinadas'* declarations cited below (note 45).

32. Vice president to militia commanders and justices of the peace, 18 July 1866, ANA/SH 351; vice president, 2 Mar. 1867, in Cardozo, *Hace cien años*, 6:11–13.

33. "Las buenas obras," *La Estrella* (Piribebuí), 24 Apr. 1869.

34. *Semanario*, 26 Jan., 12. Oct. 1867, 10 Mar., 17, 21 Apr., 7. Sept. 1869.

35. Versen, *Reisen*, 156, 159, 198, 216; Rivarola, *Polémica*, 158–62; Thompson, *Guerra del Paraguay*, 209; Masterman, *Siete años*, 88–89, 119, 158; Dionisio González Torres,

*Aspectos sanitarios de la guerra contra la Triple Alianza* (Asunción: n.p., [1968]), 17–18, 88–89.

36. Declaration of a Paraguayan soldier, in Masterman, *Siete años*, 383; *La Estrella* (Piribebuí), 27 Mar. 1869.

37. Potthast-Jutkeit, "*Paradies*," 303–4.

38. Laurent-Cochelet to Drouyn de L'Huys, Asunción, 7 Oct. 1865, in Rivarola, *Polémica*, 143.

39. ANA/CRB 4695, 4678. For details see Potthast-Jutkeit, "*Paradies*," 304–9, table 35.

40. Rodríguez Alcalá, *Residentas*, 13.

41. Most authors, especially contemporaries, do not distinguish between male and female Paraguayans. Masterman, for example, described all Paraguayans as "slaves" who did not recognize their "degradation." *Siete años*, 4–5. Before the war Alfred Demersay attributed a "blind patriotism" to Paraguayans. *Histoire physique, économique et politique du Paraguay et des établissements des Jésuites*, 2 vols. (Paris: L. Hachette, 1860), 1:398. See also Efraím Cardozo, *Paraguay Independiente* (Asunción: Carlos Schauman, 1987), 240.

42. This at least was the fate of the women who had spread the rumor that López wanted to flee the country. For their trial see ANA/CRB 4685.

43. Declaration of Susana Céspedes de Céspedes, *La Regeneración*, 31 Dec. 1869.

44. Silvia Cordal Gill, *Silvia*, ed. Roberto Quevedo and Manuel Peña Villamil (Asunción: Criterio-Ediciones, 1987), 15–17.

45. The most important and detailed ones are Dorotea Duprat de Laserre, "Aventuras y padecimientos de madama Dorotea Duprat de Laserre," in Mastermann, *Siete años*, 404–36; Cordal Gill, *Silvia*; and the memoirs of Encarnación Bedoya in Rodríguez Alcalá, *Residentas*. *La Regeneración*, Asunción's first postwar newspaper, published the declarations of some *destinadas*, including Susana Céspedes (31 Dec. 1869) and Ana María Dolores Pereira, the mother of Bishop Manuel Antonio Palacios (19 Jan. 1870).

46. Declaration of Ana María Dolores Pereira, *La Regeneración*, 19 Jan. 1870.

47. For this last phase of the war see Potthast-Jutkeit, "*Paradies*," 321–30.

48. Keith Johnston, "Recent Journeys in Paraguay," *Geographical Magazine*, Sept. 1875, 273; Cardozo, *Hace cien años*, 13:310; Centurión, *Memorias*, 4:133, 138, 143, 150. The Brazilian army's campaign diary asserts that they were murdered by Paraguayans, but this seems to be an effort to cover up the fact that the Brazilians failed to help the remaining civilians. Alfredo d'Escragnolle, Viscount of Taunay, *De campo grande a Aquidaban: Diário do exército*, 2 vols. (São Paulo: Melhoramentos, 1926), 2:165.

49. Romulo Nuñez, "Memoria del Capitán de Fragata Rómulo Núñez," *El ejército de la epopeya*, ed. Leandro Prieto Yegros (Asunción: Ediciones Cuadernos Republicanos, 1977), 372–98.

50. Alberto Moby Ribeiro da Silva, "Bailes e festas públicas em Asunción no pós-guerra da Tríplice Aliança: Mulher e resistência popular no Paraguai," *Estudos*

*Ibero-Americanos* 21, no. 1 (June 1999): 39–80, esp. 63–70; Potthast-Jutkeit, "*Paradies*," 331–34.

51. Warren, *Paraguay and the Triple Alliance*, 66–68; Hector Francisco Decoud, *Sobre los escombros de la guerra: Una década de la vida nacional, 1869–1880* (Buenos Aires: Talleres Nacionales H. Kraus, 1925), 294–98. In 1877 a newspaper reported that, based on a decree of 4 July 1876, a policeman arrested a woman because she had responded to him in Guaraní. *La Reforma*, 9 June 1877.

52. Potthast-Jutkeit, "*Paradies*," 338–45, 349–52.

53. Giacomo Bove, *Note di un viaggio nelle missione de Alto Paraná con illustrazione e tavole* (Genoa: n.p., 1885), 70.

54. Alexander Jonin, *Durch Süd-Amerika: Reise und kulturhistorischer Bilder*, vol. 1, *Die Pampa-Länder* (Berlin: Cronbach, 1895), 815.

55. Potthast-Jutkeit, "*Paradies*," 364–65, Tables 37, 38; Whigham and Potthast, "Paraguayan Rosetta Stone," 181–86.

56. Warren, *Paraguay and the Triple Alliance*, 77–78; Silva, "Bailes," 61–80.

57. *El Pueblo*, 15 Sept. 1871.

58. *La Libertad*, 27 Apr. 1874. For other examples see Potthast-Jutkeit, "*Paradies*," 374–75; and Ribeiro da Silva, "Bailes e festas," 63–67.

59. Potthast-Jutkeit, "*Paradies*," 371–79. For the prewar republic see Potthast-Jutkeit, "*Paradies*," 161–75; Potthast-Jutkeit, "Vivir bajo la dictadura del Dr. Francia: Ventajas y problemas del régimen patrimonial desde la perspectiva de las clases populares," in *El Paraguay bajo el Doctor Francia: Ensayos sobre la sociedad patrimonial (1814–1840)*, ed. Jerry W. Cooney and Thomas L. Whigham (Asunción: El Lector, 1996), 141–58; and Thomas L. Whigham, "Rosa Dominga Ocampos: A Matter of Honor in Paraguay," in *The Human Tradition in Latin America: The Nineteenth Century*, ed. Judith Ewell and William H. Beezley (Wilmington DE: Scholarly Resources, 1989), 73–81.

60. J. B. Rusch, *Die Paraguayer* (Rapperswil: H. Grasser & Sohn, 1929), 14–15.

61. This has been repeated in traditional historiography and has entered the national myth. See, for example, Philip Raine, *Paraguay* (New Brunswick: Scarecrow, 1956), 17. See also the statement of Petrona Coronel, delegate of the Movimiento Campesino Paraguayo (Paraguayan Peasants' Movement), who stated much the same in a recent interview, "Wir müssen immer ein wenig nachhelfen," in *Feministamente: Frauenbewegung in Lateinamerika*, ed. Gabi Küppers (Wuppertal: Peter Hammer Verlag, 1992), 128.

62. Potthast-Jutkeit, "*Paradies*"; Potthast-Jutkeit, "Creation of the Mestizo Family Model"; Potthast-Jutkeit, "Moral pública"; and Potthast-Jutkeit, "Ass of the Mare."

63. The first female Paraguayan intellectual was Serafina Dávalos, who received a doctoral degree in 1907 with a dissertation that included feminist ideas: "Humanismo" (Ph.D. diss., Universidad Nacional, Asunción, 1907). The best-known teachers of postwar Paraguay, however, were the daughters of immigrants, sisters Speratti and

Asunción Escalada. For a brief discussion of women's education in these years, see Potthast-Jutkeit, "*Paradies*," 374–79.

64. Figures for 2000, *Statistical Abstracts of Latin America* 38 (Los Angeles: UCLA Latin American Center, 2002), 250–53.

## 4. Patriotic Mobilization in Brazil

I thank the Social Sciences and Humanities Research Council of Canada for research funding. Earlier versions of this paper were presented at the Society for Military History Conference, University of Calgary, May 2001; and at the Conference on War and Citizenship, University of Texas at Austin, April 2003. I thank Thomas L. Whigham for his comments on earlier drafts and José Celso de Castro Alves for assistance at a key point in the research. The *Jornal do Commercio* was published in Rio de Janeiro, while *O Alabama* and *Bahia Illustrada* appeared in Salvador.

1. Francisco Otaviano de Almeida Rosa to José Antônio Saraiva, Buenos Aires, 24 Apr. 1866, in Otaviano, *Cartas*, 159.

2. Richard Graham, "Free African Brazilians and the State in Slavery Times," in *Racial Politics in Contemporary Brazil*, ed. Michael Hanchard (Durham NC: Duke University Press, 1999), 31.

3. Chiavenato, *Voluntários da Pátria*; Chiavenato, *Negro no Brasil*.

4. Cunha, *Chama*, 63, 139, 143.

5. Silva, *Prince of the People*.

6. João Batista Calógeras to Pandiá George Calógeras, Rio de Janeiro, 24 Dec. 1864, in João Batista Calógeras, *Um ministério visto por dentro: Cartas inéditas de João Batista Calógeras, alto funcionário do império*, ed. Antônio Gontijo de Carvalho (Rio de Janeiro: José Olympio, 1959), 175.

7. Richard M. Morse, *From Community to Metropolis: A Biography of São Paulo, Brazil* (New York: Octagon, 1974), 142–43; Eduardo Silva, "O Príncipe Obá, um Voluntário da Pátria," in *Guerra do Paraguai: 130 anos depois*, ed. Maria Eduarda Castro Magalhães Marques (Rio de Janeiro: Relume-Dumará, 1995), 70.

8. Decreto 3371, 7 Jan. 1865; Decreto 3508, 30 Aug. 1865, Brazil, Minister of Justice, *Coleção das Leis do Brazil* (1865); "Mappa da força . . . ," Brazil, Minister of War, *Relatório* (1872); Beattie, *Tribute of Blood*, 173–74.

9. Petitions of José Jorge Bisucheth and José Jorge Perrucho to president of Bahia, [Salvador], c. 1865, APEBA/SACP, m. 3670; president to minister of war, Salvador, 4 Aug. 1865, ANRJ/SPE/IG1, m. 125, fol. 247; J. B. Calógeras to P. G. Calógeras, Rio de Janeiro, 12 Jan. 1865, in Calógeras, *Ministério*, 197.

10. On elections and the mobilization of clienteles see Richard Graham, *Patronage and Politics in Nineteenth-Century Brazil* (Stanford CA: Stanford University Press, 1990), chap. 5. On Pernambuco see Márcio Lucena Filho, "Pernambuco e a Guerra do

Paraguai: O recrutamento e os limites da ordem" (M.A. thesis, Universidade Federal de Pernambuco, 2000), 92–93.

11. João Evangelista de Castro Tanajura to president, Curralinho, 2 Feb. 1865; and Salvador, 21 Apr. 1865, APEBa/SACP, m. 3669; Cerqueira, *Reminiscências*, 56; lieutenant colonel commanding, Second Battalion, Voluntários da Pátria, to commander of arms, Salvador, 16 May 1865 (copy), APEBA/SACP, m. 3444; *O Alabama*, 25 May 1865.

12. On these offers see "Registro de Donativos," APEBA/SACP, m. 3675–1, fols. 86r–146r. The meeting with merchants is reported in president to minister of war, Salvador, 24 Oct. 1865, ANRJ/SPE/IG1, m. 125, fols. 276r–77r. Numerous other such donations to the war effort can be found in APEBa/SACP, m. 3669; and "Relação dos donativos feitos ao Estado para as despezas da guerra, bem como para acquisição de Voluntários da Pátria . . . ," 20 Apr. 1866, appendix to Brazil, Minister of War, *Relatório* (1866). Such donations have been analyzed by Sílio Bocanera Júnior, "A Bahia na Guerra do Paraguai," *Revista do Instituto Geográfico e Histórico da Bahia* 72 (1945), 141–88; Salles, *Guerra do Paraguai*, 98–105; and Marcelo Santos Rodrigues, "Os (in)voluntários da Pátria na Guerra do Paraguai (a participação da Bahia no conflito)" (M.A. thesis, Universidade Federal da Bahia, 2001), 55–56. Much the same story can be told for other provinces. See Carneiro, *Paraná*, 119–25; Zildete Inácio de Oliveira Martins, *A participação de Goiás na Guerra do Paraguai* (Goiâna: UFG Editora, 1983), 70–73; Lucena Filho, "Pernambuco," 89–91; and Adauto M. R. da Câmara, *O Rio Grande do Norte na Guerra do Paraguai* (Natal: Tipografia Galhardo, 1951), 24–27.

13. J. B. Calógeras to P. G. Calógeras, Rio de Janeiro, 22 Jan. 1865, in Calógeras, *Ministério*, 202.

14. Feliciana Maria de Brito Lopes Alves to president, Salvador, 31 Oct. 1865, APEBa/SACP, m. 3669.

15. June Hahner, *Emancipating the Female Sex: The Struggle for Women's Rights in Brazil, 1850–1940* (Durham NC: Duke University Press, 1990), 63; Francisco Augusto Pereira da Costa, *Cronologia histórica do Estado do Piauí*, 2d ed., 2 vols. (Rio de Janeiro: Artenova, 1974), 2:501–5.

16. Gustavo Adolpho de Menezes to commander of arms, Salvador, 3 May 1864, ANRJ/SPE/IG1, m. 125, fol. 203.

17. Felisberto José Pinho to president, Monte Santo, 6 May 1865, APEBa/SACP, m. 3669.

18. For Salvador this trajectory can easily be traced in the January 1865 issues of *O Alabama*. For another province see Câmara, *Rio Grande do Norte*, 21.

19. Commander of arms to president, Salvador, 21 Aug. 1865, APEBA/SACP, m. 3454; 19 Oct. 1865, APEBA/SACP, m. 3411; Silva, *Recordações*, 23; Artur Silveira da Mota Jaceguai, *Reminiscências da Guerra do Paraguai* (Rio de Janeiro: Officina Graphica "A Noite," 1935), 154; Gilberto Freyre, *Order and Progress: Brazil from Monarchy to Republic*, ed. and trans. Rod W. Horton (Berkeley: University of California Press, 1986), 175.

20. Bahia, President, *Relatório* (1866), 16–17.

21. Manoel Pinto de Souza Dantas to Saraiva, Salvador, 24 Aug. 1865, Arquivo do Instituto Histórico e Geográfico Brasileiro, lata 272, pasta 31, doc. 20.

22. On this point see also Salles, *Guerra do Paraguai*, 61, 63.

23. I trace these changes in army recruitment policy in Hendrik Kraay, *Race, State, and Armed Forces in Independence-Era Brazil: Bahia, 1790s–1840s* (Stanford CA: Stanford University Press, 2001), 76–80, 187, 198–200, 225–26.

24. Only 17.1 percent of 936 desertion notices dating from 1830 to 1887 contained information on the soldier's race. See the Bahian commander of arms's correspondence in APEBa/SACP, BNRJ/SM.

25. Quirino Antônio do Espírito Santo to president, Salvador, 26 Jan. 1865, in *O Alabama*, 6 Feb. 1865.

26. On the subscriptions see letter from Bahia, 5 Feb. 1865, in *Jornal do Commercio*, 10 Feb. 1865; letter from Bahia, 14 Feb. 1865, in *Jornal do Commercio*, 21 Feb. 1865 (supplement); and Pedro Francelino to president, Salvador, 6 Apr. 1865, APEBa/SACP, m. 3137.

27. Bahia, President, *Relatório* (1866), 16–17; "Mappa demonstrativo do pessoal das Companhias de Zuavos, Couraças e Sapadores organizado pelo Coronel Comandante Superior Joaquim Antonio da Silva Carvalhal," 13 Nov. 1871, APEBa/SACP, m. 3675.

28. Henri Dutailly, "Les premiers Zouaves (1830–1841)," *Revue Historique des Armées* 5, no. 4 (1978): 43–52; Lee A. Wallace, "Coppens' Louisiana Zouaves," *Civil War History* 8, no. 3 (1962): 269–92; Gerald E. Wheeler, "D'Epineuil's Zouaves," *Civil War History* 2, no. 4 (1956): 93–100; Jean Guenel, *La dernière guerre du pape: Les Zouaves Pontificaux au secours du Saint-Siège* (Rennes: Presses Universitaires de Rennes, 1998).

29. Cunha, *Chama*, 73. This explanation originates with the early-twentieth-century military historian Gustavo Barroso. See Paulo de Queiroz Duarte, *Os Voluntários da Pátria na Guerra do Paraguai*, 4 vols. (Rio de Janeiro: Biblioteca do Exército, 1981–89), vol. 2, tomo 5, pp. 185–86.

30. On the creation of the black company in Pernambuco see Lucena Filho, "Pernambuco," 66–67.

31. On independence in Bahia see Kraay, *Race, State, and Armed Forces,* chap 5. Rodrigues also notes the importance of independence rhetoric in Bahia's mobilization. "(In)voluntários," 18, 43, 51.

32. "Estatutos da Sociedade Veteranos da Independencia," APEBa/SACP, m. 3802.

33. *O Alabama*, 24 Jan. 1865; letter from Bahia, 1 Apr. 1868, in *Jornal do Commercio*, 10 Apr. 1868; *O Alabama*, 21 Mar. 1868.

34. On the Couraças' creation see *O Alabama*, 3, 12 Aug., 4 Nov. 1865.

35. Petition of Domingos Mundim Pestana to emperor, Salvador, 21 Jan. 1841, AHEX/RQ, D-26-709; Service Record of Joaquim Antônio da Silva Carvalhal, AHEX/RQ, JJ-119-3115.

36. Respectively, Joaquim Maurício Ferreira and José Baltazar da Silveira. On these men as independence veterans, see *Jornal do Commercio*, 7 Jan. 1865; and Kraay, *Race, State, and Armed Forces*, 121, 174.

37. André Pinto Rebouças, *Diário e notas autobiográficas: Texto escolhido e anotações*, ed. Ana Flora and Inácio José Veríssimo (Rio de Janeiro: José Olympio, 1938), 65 (31 Mar. 1865).

38. *O Alabama*, 1 Mar. 1866, 7 May 1868, 14 June 1866; files on Quirino and José Eloy Bury, ANRJ/FGP.

39. Quoted in Duarte, *Voluntários*, vol. 2, tomo 5, p. 189.

40. This discussion summarizes the analysis of the black militia in Kraay, *Race, State, and Armed Forces*, passim; it is more concisely presented in Hendrik Kraay, "The Politics of Race in Independence-Era Bahia: The Black Militia Officers of Salvador, 1790–1840," in *Afro-Brazilian Culture and Politics: Bahia, 1790s-1990s*, ed. Hendrik Kraay (Armonk NY: M. E. Sharpe, 1998), 30–56.

41. Evaldo Cabral de Mello, *Rubro veio: O imaginário da restauração pernambucana*, 2d ed. (Rio de Janeiro: Topbooks, 1997), 34, 50, 53–54, 195–96, 220–24; Lucena Filho, "Pernambuco," 66–67.

42. "Despedida do organisador da 2.a Comp.a de Zuavos Bahianos, Joaquim Antonio da Silva Carvalhal," 1 May 1865, BNRJ/SM, II-34, 5, 47.

43. "Hymno dos Zuavos Bahianos," *O Alabama*, 1 Mar. 1865. In the early twentieth century Manoel Raimundo Querino recorded a slightly different version of this song. *A Bahia de outrora* (Salvador: Progresso, 1955), 185–86.

44. Letters from Bahia, in *Jornal do Commercio*, 7 Mar., 6 Apr. 1865. On Gomes see Kraay, *Race, State, and Armed Forces*, 103, 224, 233–39.

45. Manoel [Raimundo] Querino, "Os homens de côr preta na história," *Revista do Instituto Geográfico e Histórico da Bahia* 48 (1923): 363.

46. Petition of Felippe Jose da Exaltação Maniva to emperor, Rio de Janeiro, 7 June 1874, AHEX/RQ, F-18-672.

47. Count of Eu, *Viagem militar ao Rio Grande do Sul* (São Paulo: Companhia Editora Nacional, 1936), 135; Carvalhal to president, Salvador, 13 Sept. 1865, APEBA/SACP, m. 3454. On guard qualifications see Kraay, *Race, State, and Armed Forces*, 225–26.

48. Petition of Maniva to emperor, 5 Sept. 1837, AHEX/RQ, F-18-672; petition of Constantino Luiz Xavier Bigode to minister of empire, Salvador, 12 June 1875, AHEX/RQ, C-60-1707; *O Alabama*, 23 Sept. 1865, 19 Nov. 1868.

49. Kraay, *Race, State, and Armed Forces*, 91.

50. Quirino to commander of arms, Salvador, 24 Feb. 1865, APEBA/SACP, m. 6463.

51. Silva, *Prince of the People*, 22–23.

52. Petition of Andre Fernandes Galliza to president, c. June 1865, APEBA/SACP, m. 3438; commander of arms to president, Salvador, 21 Aug. 1865, APEBA/SACP, m. 3454.

53. Letter from Bahia, 13 Sept. 1865, in *Jornal do Commercio*, 22 Sept. 1865; Abílio Cesar Borges to president, Salvador, 21 Dec. 1865, APEBA/SACP, m. 3669.

54. Commander of arms to president, Salvador, 2 Nov. 1865, APEBA/SACP, m. 3424.

55. Commander of arms to president, Salvador, 10 Aug. 1865, APEBA/SACP, m. 3438; 26 July 1865, APEBA/SACP, m. 3448; 24 Oct. 1865, APEBA/SACP, m. 3411.

56. *O Alabama*, 1, 22, and 31 Aug. 1865; João Francisco Barbosa de Oliveira to commander of arms, Salvador, 5 June 1865, APEBa/SACP, m. 3444; commander of arms to chief of police, 11 Sept. 1865, APEBa/SACP, m. 6463; *O Alabama*, 11 Sept. 1865.

57. These cases can be followed in petition of Florencio da Silva e Oliveira to president, c. 1865, APEBa/SACP, m. 3696; *O Alabama*, 2, 4 Sept., 4 Oct. 1865; acting commander of arms to president, Salvador, 9 Sept. 1865, APEBa/SACP, m. 3432. On reclaiming fugitive slaves from the army, see Hendrik Kraay, "'The Shelter of the Uniform': The Brazilian Army and Runaway Slaves, 1800–1888," *Journal of Social History* 29, no. 3 (spring 1996): 637–57.

58. *O Alabama*, 6 June 1865. In these respects the Zuavos differed little from other Brazilian soldiers. Kraay, *Race, State, and Armed Forces*, chaps. 3, 7; Beattie, *Tribute of Blood*, chap. 7.

59. Kraay, "Reconsidering Recruitment," 1–33.

60. Letters from Bahia, 26 Mar., 10 Apr. 1865, in *Jornal do Commercio*, 6, 15 Apr. 1865.

61. Thomas H. Holloway, "'A Healthy Terror': Police Repression of Capoeira in Nineteenth-Century Rio de Janeiro," *Hispanic American Historical Review* 69, no. 4 (Nov. 1989): 637–76; Carlos Eugênio Líbano Soares, *A capoeira escrava e outras tradições rebeldes no Rio de Janeiro (1808–1850)* (Campinas: Editora da UNICAMP, 2001); Soares, *A negregada instituição: Os capoeiras na Corte imperial, 1850–1890* (Rio de Janeiro: Access, 1999); Maya Talmon Chvaicer, "The Criminalization of *Capoeira* in Nineteenth-Century Brazil," *Hispanic American Historical Review* 82, no. 3 (Aug. 2002): 525–27.

62. Querino, *Bahia*, 78–80.

63. *O Alabama*, 22 June 1867, p. 1.

64. Letter from Bahia, 29 Sept. 1869, in *Jornal do Commercio* (primeira folha), 15 Oct. 1869.

65. Letter from Bahia, 5 July 1865, in *Jornal do Commercio*, 11 July 1865.

66. In addition to fig. 3, see *Bahia Illustrada*, 11 July, 1 Sept. 1867.

67. *O Alabama*, 11 Mar., 14 Sept. 1865.

68. Will of Carvalhal, 17 June 1878, APEBa/SJ, Livros de Registro de Testamentos, vol. 55, fols. 10v–11r.

69. Carvalhal to president, Salvador, 14 Mar. 1865, APEBa/SACP, m. 3454; petition of Carvalhal to president, [Salvador], c. 1866, APEBa/SACP, m. 3671; "Registro de donativos," APEBa/SACP, m. 3675-1, fols. 93v–94r; *Bahia Illustrada*, 1 Dec. 1867; file on Innocencio da Costa Lima, ANRJ/FGP; *O Alabama*, 17 July 1869; "Despedida," *O Alabama*, 4 May 1865; "Despedidas," *Jornal do Commercio*, 10 May 1865.

70. Carvalhal to president, Salvador, 31 July 1865, APEBa/SACP, m. 3454; petition of Silvana Porcina de S. José to president, Salvador, 18 Sept. 1866 (with supporting documentation), APEBa/SACP, m. 3674; "O Coronel Joaquim Antonio da Silva Carvalhal," *Bahia Illustrada*, 5 May 1867.

71. *O Alabama*, 17 July, 5 Sept. 1868.

72. P. de S., *Memorias da viagem de Suas Magestades Imperiaes á provincia da Bahia* (Rio de Janeiro: Typographia Industria Nacional de Cotrim & Campos, 1867), 112–13; Júlio de Santana Braga, *Sociedade Protetora dos Desvalidos: Uma irmandade de cor* (Salvador: Ianamá, 1987), 73. On the Sociedade Protetora dos Desvalidos see also Mieko Nishida, "From Ethnicity to Race and Gender: Transformations of Black Lay Sodalities in Salvador, Brazil," *Journal of Social History* 32, no. 2 (winter 1998): 339–41.

73. *O Alabama*, 18 Sept. 1869, 7 Sept. 1870.

74. *O Alabama*, 18 Jan. 1865.

75. Petition of Carvalhal to president, c. 1866, APEBa/SACP, m. 3671; *O Alabama*, 11 Sept., 11 Dec. 1866; commander of arms to president, Salvador, 23 Feb. 1867, APEBa/SACP, m. 3414. The social composition of the Sapador ranks can be inferred from commander of arms to chief of police, Salvador, 10 Feb. 1867, APEBa/SACP, m. 6464. On slave recruitment in Bahia see Kraay, "Slavery, Citizenship, and Military Service," 228–56.

76. Petitions of Francisco Antônio de Carvalhal Menezes e Vasconcelos (and supporting documents, including a list of these volunteers), AHEX/RQ, F-48-1617.

77. *Bahia Illustrada*, 3, 10 Nov., 1 Dec. 1867.

78. *O Alabama*, 2 Nov. 1867; letters from Bahia, 4, 24 Nov. 1867, in *Jornal do Commercio*, 12 Nov., 2 Dec. 1867.

79. Commander of arms to president, Recife, 29 July 1867, Arquivo Público do Estado de Pernambuco, CA 81, fol. 207. Maniva probably failed to raise this company, for he never claimed to have successfully done so even as he trumpeted his other services. See his petitions file, AHEX/RQ, F-18-672.

80. Most of Paulo de Queiroz Duarte's institutional history of the Zuavos is consistent with the personnel records I located. But Duarte was unable to trace the later Zuavo companies, the Fifth through the Eleventh, which embarked from Salvador in late 1865 and early 1866. See Duarte, *Voluntários*, vol. 2, tomo 5, pp. 184–204. The following account differs significantly from that of Eduardo Silva, who incorrectly assumed that the Third Zuavos, in which Galvão served, remained with the Voluntários da Pátria battalion with which it had embarked from Salvador, implying (also incorrectly) that Galvão saw combat in May 1866. *Prince*, 26–34.

81. "Gazetilha," *Jornal do Commercio*, 22 May 1865.

82. Quoted in Duarte, *Voluntários*, vol. 2, tomo 5, p. 189.

83. Duarte, *Voluntários*, vol. 2, tomo 5, p. 190; Whigham, *Paraguayan War*, 346; Augusto Tasso Fragoso, *História da guerra entre a Tríplice Aliança e o Paraguai*, 5 vols., 2d ed. (1934; Rio de Janeiro: Imprensa do Estado Maior do Exército, 1956–60), 2:225 n. 115; Eu, *Viagem*, 135.

84. Duarte, *Voluntários*, vol. 2, tomo 5, pp. 189–95.

85. Otaviano to Ângelo Muniz da Silva Ferraz, Buenos Aires, 7 Feb. 1866 (secret), in Otaviano, *Cartas*, 150–51. Galvão failed to obtain his request, and on 5 Mar. 1866 he was formally removed from his post on health grounds. Atestado, Secretaria do Comando das Armas, Salvador, 6 May 1871, AHEX/RQ, C-17-539.

86. Files on Galliza and Maniva, ANRJ/FGP.

87. Duarte, *Voluntários*, vol. 2, tomo 5, pp. 195–94; "Correspondenica encyclo-pedica de Alabama,"Tuyutí, 2 Aug. 1866, *O Alabama*, 4 Sept. 1866. The assignment of Zuavos to hospitals is mentioned by two contemporaries. See Cerqueira, *Remi-niscências*, 104; André [Pinto] Rebouças, *Diário: A Guerra do Paraguai (1866)*, ed. Maria Odila Silva Dias (São Paulo: Instituto de Estudos Brasileiros, 1973), 71.

88. Duarte, *Voluntários*, vol. 2, tomo 5, pp. 197–98, 203–4.

89. Cerqueira, *Reminiscências*, 104.

90. The foregoing composite account derives from the following sources: Atestado, Antonio Martins d'Amorim Rangel, Rio de Janeiro, 7 July 1873, AHEX/RQ, F-18-672; file on Marcolino José Dias, ANRJ/FGP; *O Alabama*, 29 Sept. 1866; Rozendo Moniz, "À victoria do Curuzu," 20 Sept. 1866, in *Jornal do Commercio*, 6 Oct. 1866; Querino, "Homens," 362; João Varella, *Da Bahia que eu vi* (Salvador: Tipografia do Povo, 1935), 16.

91. Files on Firmino José das Dores, José Soares Cupim Júnior, Militão de Jesus Pires, and Nicolau da Silveira, ANRJ/FGP.

92. "Vista de interior de Curuzú mirado de aguas arriba (norte a sur) el 20 de setiembre de 1866," 1891, Museu Nacional de Bellas Artes (Buenos Aires), reproduced in Marta Gil Solá and Marta Dujovne, *Cándido López* (Buenos Aires: Associación Amigos del Museo Nacional de Bellas Artes de Buenos Aires, 1971), 25, 26.

93. Files on Militão, Barbosa, Inocêncio, and Manoel do Nascimento e Almeida (killed), ANRJ/FGP; Procuração, Nicolau Beraldo Ribeiro de Navarro, Curupayty, 9 Dec. 1868, BNRJ/SM, Documentos Biográficos, C.988.38.

94. In addition to the illustrations cited in note 66 above, see Captain Marcolino's photograph in Varella, *Da Bahia*, 13.

95. Petition of Barbosa to emperor, Rio de Janeiro, 27 Sept. 1873, AHEX/RQ, JZ-8-2233. Querino incorrectly notes that he died in Paraguay. "Homens," 363.

96. File on Bigode, ANRJ/FGP; Querino, "Homens," 363.

97. *O Alabama*, 28 May, 1 June 1870.

98. *O Alabama*, 29 Mar., 31 July 1870.

99. Petition of Bigode to minister of empire, Salvador, 12 June 1875 (and sup-porting documents), AHEX/RQ, C-60-1707.

100. Varella, *Da Bahia*, 13, 14–15; Braga, *Sociedade*, 75.

101. Silva, *Prince of the People*, 37–41; petitions of Maniva, AHEX/RQ, F-18-672; Barbosa, AHEX/RQ, JZ-8-2233; Balbino Nunes Pereira, AHEX/RQ, B-4-138.

102. See the petitions, dated 31 Mar. 1871, 27 Mar. 1872, and 16 May 1874, in AHEX/RQ, C-17-539. None contain the usual supporting documentation, though army officials repeatedly requested that he provide it. Writing in 1895, Alexandre José de Mello Moraes Filho commented that Obá's companions in Rio de Janeiro insisted that he had a praiseworthy service record. *Festas e tradições populares do Brasil*, 3d ed. (Rio de Janeiro: F. Briguiet, 1946), 543.

103. Querino, "Homens."

104. Silva, *Prince of the People*, chap. 7.
105. Nelson Werneck Sodré, *A história militar do Brasil*, 3d ed. (Rio de Janeiro: Civilização Brasileira, 1979), 143.
106. Centeno, *Blood and Debt*, 31.

## 5. Benjamin Constant

Translated by Hendrik Kraay.

1. The classic Brazilian military history of the war is Tasso Fragoso, *História da guerra*, 2d ed. The most recent scholarly Brazilian study of the war is Doratioto, *Maldita guerra*.
2. Benjamin Constant to [?], n.d. (draft), MCBC/ABC, BC/Doc. Of./C.P. 000.00.00.
3. Lemos, *Cartas da guerra*.
4. Renato Lemos, *Benjamin Constant: Vida e história* (Rio de Janeiro: Topbooks, 1999).
5. Some of these letters, extracts of which were published by his first biographer, no longer exist in the Benjamin Constant archive. See Raimundo Teixeira Mendes, *Benjamin Constant: Esboço de uma apreciação da vida e da obra do Fundador da República Brasileira*, 2 vols. (Rio de Janeiro: Apostolado Positivista do Brasil, 1894), 2:64–150.
6. Bell I. Wiley, *The Life of Johnny Reb: The Common Soldier of the Confederacy* ([1943]; Baton Rouge: Louisiania State University Press, 1993); and Wiley, *The Life of Billy Yank: The Common Soldier of the Union* ([1952]; Baton Rouge: Louisiania State University Press, 1992). I thank Ricardo Salles for calling my attention to these sources.
7. Ricardo Salles, "Memórias de guerra: Guerra do Paraguai e narrativa nacional," *História* (São Paulo) 16 (1997): 138.
8. For different perspectives on this issue see Wilma Peres Costa, *A espada de Dâmocles*; and Izecksohn, *Cerne da discórdia*.
9. Benjamin Constant to Antônio Tibúrcio Ferreira de Sousa, Rio de Janeiro, n.d., MCBC/ABC, BC/Magalhães, BC/IPB 867.00.00.
10. Benjamin Constant to Antônio Tibúrcio Ferreira de Sousa, n.d., MCBC/ABC, BC/Magalhães, BC/IPB 867.00.00.
11. Benjamin Constant to Cláudio Luís da Costa, Corrientes, 3 Oct. 1866, in Lemos, *Cartas da guerra*, 49.
12. Benjamin Constant to Maria Joaquina Botelho de Magalhães, Potrero Piris Camp, 1 Nov. 1866, in Lemos, *Cartas da guerra*, 57.
13. On this point see Auguste Comte, *Opúsculos de filosofia social*, trans. Ivan Lins and J. F. de Souza (Porto Alegre: Globo; São Paulo: Editora da Universidade de São Paulo, 1972), 4–13.
14. Benjamin Constant to Maria Joaquina, Tuyutí, 13 Dec. 1866, in Lemos, *Cartas da guerra*, 66.

15. Benjamin Constant to Maria Joaquina, Tuyutí, 1 June 1867, in Lemos, *Cartas da guerra*, 164.

16. Benjamin Constant to Maria Joaquina, Itapirú, 19 Dec. 1866, in Lemos, *Cartas da guerra*, 72.

17. Dionísio Cerqueira, *Reminiscências da Campanha do Paraguai* (Rio de Janeiro: Gráfica Laemmert, 1948), 193.

18. Benjamin Constant to Maria Joaquina, Itapirú, 19 Dec. 1866, in Lemos, *Cartas da guerra*, 72.

19. Rebouças, *Diário e notas autobiográficas*, 70.

20. Alfredo d'Escragnolle Taunay, *Memórias* (Rio de Janeiro: Biblioteca do Exército, 1960), 137.

21. Cerqueira, *Reminiscências*, 64.

22. Taunay, *Memórias*, 102–3.

23. Benjamin Constant to Costa, Corrientes, 11 Apr. 1867, in Lemos, *Cartas da guerra*, 155 (see the text of this letter in the appendix to chap. 5).

24. Cerqueira, *Reminiscências*, 134.

25. Benjamin Constant to Maria Joaquina, Paso Verde, 25 Sept. 1866, in Lemos, *Cartas da guerra*, 36.

26. Benjamin Constant to Maria Joaquina, Paso Verde, 25 Sept. 1866, in Lemos, *Cartas da guerra*, 39, 40.

27. Benjamin Constant to Maria Joaquina, Corrientes, 3 Oct. 1866, in Lemos, *Cartas da guerra*, 45.

28. Benjamin Constant to Maria Joaquina, Paso Verde, 25 Sept. 1866, in Lemos, *Cartas da guerra*, 41.

29. Benjamin Constant to Costa, Corrientes, 11 Apr. 1867, in Lemos, *Cartas da guerra*, 154 (see the text of this letter in the appendix to chap. 5).

30. Benjamin Constant to Costa, Corrientes, 20 Apr. 1867, in Lemos, *Cartas da guerra*, 163.

31. Benjamin Constant to Costa, Corrientes, 20 Apr. 1867, in Lemos, *Cartas da guerra*, 163.

32. Benjamin Constant to Maria Joaquina, on board *Cuevas*, 7 July 1867, in Lemos, *Cartas da guerra*, 192.

33. Benjamin Constant to Maria Joaquina, Tuyutí, 20 Mar. 1867, in Lemos, *Cartas da guerra*, 131–33.

34. Benjamin Constant to Costa, Corrientes, 3 Oct. 1866, in Lemos, *Cartas da guerra*, 49.

35. Benjamin Constant to Costa, Corrientes, 11 Apr. 1867, in Lemos, *Cartas da guerra*, 156 (see the text of this letter in the appendix to chap. 5).

36. Cerqueira, *Reminiscências*, 286.

37. See his letter of 23 January 1867 in the appendix to chap. 5.

38. Benjamin Constant to Maria Joaquina, Corrientes, 3 Feb. 1867, in Lemos, *Cartas da guerra*, 96.

39. Álvaro Joaquim de Oliveira to Benjamin Constant, Tuyucué, 2 Sept. 1867, in Lemos, *Cartas da guerra*, 96. On the Liberal Party's view of the war see Raimundo Magalhães Júnior, *Deodoro: A espada contra o império*, 2 vols. (São Paulo: Companhia Editora Nacional, 1957), 1:87.

40. Benjamin Constant to Maria Joaquina, Corrientes, 3 Feb. 1867, in Lemos, *Cartas da guerra*, 97.

41. Benjamin Constant to Maria Joaquina, Tuyutí, 1 June 1867, in Lemos, *Cartas da guerra*, 165.

42. Cerqueira, *Reminiscências*, 161.

43. John Schulz, "O Exército e o império," in *História Geral da Civilização Brasileira*, ed. Sérgio Buarque de Holanda and Pedro Moacir Campos (São Paulo: Difel, 1971), tomo 2, vol. 4, p. 237.

44. Benjamin Constant to Maria Joaquina, on board *Cuevas*, 7 July 1867, in Lemos, *Cartas da guerra*, 193.

45. Benjamin Constant to Maria Joaquina, on board *Cuevas*, 7 July 1867, in Lemos, *Cartas da guerra*, 194.

46. Benjamin Constant to Maria Joaquina, Potrero Piris, 1 Nov. 1866, in Lemos, *Cartas da guerra*, 56.

47. Benjamin Constant to Maria Joaquina, Potrero Piris, 29 Nov. 1866, in Lemos, *Cartas da guerra*, 64 (see also the letter of 23 January 1867 in the appendix to chap. 5).

48. Benjamin Constant to Maria Joaquina, Tuyutí, 9 [?] 1867, in Lemos, *Cartas da guerra*, 115. In this letter Benjamin Constant is referring to the Brazilian custom in which children ask for and receive a blessing from their parents.

49. Benjamin Constant to Costa, Tuyutí, 23 Mar. 1867, in Lemos, *Cartas da guerra*, 134.

50. Benjamin Constant to Costa, Corrientes, 5 Apr. 1867, in Lemos, *Cartas da guerra*, 151.

51. Benjamin Constant to Costa, Tuyutí, 7 Mar. 1867, in Lemos, *Cartas da guerra*, 129.

52. Benjamin Constant to Costa, Corrientes, 2 Apr. 1867, in Lemos, *Cartas da guerra*, 142.

53. Benjamin Constant to Maria Joaquina, Corrientes, 12 Apr. 1867, in Lemos, *Cartas da guerra*, 157.

54. Benjamin Constant to Maria Joaquina, Tuyutí, 7 June 1867, in Lemos, *Cartas da guerra*, 175.

55. Benjamin Constant to Maria Joaquina, Tuyutí, 5 June 1867, in Lemos, *Cartas da guerra*, 169.

56. João Cruz Costa, *Contribuição à história das idéias no Brasil* (Rio de Janeiro: José Olympio, 1956), 144.

57. Nabuco, *Um estadista do Império*, 439–40. On this point see also Lemos, *Benjamin Constant*, 177–83; and Celso Castro, *Os Militares e a República: Um estudo sobre cultura e ação política* (Rio de Janeiro: Jorge Zahar Editor, 1995).

58. Benjamin Constant to Maria Joaquina, Paso Verde, 25 Sept. 1866, in Lemos, *Cartas da guerra*, 41.

59. Benjamin Constant to Costa, Corrientes, 20 Apr. 1867, in Lemos, *Cartas da guerra*, 163.

60. José Murilo de Carvalho, "Forças Armadas na Primeira República: O poder desestabilizador," *História Geral da Civilização Brasileira*, ed. Boris Fausto (São Paulo: DIFEL, 1977), tomo 3, vol. 2, p. 197.

61. Benjamin Constant Botelho de Magalhães to Cláudio Luís da Costa, Itapirú, 23 Jan. 1867, in Lemos, *Cartas da guerra*, 90–93.

62. Olímpia Gonçalves Dias, sister of Benjamin Constant's wife and widow of the romantic poet Antônio Gonçalves Dias.

63. Friend of Cláudio Luís da Costa's family and a resident (*agregada*) in their house.

64. Count Wilhelm of Schaumburg-Lippe (1724–65), a German officer contracted by Portugal to train its army and author of the Articles of War still in force at the time of the Paraguayan War. The "terrifying cries" that Benjamin Constant mentions is an allusion to the articles, which specify death for soldiers who in battle shout "The enemy has surrounded us," "We are cut off," or "Escape if you can." See "Regulamento de infantaria e artilharia de 1763," in Wenceslao Freire de Carvalho, *Promptuário dos processos militares*, 2d ed. (Rio de Janeiro: Imp. Nacional, 1887), 302.

65. [Benjamin Constant's footnote]. Maybe our battalions will shoot at each other to see whether they can thus finish off the Paraguayans.

66. The Marquis of Caxias, commander of the Brazilian forces.

67. Marshal Alexandre Gomes de Argolo Ferrão, the future Viscount of Itaparica.

68. Nickname of Maria Joaquina Botelho de Magalhães, wife of Benjamin Constant.

69. Maj. Antônio Tibúrcio Ferreira de Sousa, friend of Benjamin Constant.

70. Benjamin Consant to Costa, Corrientes, 11 Apr. [1867] in Lemos, *Cartas da guerra*, 152–56.

## 6. The War and Political Culture

An earlier version of this paper was presented at the Society for Military History Conference, University of Calgary, May 2001. My thanks to Thomas L. Whigham, Hendrik Kraay, and Zayde Antrim for their comments on this chapter and to Paulo Roberto Staudt Moreira for his friendship and generosity during years of research in Porto Alegre.

1. Joaquim Nabuco, *Um estadista do império*, 5th ed., 2 vols. ([1897–98]; Rio de Janeiro: Topbooks, 1997), 1:533–34 n. 81. Franciso Doratioto confirms the avarice of Gaúcho speculators. *Maldita guerra*, 178–79.

2. Antonio Eleutherio de Camargo, *Quadro estatistico e geographico da Provincia de S. Pedro do Rio Grande do Sul* (Porto Alegre: Typ. do *Jornal do Commercio*, 1868), 79.

3. Newton Luis Garcia Carneiro, *A identidade inacabada: O regionalismo político no Rio Grande do Sul* (Porto Alegre: EDIPUCRS, 2000), 146–84; Helga I. L. Piccolo, *Vida política no século 19: Da descolonização ao movimento republicano* (Porto Alegre: Editora da UFRGS, 1991).

4. José Murilo de Carvalho, *Os bestializados: O Rio de Janeiro e a república que não foi* (São Paulo: Companhia das Letras, 1987), 51; Silva, *Prince of the People*, 38–40; Silva, "O Príncipe Obá," 65–76.

5. Compare the claims on citizenship by peasants who had fought in national and international wars in Mexico and Peru as analyzed by Florencia E. Mallon, *Peasant and Nation: The Making of Postcolonial Mexico and Peru* (Berkeley: University of California Press, 1995).

6. For example, *processo* 1204, *réu* Inocente José de Vargas, m. 41, APERGS.

7. Duarte, *Voluntários*, vol. 1, tomo 1, p. 218.

8. Salles, *Guerra do Paraguai*, 81.

9. On the conscription of voluntários and other soldiers, see, for instance, the lists of slaves offered as substitutes in Pelotas, "Livro para lançamento ordinário do 1.o Cartório de Pelotas, 1867 a 1868," J-69, AHRGS; and nationally, Beattie, *Tribute of Blood*, chap. 2; and Jorge Prata de Souza, *Escravidão ou morte: Os escravos brasileiros na Guerra do Paraguai* (Rio de Janeiro: Mauad and ADESA, 1996).

10. As Peter M. Beattie has argued, that effort had much to overcome. The Brazilian military's rank and file had a poor reputation as the repository of criminals and sexually "dishonorable" individuals. *Tribute of Blood*; Beattie, "The House, the Street, and the Barracks: Reform and Honorable Masculine Social Space in Brazil, 1864–1945," *Hispanic American Historical Review* 76, no. 3 (Aug. 1996): 439–73.

11. Manoel Paranhos de S. Vellozo to Diogo Antonio Feijó, Rio Pardo, 19 Feb. 1836, BNRJ/SM, II-32, 3, 5, n. 1. The Farroupilha Revolution began as a protest against imperial tariffs and other policies seen as hampering the pastoral economy of Rio Grande do Sul. It escalated into the declaration of a separate republic before its "pacification" in 1845. Spencer Leitman, *Raízes sócio-econômicas da Guerra dos Farrapos: Um capítulo da história do Brasil no século XIX* (Rio de Janeiro: Edições Graal, 1979).

12. See the *atos* of 16 Feb. 1866, 16 June 1866, and 11 Jan. 1867, Legislação, cód. 584, AHRGS; and the correspondence of authorities in Cruz Alta, who worried that the removal of their National Guard detachment would lead to slave rebellion: subdelegate, Fifth District, to president of Rio Grande do Sul, Cruz Alta, 4 July 1865, Subdelegacia de Polícia, m. 7, AHRGS.

13. Brazil, Directoria Geral de Estatísticas, *Recenseamento da população do Brazil a que se procedeu no dia 1 de agosto de 1872*, 21 vols. (Rio de Janeiro: Leuzinger & Filhos, 1873–76), 19:1.

14. Helga I. L. Piccolo provides a useful annotated catalog of slave insurrections in 1835–68, *A resistência escrava no Rio Grande do Sul* (Porto Alegre: Curso de Pós-Graduação em História, Universidade Federal do Rio Grande do Sul, 1992).

15. Consul to secretary of state, Rio Grande, 18 Feb. 1865, "Despatches from United States Consuls in Rio Grande do Sul, 1829–97," National Archives and Records Administration, Washington DC, T4, roll 4.

16. See the reports reprinted in Piccolo, *Resistência*, 42–43.

17. Police delegate to president, Porto Alegre, 2 and 7 Feb. 1865, Delegacia de Polícia, m. 7, AHRGS; police delegate to chief of police, São Gabriel, 6 Nov. 1870, Delegacia de Polícia, m. 27, AHRGS; subdelegate, Second District, to president, Bagé, 22 Mar. 1865, Subdelegacia de Polícia, m. 1, AHRGS; subdelegate, First District, to president, Arroio Grande, 22 Feb. 1865, Subdelegacia de Polícia, m. 1, AHRGS; Rio Grande do Sul, President, *Relatório* (1865), 21; police delegate to police chief, São Gabriel, 6 Nov. 1870, Delegacia de Polícia, m. 27, AHRGS.

18. Police delegate to president, Porto Alegre, 19, 22, 26 Nov. 1864, Secretaria de Polícia, m. 8, AHRGS; commander, Navy Apprentices' Company, to president, Santa Isabel, 25 Feb., 23 Mar. 1865, Marinha, Companhia de Aprendizes Marinheiros, m. 72, lata 536, AHRGS.

19. President to minister of justice, Porto Alegre, 27 Dec. 1864 (secret), Correspondência do Presidente da Província, cód. A-2.16, AHRGS; Police Delegate to president, Porto Alegre, 17 Dec. 1864, Secretaria de Polícia, m. 8, AHRGS. On the Germans' offer see police delegate to president, Porto Alegre, 23 Dec. 1864, Secretaria de Polícia, m. 8, AHRGS. For other rumors judged false compare Rio Grande do Sul, President, *Relatório* ([1859]), 3–4 [on Capivary, Encruzilhada, and Herval]; (1854), 4–5 [on Rio Grande]; and "Interrogatório feito a Feliciano Gonçalves Botelha," 18 June 1859, Polícia, Inquéritos, m. 2, AHRGS.

20. Police delegate to president, Jaguarão, 2, 7 Feb. 1865, Delegacia de Polícia, m. 7, AHRGS.

21. Chief of police to president, Porto Alegre, 16, 21 Oct., 4 Nov. 1868, Secretaria de Polícia, m. 12, AHRGS.

22. Chief of police to vice president, Porto Alegre, 27 June 1868, Secretaria de Polícia, m. 11, AHRGS; acting chief of police to vice president, Porto Alegre, 28 Aug. 1868, Secretaria de Polícia, m. 12, AHRGS. Piccolo reprints several key documents in *Resistência*, 44–47. Rui Vieira da Cunha provides a basic narrative of events. "Escravos rebeldes em Porto Alegre," *Mensário do Arquivo Nacional* 9, no. 8 (Aug. 1978): 9–14.

23. Given the size and popularity of the festivities of that holiday, his calculations may well have been correct. On Espírito Santo celebrations in Porto Alegre see Gaston Mazeron Hasslocher, *Notas para a história de Porto Alegre* (Porto Alegre: Barcellos, Bertaso & Cia., 1928), 27–29.

24. Chief of police to vice president, Porto Alegre, 27 June 1868, Secretaria de Polícia, m. 11, AHRGS.

25. Other parts of Brazil, of course, bordered on foreign countries, but many of those regions were in interior zones still weakly integrated into the empire in the nineteenth century. One other exception to that tendency was Mato Grosso; bordering on Paraguay, it had been part of the gold cycle that dominated the eighteenth-century Brazilian economy. On the effects of the militarized frontier and the Paraguayan War on master-slave relations in Mato Grosso's capital, see Luiza Rios Ricci Volpato, *Cativos do sertão: Vida cotidiana e escravidão em Cuiabá em 1850–1888* (São Paulo: Editora Marco Zero; Cuiabá: Editora da Universidade Federal de Mato Grosso, 1993).

26. Requerimentos, Grupo Escravos, m. 60, 1829, AHRGS; Requerimentos, Grupo Justiça, m. 62, 1830, AHRGS.

27. "Auto de Perguntas feito a escravos fugidos," Passo Fundo, 16 Aug. 1878, Delegacia de Polícia de Cruz Alta, Delegacia de Polícia, m. 4B, AHRGS. On escaped slaves in foreign military forces, see police delegate to police chief, São Gabriel, 26 Jan. 1866, Delegacia de Polícia, m. 27, AHRGS; and "Relação dos escravos fugidos para o Estado Oriental, pertencentes a diversas pessoas desta província" and "Relação de escravos fugidos para a República do Paraguay, pertencentes a diversas pessoas desta província" (both 1850), lata 531, m. 1, Estatística, AHRGS.

28. Unnumbered *processo, réu* José Soares Pinto, Justiça, Processos, lata 101, AHRGS; Michael G. Mulhall, *Rio Grande do Sul and Its German Colonies* (London: Longmans, Green, 1873), 169. Brazilian law was less generous than Mulhall implies; only those slaves whose masters voluntarily took them outside of the empire were to gain their freedom. Antônio Marques Perdigão Malheiro, *A escravidão no Brasil: Ensaio Histórico, Jurídico, Social,* 3d ed., 2 vols. (Petrópolis: Vozes, 1976), 1:99.

29. *Annaes da Assembléa Legislativa da Provincia de São Pedro do Sul: 12.a legislatura* (Porto Alegre: Typographia do *Jornal do Commercio,* 1867), 26–28, 108–11, 121–23, 138–44, 166–70. Compare promotor público to president, Porto Alegre, 18 Dec 1858, Justiça, Porto Alegre, m. 27, AHRGS.

30. Police delegate to chief of police, São Gabriel, 26 Jan. 1866, Delegacia de Polícia, m. 27, AHRGS.

31. Judy Bieber, "Slavery and Social Life: Attempts to Reduce Free People to Slavery in the Sertão Mineiro, Brazil, 1850–1871," *Journal of Latin American Studies* 26, no. 3 (Oct. 1994): 597–617.

32. Joan E. Meznar, "The Ranks of the Poor: Military Service and Social Differentiation in Northeast Brazil, 1830–1875," *Hispanic American Historical Review* 72, no. 3 (Aug. 1992): 344.

33. Meznar, "Ranks." Compare also Silva, *Prince of the People,* 19–25; Beattie, *Tribute of Blood,* chaps. 1–2; and J. Carlos, "Memoria sobre a organisação da Guarda Nacional na Província de São Pedro do Rio-grande do Sul," 1863, BNRJ/SM, 16, 1, 16.

34. Police delegate to chief of police, Conceição do Arroio, 7 Apr. 1870, Delegacia de Polícia de Conceição do Arroio, m. 4, AHRGS.

35. President to chief of police, Porto Alegre, 27 Mar. 1871, Correspondência dos Governantes, m. 111, AHRGS.

36. On the preference for recruiting vagrants, see especially circular from chief of police, 16 June 1857, Polícia/Correspondência, Chefatura de Polícia, m. 11, AHRGS. Compare also Paulo Roberto Staudt Moreira, "Entre o deboche e a rapina: Os cenários sociais da criminalidade popular em Porto Alegre (1868–1888)" (M.A. thesis, Universidade Federal do Rio Grande do Sul, 1993), 34–39; and chief of police to port captain, Porto Alegre, 11 Sept. 1854; and acting chief of police to port captain, Porto Alegre, 11 May 1854, both in Polícia, cód. 243, AHRGS.

37. For a particularly thorough and balanced consideration of this issue, see Kraay, "'Shelter of the Uniform,'" 637–57.

38. Petition of Florencia Maria de Jesús to president, 3 July 1863, Requerimentos, Escravos, m. 101, AHRGS; port captain to president, Porto Alegre, 11 Sept. 1880, and annexed documents, Requerimentos, Polícia, m. 196, AHRGS; president to chief of police, Porto Alegre, 1 Sept. 1869, Polícia, cód. A.552, AHRGS; chief of police to president, Porto Alegre, 5 Jan. 1869, and annexed documents, Secretaria de Polícia, m. 13, AHRGS.

39. Martiniano's case appears in chief of police to president, Porto Alegre, 22 Aug. 1862, Secretaria de Polícia, m. 4, AHRGS. Compare president to chief of police, Porto Alegre, 19 Oct. 1871, Correspondência dos Governantes, m. 112, AHRGS; subdelegate, First District, to commander of arms, Porto Alegre, 26 Dec. 1854, Polícia, Subdelegacia de Políca, Porto Alegre, m. 5, AHRGS; petition of Rosa Antonia da Cunha Ferreira to president, 21 May 1862, Requerimentos, Escravos, m. 99, AHRGS; and police secretary to chief of police, Porto Alegre, 2 Nov. 1867, Chefatura de Polícia, m. 6, AHRGS. On looking for runaways in naval and army arsenals, see police secretary of Corte to chief of police of Rio Grande do Sul, Rio de Janeiro, 17 May 1867, Chefatura de Polícia, m. 6, AHRGS; and Mário Maestri Filho, *O escravo no Rio Grande do Sul: A charqueada e a gênese do escravismo gaúcho* (Porto Alegre: Escola Superior de Teologia São Lourenço de Brindes; Caxias do Sul: Editora da Universidade de Caxias do Sul, 1984), 123. After the war authorities may have been more likely to imprison unclaimed slave-soldiers. See chief of police to president, Fourth District, Passo Fundo, 24 Feb. 1876, Polícia, cód. 78, AHRGS.

40. On the troubled use of the military as a penal institution, see Beattie, *Tribute of Blood*, chap. 6.

41. Subdelegate, Fifth District, to president, Cruz Alta, 4 July 1865, Subdelegacia de Polícia, m. 7, AHRGS; delegate to chief of police, Jaguarão, 8 Oct. 1870, Delegacia de Polícia, m. 7, AHRGS; petition from residents of Villa de Piratiny to president, 4 Feb. 1865, Requerimentos, Polícia, m. 124, AHRGS; subdelegate to chief of police, Capivary, 10 Jan. 1866, Delegacia de Polícia, m. 20, AHRGS; president to chief of police, 3 June 1868, Polícia, cód. A.552, AHRGS; "Auto de perguntas feito a João Vargas Correia," 16 Sept. 1873; Moreira, "Entre o deboche," 13–18.

42. "Auto de perguntas feito a Benedicto Santa Anna de Arruda," 7 Feb. 1867, Delegacia de Polícia, Porto Alegre, m. 12, AHRGS.

43. Roger Alan Kittleson, "The Problem of the People: Popular Classes and the Social Construction of Ideas in Porto Alegre, Brazil, 1846–1893" (Ph.D. diss., University of Wisconsin–Madison, 1997), esp. chap. 3. See also João José Reis and Eduardo Silva, *Negociação e conflito: A resistência negra no Brasil escravista* (São Paulo: Companhia das Letras, 1989); Sidney Chalhoub, *Visões da liberdade: Uma história das últimas décadas da escravidão na corte* (São Paulo: Companhia das Letras, 1990); and Silvia Hunold Lara, *Campos da violência: Escravos e senhores na Capitania do Rio de Janeiro, 1750–1808* (Rio de Janeiro: Paz e Terra, 1988).

44. Porto Alegre's city council began renaming prominent streets and squares in honor of Paraguayan War heroes and victories as early as 1865. Sérgio da Costa Franco, *Porto Alegre: Guia histórico*, 2d ed. (Porto Alegre: Editora da Universidade Federal do Rio Grande do Sul, 1992), 135, passim.

45. *Processo* 1270A, *réu* Antonio José Godinho, m. 45, APERGS.

46. *Processo* 1270A, *réu* Antonio José Godinho, m. 45, APERGS. Contemporary chroniclers often considered police and army soldiers stationed in Porto Alegre to be as much a threat to public order as a guarantee of it. Achylles Porto Alegre, for instance, wrote of the nineteenth century, "soldiers were in general bad elements, drunks, disorderly, and knife-artists." *Porto Alegre, Paizagens mortas* (Porto Alegre: Livraria do Globo, 1922), 24; Porto Alegre, *História popular de Porto Alegre*, 2d ed. (Porto Alegre: Unidade Editorial Porto Alegre, 1994), 68–69. See also Moreira, "Entre o deboche," 10–29, passim; and Cláudia Mauch, "Ordem pública e moralidade: Imprensa e policiamento urbano em Porto Alegre na década de 1890" (M.A. thesis, Universidade Federal do Rio Grande do Sul, 1992).

47. *Processo* 1322, *réu* João Alves Pedroso, m. 48, APERGS. Compare Paulo Roberto Staudt Moreira, *Faces da liberdade, máscaras do cativeiro: Experiências de liberdade e escravidão, percebidas através das cartas de alforria—Porto Alegre (1858–1888)* (Porto Alegre: Arquivo Público do Estado/EDIPUCRS, 1996), 69–71. On authorities' general concern about such veterans, see Circular to Delegates, 3 Nov. 1870, Polícia, cód. 241, AHRGS. On other soldiers' hostility to foreigners see chief of police to president, Porto Alegre, 8 Apr. 1879, Polícia, cód. 88, AHRGS.

48. Salles, *Guerra do Paraguai*, 63.

49. *Processo* 1499, *réu* Salome Suzano Escalara, m. 58, APERGS; and compare *processo* 1234, *réu* Miguel Alves de Carvalho, m. 43, APERGS.

50. *Processo* 1219, *réu* Serafim Floriano, m. 42, APERGS.

51. *Processo* 1209, *réu* Propício José de Magalhães, m. 42, APERGS; and compare *processo* 1215, *réu* Felisbino Gonçalves da Silva, m. 42, APERGS.

52. Hebe Maria Mattos de Castro, *Das cores do silêncio: Os significados da liberdade no sudeste escravista—Brasil século XIX* (Rio de Janeiro: Arquivo Nacional, 1995), 35, passim; Hebe Maria Mattos, *Escravidão e cidadania no Brasil monárquico* (Rio de Janeiro: Jorge Zahar, 2000), 17.

53. *Processo* 1293, *réu* Manoel Florencio da Conceição, m. 46, APERGS.

54. *Processo* 1417, *réu* Francisco Mambretti, m. 54, APERGS.

55. Moreira, "Entre o deboche," 80–121.

56. *Processo* 1737, *réu* Francisco Barbosa Forquine, m. 70, APERGS; chief of police to delegate, Porto Alegre, 12 Oct. 1870, Polícia, cód. 241, AHRGS.

57. Circular to Delegate, 3 Nov. 1870, Polícia, cód. 241, AHRGS; chief of police to sudelegate, Belém, 23 Sept. 1871, Polícia, cód. 241, AHRGS.

58. *Processo* 1358, *réu* Ildefonso Ferreira de Azevedo Lopes, m. 51, APERGS.

59. *O Mercantil* (Porto Alegre), 31 May 1878.

60. Police delegate to commander of detachment of Sixth Infantry Battalion, Pelotas, 31 Dec. 1871, Delegacia de Polícia, m. 10, AHRGS.

61. *Processo* 1551, *réus* Rezendo Rodrigo Homem de Carvalho and José Vieira Pacheco, m. 61, APERGS. See also *processo* 1589, *réus* Alfredo Alves Teixeira and Querino José de Oliveira, m. 63, APERGS; *processo* 1477, *réu* Faustino Antonio Barbosa, m. 57, APERGS.

62. *Processo* 1181, *réus* Joaquim Alvaro et al., m. 40, APERGS.

63. See Fernando Uricoechea, *The Patrimonial Foundations of the Brazilian Bureaucratic State* (Berkeley: University of California Press, 1980), chap. 6.

64. In this respect they share parallels to the defense of *fueros* (military corporate jurisdictions) in nineteenth-century Mexico. Fernando Escalante Gonzalbo, *Ciudadanos imaginarios* (Mexico: El Colegio de Mexico, 1992), 171. More generally see William A. DePalo Jr., *The Mexican National Army, 1822–1852* (College Station: Texas A&M University Press, 1997).

65. Ilmar Rohloff de Mattos, *O tempo saquarema: A formação do estado imperial*, 2d ed. (São Paulo: Editora Hucitec, 1990).

66. Quoted in Helga I. L. Piccolo, "Porto Alegre em 1873: A imprensa liberal da capital como fonte de estudo para a política provincial," *Revista do Instituto de Filosofia e Ciências Humanas* 4 (1976): 226. See also Carneiro, *Identidade*, 146–57; Rio Grande do Sul, President, *Relatório* (1866), 3; Beattie, *Tribute of Blood*, 72, 90; and Assembléia Legislativa Provincial, 19 Oct. 1857, *Correio do Sul* (Porto Alegre) 21 Oct. 1857.

67. Eduardo Silva, *As queixas do povo* (Rio de Janeiro: Paz e Terra, 1988), 35.

## 7. Uruguay and the Paraguayan War

1. The term "Oriental" refers to Uruguayans. It derives from the formal name of the country, "Oriental Republic of Uruguay," and was used in preference to "Uruguayan" throughout the nineteenth century.

2. See Eduardo Acevedo, *Anales históricos del Uruguay*, 6 vols. (Montevideo: Barreiro y Ramos, 1933–36), 2:31. Unless otherwise indicated, factual information for this study has been taken from Acevedo's *Anales* and Juan E. Pivel Devoto and Alcira Raineri de Pivel, *Historia de la República Oriental del Uruguay (1830–1930)* (Montevideo:

Raúl Artagaveitia Editor, 1945). A combined use of these two excellent works, written by a Colorado and two Blanco authors respectively, allows a balanced assessment of Uruguayan history until the 1930s.

3. A good description of *montonera* war can be found in José María Paz, *Memorias póstumas: Comprende sus campañas, servicios y padecimientos, desde la Guerra de la Independencia, hasta su muerte, con variedad de otros documentos inéditos y de alta importancia*, 3 vols. ([1855]; reprint, Buenos Aires: La Cultura Argentina, 1917), 1:245–53.

4. "Manifiesto del General Venancio Flores a sus compatriotas. Norte del Río Negro," 1 Aug. 1863, in Antonio H. Conte, *La cruzada libertadora: Recopilación de datos y documentos* (Montevideo: Imprenta y Librería del Plata, 1891), 100–105.

5. Decrees of 9, 17 Mar. 1865, in Pedro de León, *Recopilación de decretos militares desde el año 1828 hasta 1889*, 2 vols. (Montevideo: Tipografía de la Escuela Nacional de Artes y Oficios, 1889–90), 2:227–30; decrees of 10, 29, 31 Mar., 10 Apr. 1865, BHEME 127 (1970), 86–87, 95–98.

6. This chapter includes several references to articles published in Colorado newspapers as well as to debates among them taken from *El Siglo* (Montevideo), Feb. 1865–Dec. 1869; *La Tribuna* (Montevideo), Mar. 1865–Dec. 1869; *El Orden* (Montevideo), Apr.–Dec. 1868; and *La Soberanía Popular* (Montevideo), May–Sept. 1869.

7. Decrees of 5, 19 May 1865, in De León, *Recopilación*, 2:232–33, 235–36; decrees of 17, 31 Mar., 1 Apr., 20 May, 14 June 1865, BHEME 127 (1970), 89–90, 96, 98, 111–12, 123.

8. "Informe de Manuel Martínez a la Comisión Histórica del Centro de Guerreros del Paraguay," Montevideo, 26 Mar. 1916, MHN, vol. 88.

9. Decree of 9 May 1865 [ratifying the Triple Alliance treaty], in Antonio H. Conte, *Gobierno provisorio del Brigadier General Venancio Flores y Guerra del Paraguay: Recopilación de documentos históricos, datos, correspondencias y extractos de la prensa desde febrero de 1865 hasta la terminación de la Guerra del Paraguay*, 2 vols. (Montevideo: Imprenta Latina, 1897–1900), 1:108–9.

10. Juan Bautista Alberdi, "Texto y comentario del tratado secreto de la Triple Alianza contra el Paraguay," *Cuadernos de Marcha*, 1st ser., 35 (Mar. 1970): 30–33.

11. This is indicated by a comparison of several sources, which include a list of the "crusaders" of 1863, published by *La Tribuna* (Buenos Aires) 10 May 1863; lists of deserters published by the Uruguayan government from 1863 to 1865 and reproduced in De León, *Recopilación*, 2:163–63; Conte, *Cruzada*, 124–25; and BHEME 126 (1970), 22, 24–26; BHEME 127 (1970), 7–27, passim; lists of promotions granted by Flores during the crusade and in 1866 BHEME 127 (1970), 96–126; BHEME 145–48 (1975), 204–8; and the following service records held in AEME (numbers indicate bundle and folder respectively): Cándido Acuña (1-31), Fausto Aguilar (2-9), Francisco Belén (183-86), Carlos Clark y Obregón (65-1), Ernesto Courtin (188-44), Angel Farías (18-35), Casimiro García (21-38), Carlos Gaudencio (21-36), Genuario González

(198-17), Gabino Monegal (31-46), Melitón Muñoz (33-36), Miguel A. Navajas (36-11), Eduardo T. Olave (36-38), Simón Patiño (41-27), Luis Eduardo Pérez (40-30), Pedro P. Solano (49-21), Zenón de Tezanos (75-13), Alfredo Trianón (50-16), and Feliciano Viera (52-33).

12. José Luciano Martínez, *Vida militar de los Generales Enrique y Gregorio Castro* (Montevideo: Dornaleche y Reyes, 1901), 162.

13. This monthly subsidy consisted formally of 30,000 gold pesos. Informally, however, Brazil had paid 150,000 since May 1865 and during Flores's command of the Oriental Division. A thorough discussion of this matter can be found in Acevedo, *Anales*, 3:478. See also Martin de Maillefer, "Los informes de Maillefer," *Cuadernos de Marcha*, 1st ser., 35 (Mar. 1970): 95.

14. See Alfredo Lepro, *Años de forja: Venancio Flores* (Montevideo: Editorial Alfa, 1962), 9–18; and Washington Lockhart, *Venancio Flores: Un caudillo trágico* (Montevideo: Ediciones de la Banda Oriental, 1976), 5–13.

15. Col. Juan Pablo Rebollo, another landlord-warrior, reorganized these forces in 1864 under the name "Florida Battalion." Service records, AEME, Gregorio Castro (11-32, Nicomedes Castro (13-27), and Juan Pablo Rebollo (44-4); Martínez, *Vida militar*, 406–14.

16. Service records, AEME, Nicasio Borges (18-33), Francisco Elías (192-87), Nicasio Galeano (24-8), Simón Martínez (35-8), Fidelis Paes da Silva (39-18), Máximo Pérez (94-12), Wenceslao Regules (45-25), Atanasildo Saldanha (46-14), and José Gregorio Suárez (219-4). Further information on these officers can be found in José M. Fernández Saldaña, *Diccionario uruguayo de biografías, 1810–1940* (Montevideo: Amerindia, 1945).

17. Service record, AEME, León de Palleja (40-26); Edison Alonso Rodríguez, "León de Palleja," *BHEME* 108–11 (1966), 289–94; service record, AEME, José Antonio Costa (58-24); "General José Antonio Costa," in Jacinto R. Yaben, *Biografías argentinas y sudamericanas*, 5 vols. (Buenos Aires: Editorial Metrópolis, 1938–40), 2:84–85; service records, AEME, Fortunato Flores (19-16) and Eduardo Flores (77-13).

18. See Martínez, "José Cándido Bustamante," *Revista Nacional* (Montevideo), 1st ser., 21, no. 63 (Mar. 1943): 393–404. The Oriental Division also included individuals who later became presidents of the country, such as Julio Herrera y Obes (Flores's personal secretary during the campaign) and Lt. Lorenzo Latorre, who inaugurated an era of militarism in the country from 1876 to 1886. Some other officers and even sergeants in the division would dominate the Uruguayan military scene during the following three decades, some of them remaining in command positions even in the first decades of the twentieth century. This is indicated by a comparison between three army rosters published from 1888 to 1917, the "Escalafón militar de la Inspección General de Armas para 1888," AEME; Estado Mayor del Ejército (Uruguay), *Escalafón Militar para 1895* (Montevideo: Imprenta Militar, 1895); and *Escalafón de los Oficiales del Ejército* (Montevideo: Imprenta Militar, 1917). Such was the case, for example,

of Capt. Pedro Callorda and Lt. Eduardo Vázquez, who headed the ministry of war in 1890 and 1903 respectively, and of Sgt. Cándido Robido, another chronicler of the Oriental Division, who became a noted expert on military affairs in the 1920s. Service records, AEME, Lorenzo Latorre (23-23), Pedro Callorda (13-32), Eduardo Vázquez (52-25), and Cándido Robido (62-24).

19. León de Palleja, *Diario de la campaña de las fuerzas aliadas contra el Paraguay*, 2 vols. ([1865–66]; reprint, Montevideo: Ministerio de Instrucción Pública y Previsión Social, 1960), 2:8–9.

20. Palleja, *Diario*, 1:93.

21. Gen. Enrique Castro to President Lorenzo Batlle, Asunción, 19 Mar. 1869, BHEME 145–48 (1975), 125.

22. The idiosyncratic way of life of the Uruguayan gauchos is well described in Fernando O. Assunção, *El gaucho: Estudio socio-cultural*, 2 vols. (Montevideo: Dirección General de Extensión Universitaria, 1978–79); Daniel Vidart, *El gaucho* (Montevideo: Arca, 1968); and Guillermo Vázquez Franco, *Economía y sociedad en el latifundio colonial* (Montevideo: Forum, 1986), 63–83, 111–15. See also Richard W. Slatta, *Gauchos and the Vanishing Frontier* (Lincoln: University of Nebraska Press, 1992).

23. Palleja, *Diario*, 1:16–17, 78, 88.

24. BHEME 145–48 (1975), 6–9, 11–26, 50–53, 102–8, 174, 179, 201, 207.

25. Palleja, *Diario*, 1:29–30.

26. After the battle of Yataí and the incorporation of Paraguayan prisoners into the Oriental Division, Palleja estimated the division's strength at 1,221 effectives, which means that only 721 Uruguayans remained. *Diario*, 1:92. See also Whigham, *Paraguayan War*, 364–73.

27. Palleja, *Diario*, 1:331, 324.

28. Palleja, *Diario*, 1:207–9, 276.

29. BHEME 145–48 (1975), 179–80, 186–87.

30. BHEME 145–48 (1975), 209–15. Other punishments included turning over deserters to the Brazilian fleet, famed for its rigorous discipline. BHEME 145–48 (1975), 184, 202–3.

31. Palleja, *Diario*, 1:307; BHEME 145–48 (1975), 58, 66, 68, 96, 188–92.

32. Palleja, *Diario*, 1:32–38, 63–80, passim, 98–101, 270; BHEME 145–48 (1975), 1–2, 192, 200.

33. Palleja, *Diario*, 2:81.

34. Unless otherwise indicated, the following account of the Oriental Division's campaign is based on Palleja, *Diario*; Martínez, *Vida militar*; and on military orders and reports published in BHEME 145–48 (1975). A history of this campaign has never been written. Only some references, mainly taken from Palleja, can be found in general works such as those of Acevedo and Pivel as well as in Antonio Díaz's interesting and controversial *Historia política y militar de las Repúblicas del Plata: Desde el año de 1828 hasta el de 1866*, 13 vols. (Montevideo: Editores Hoffman y Martínez and *El*

*Siglo*, 1877–78). Possibly to avoid rekindling the heated disagreement that Blancos and Colorados held regarding Uruguayan participation in the war, historians have preferred not to tackle the subject.

35. Decrees of 17, 31 May, 1 June 1865, in De León, *Recopilación*, 2:234, 244–45; Florencio César González, *Ejército del Uruguay: Apuntes históricos* (Montevideo: Dornaleche y Reyes, 1908), 41, 44.

36. Flores blamed Palleja's overconfidence for these casualties. Recent research, however, indicates that Flores ordered Palleja to advance without sufficient artillery cover. See Ernesto Puiggrós, "El combate de Yatay en la Guerra de la Triple Alianza," *BHEME* 275–78 (1989), 43, 71.

37. "Informe de Manuel Martínez," which estimates the number of Paraguayans at 1,500. Palleja calculates 1,879. *Diario*, 1:170.

38. Palleja, *Diario*, 1:349.

39. Flores to María García de Flores, Campamento de San Francisco, 3 May 1866, in Conte, *Gobierno provisorio*, 1:412–13.

40. Service record, AEME, Francisco Caraballo (11-13); *BHEME* 128–31 (1971), 10–11.

41. President Batlle's 1869 address to Congress, quoted in Acevedo, *Anales*, 3:516.

42. Castro to Batlle, Angostura, 15 Oct. 1868; and Castro to Suárez, n.p., 21 Nov. 1868, *BHEME* 145–48 (1975), 45–46, 59–60.

43. Castro to Suárez, n.p., 5 Jan. 1869, *BHEME* 145–48 (1975), 92–93.

44. Castro to Suárez, Angostura, 30 Dec. 1868, *BHEME* 145–48 (1975), 87–88.

45. Castro to Batlle, Asunción, 22 Jan. 1869, *BHEME* 145–48 (1975), 99–100.

46. Castro to Suárez, n.p., 17 Jan. 1869; and Asunción, 5 Feb. 1869, *BHEME* 145–48 (1975), 98, 104–6.

47. Batlle to Castro, Montevideo, 2 Jan. 1869, in Martínez, *Vida militar*, 250–51.

48. Castro to Batlle, Angostura, 30 Dec. 1868, *BHEME* 145–48 (1975), 85–86.

49. Castro to Suárez, Asunción, 15 Mar. 1869, *BHEME* 145–48 (1975), 120–22.

50. Castro to Batlle, Cerro León, 29 Nov. 1869, *BHEME* 145–48 (1975), 25.

51. Promotions granted to the Oriental Division in Mar. and Aug. 1866, *BHEME* 145–48 (1975), 204–9; and *BHEME* 128–31 (1971), 69–71; Apr. and Nov. 1867, *BHEME* 132–35 (1972), 19, 47–48; and Aug. 1868, *BHEME* 136–39 (1974), 17–20, 23. All prove that almost all Uruguayan survivors from the Paraguayan War were officers or had been promoted to officer grade before the government withdrew the division.

52. Hundreds of Blanco officers and soldiers appearing in military rosters in 1864 disappeared from view. Their names can be found in *BHEME* 127 (1970), 40, 74.

53. See Flores's February 1868 address to the Uruguayan Congress in Acevedo, *Anales*, 3:420. For the opinion of the Floristas on the necessity of dictatorship, see José Román Mendoza, prologue to Conte, *Gobierno provisorio*, 1:5–6.

54. José P. Barrán and Benjamín Nahum, *Historia rural del Uruguay moderno*, 7 vols. (Montevideo: Ediciones de la Banda Oriental, 1967–78), 1:189, 221.

## 8. Federalism and Opposition

1. De la Fuente, *Children of Facundo*. On state formation in Argentina see also Oscar Oszlak, *La formación del estado argentino* (Buenos Aires: Editorial de Belgrano, 1985); Tulio Halperín Donghi, *Proyecto y construcción de una nación (1846–1880)* (Buenos Aires: Ariel, 1995); and David Rock, *State Building and Political Movements in Argentina, 1860–1916* (Stanford CA: Stanford University Press, 2002).

2. I use "gaucho" in a denotative sense: Argentine gauchos were members of the rural lower classes regardless of their position in the economy. They could be peasants ("labradores"), peons, artisans, or even miners as well as cowboys. I examine the range of contemporary meanings attributed to "gaucho" in de la Fuente, *Children of Facundo*, 75–77.

3. Joaquín González to Tristán Dávila, Nonogasta, 13 Nov. 1855, AFZ/CTD.

4. Rock, *State Building*, 42–43.

5. Marcelino Reyes, *Bosquejo histórico de la provincia de La Rioja, 1543–1867* (Buenos Aires: H. Cattáneo, 1913), 226; *Primer Censo de la República Argentina, verificado en los días 15, 16 y 17 de setiembre de 1869* (Buenos Aires: Impr. del Porvenir, 1872), 420–34.

6. Testimony of Manuel Ibarra (age seventy, 1921), in Olga Fernández Latour, *Cantares históricos de la tradición argentina* (Buenos Aires: Instituto Nacional de Investigaciones Folklóricas, 1960), 253; Exequías Bringas to Nicolás Barros, 1 July 1865, AHLR/CNB, dossier 12, fols. 8–9.

7. Restituta de Dávila to T. Dávila, Campañas, 5 Nov. 1865, AFZ/CTD.

8. Wenceslao Paunero to Bartolomé Mitre, San Juan, 27 July 1867, MM/AIM-7300.

9. Reyes, *Bosquejo*, 232.

10. Dálmiro Hernández to Paunero, San Luis, 17 July 1867, MM/AIM-7300.

11. José M. de la Fuente to Mitre, Córdoba, 2 Nov. 1866, MM/AIM-6173 [emphasis in original].

12. For an analysis of these terms, see de la Fuente, *Children of Facundo*, 77–78.

13. "Causa criminal seguida de oficio contra los reos presentes Don Manuel Vicente Bustos [y otros]," 1865, cuaderno 2, AJFLR, Penal, leg. 1, fols. 113–14.

14. Julio Campos to Mitre, Rioja, 1 Sept. 1865, MM/AIM-6584 [emphasis in original].

15. Campos to T. Dávila, Rioja, 16 July 1865, in Pedro De Paoli and Manuel Mercado, *Proceso a los montoneros y Guerra del Paraguay* (Buenos Aires: Eudeba, 1974), 64–65.

16. Paunero to Mitre, San Juan, 27 July 1867, MM/AIM-7300.

17. Collected in Corral de Isaac, La Rioja, 1921 (informant: Juan Ibáñez, age seventy-four), in Fernández Latour, *Cantares*, 248.

18. CFED, La Rioja, dossier 81, Punta de Los Llanos, "Las Montoneras," 1921 (informant: Manuel Antonio Díaz, age seventy).

19. De Paoli and Mercado, *Proceso*, 80.

20. Ramón Gil Navarro Ocampo to Justo José de Urquiza, Córdoba, 11, 14 Feb. 1867, AFSB/CRGNO.

21. Reyes, *Bosquejo*, 226.

22. "Causa criminal seguida de oficio . . . ," 1865, AJFLR, Penal, leg. 1, fol. 96.

23. De Paoli and Mercado, *Proceso*, 68–69.

24. "Causa criminal seguida de oficio . . . ," fols. 113–14. On the new taxes see de la Fuente, *Children of Facundo*, 176–80.

25. Felipe Varela, *Manifiesto del Jeneral Felipe Varela a los pueblos americanos sobre los acontencimientos políticos de la República Arjentina en los años 1866 y 1867*, ed. Rodolfo Ortega Peña and Eduardo Luis Duhalde (Buenos Aires: Editorial Sudestada, 1968), 80–82, 87.

26. Filemón Posse to José Posse, Catamarca, 4 May 1865, in *Archivo del General Mitre: Documentos y correspondencia*, 28 vols. (Buenos Aires: Biblioteca de "La Nación," 1911–14), 26:132.

27. Whigham, *Paraguayan War*, 266–67, 274–76, 401–2.

28. "Correspondencia para la Regeneración," *La Regeneración* (La Rioja), 18 Feb. 1865.

29. Paunero to Mitre, Córdoba, 31 Dec. 1861, *Archivo del General Mitre*, 10:259.

30. "Causa criminal contra Toribio Urrutia (chileno) por participación con los rebeldes encabezados por Felipe Varela," 1867, AJFLR, Penal, leg. 2.

31. CFED, Catamarca, dossier 322, Huaco (Belén), 1921 (informant: Segundo Acosta, age seventy-five). Fernández Latour found three other fragmentary versions of the same song, all in Catamarca. *Cantares*, 264–65.

32. Reyes, *Bosquejo*, 227–28.

33. CFED, Santa Fe, San Lorenzo, dossier 67, "Guerra del Paraguay," 1921, fol. 21 (informant: Secundino Márquez, age seventy-eight).

34. "Causa criminal contra Agustín Molina, por rebelión," 1872, AJFLR, Penal, leg. 5, fols. 6–8, 18–20.

35. William C. Davis, *The Last Conquistadores: The Spanish Intervention in Peru and Chile, 1863–1866* (Athens: University of Georgia Press, 1950), 222, 266–67. For a good analysis of the French intervention in Mexico see Brian Hamnett, *Juárez* (Essex: Longman, 1994).

36. Victorino Lastarria to Mitre, Santiago, 15 Aug. 1864; and Benjamin Vicuña Mackenna to Mitre, n.p., 25 May 1865, *Archivo del General Mitre*, 27:95–97, 100–101.

37. Davis, *Last Conquistadores*, 13.

38. Davis, *Last Conquistadores*, 267. See also the correspondence between Mitre and V. Lastarria, the Chilean emissary to Buenos Aires, from October 1865 to October 1866, in *Archivo del General Mitre*, 27:111–25.

39. Provisional government of La Rioja to governor of San Juan, La Rioja, 8 Mar. 1867, AHLR, Carpeta de Fotocopias 1, doc. 110, fol. 179.

40. Varela, *Manifiesto*, 71, 74, 79, 80, 120.

41. Domingo B. Dávila, "Orígenes nacionales: Narraciones riojanas," *Revista de Derecho, Historia y Letras* (Buenos Aires) 5 (1899): 19.

42. Antonio Zinny, *Historia de los gobernadores de las provincias argentinas*, 3 vols. (Buenos Aires: C. Casavalle, 1882), 3:444–45.

43. Ocampo to Urquiza, Córdoba, 1 Mar. 1867, AFSB/CRGNO.

44. CFED, Catamarca, dossier 322, Huaco (Belén), 1921 (informant: Segundo Acosta, age seventy-five).

45. Guillermo San Román to Guillermo Rawson, Rioja, 21 Dec. 1866; and Ocampo to José María Linares, Vinchina, 20 Dec. 1866, MM/AP-7-3-8-682.

46. "Causa criminal contra Toribio Urrutia . . . ," 1867, AJFLR, Penal, leg. 2.

47. On these points see Oszlak, *Formación del estado argentino*.

48. For critical assessments of Latin American *caudillismo*, see John Chasteen, *Heroes on Horseback: A Life and Times of the Last Gaucho Caudillos* (Albuquerque: University of New Mexico Press, 1995); and Charles Walker, *Smoldering Ashes: Cuzco and the Creation of Republican Peru, 1780–1940* (Durham NC: Duke University Press, 1999).

49. Gilbert Joseph and Daniel Nugent, eds., *Everyday Forms of State-Formation: Revolution and the Negotiation of Rule in Modern Mexico* (Durham NC: Duke University Press, 1994).

50. Mallon, *Peasant and Nation*.

## 9. Images of War

Translated by Mirta Alloni; revisions by Thomas L. Whigham and Hendrik Kraay.

1. Few scholars have studied Paraguayan War photography. See André Toral, "Entre retratos e cadáveres: A fotografia na Guerra do Paraguai," *Revista Brasileira de História* 19, no. 38 (1999): 283–310; Miguel Angel Cuarterolo, *Soldados de la memoria: Hombres e imágenes de la guerra del Paraguay* (Buenos Aires: Editorial Planeta, 2000).

2. On this early history of photography, see Miguel Angel Cuarterolo, *Los años del daguerrotipo: Primeras fotografías argentinas, 1843–1870* (Buenos Aires: Fundación Antorchas, 1995). On the history of photography in Latin America more generally, see Robert M. Levine, *Images of History: Nineteenth and Early Twentieth-Century Photographs as Historical Documents* (Durham NC: Duke University Press, 1989); Levine, *Windows on Latin America: Understanding Society through Photographs* (Coral Gables: North-South Center, University of Miami, 1987).

3. On the wet-collodion process and its effect on photojournalism, see Carlos Abreu, *La fotografía periodística: Una aproximación histórica* (Caracas: Consejo Nacional de la Cultura, 1992); James Horan, *Mathew Brady: Historian with a Camera* (New York: Crown, 1955); Beaumont Newhall, *Historia de la fotografía desde sus orígenes hasta nuestros días* (Barcelona: Gustavo Gili, 1983).

4. *La República* (Montevideo), 9 June 1861.

5. Cuarterolo, *Soldados de la memoria*, 28.

6. Giselle Freund, *La fotografía como documento social* (Barcelona: Gustavo Gili, 1993), 13.

7. Gilberto Freyre, Fernando Ponce de León, and Pedro Vazquez, *O retrato brasileiro* (Rio de Janeiro: Funarte, 1983), 97.

8. *El Avisador, guía general de comercio de Buenos Ayres y de forasteros, 1866–1868* (Buenos Aires: Wenceslao R. Soleyra, 1866).

9. Photographic album containing 180 original *cartes de visite*, CM&MC.

10. Juan Antonio Varese, "La Guerra Ilustrada," *El País* (Montevideo), 21 May 1989.

11. Vicente Gesualdo, *Historia de la fotografía en América* (Buenos Aires: Ed. Sui Generis, 1990), 234–36.

12. *La Tribuna* (Buenos Aires), 18 Apr. 1865.

13. Benjamín Canard to Antonio Ballesteros, Ayui, 18 Aug. 1865, in Canard, Cascallar, and Gallegos, *Cartas sobre la Guerra del Paraguay* (Buenos Aires: Academia Nacional de la Historia, 1999), 42.

14. Domingo Fidel Sarmiento to Benita Martinez Pastoriza, Ayui Chico, 30 July 1865, in Miguel Angel de Marco, *La Guerra del Paraguay* (Buenos Aires: Editorial Planeta, 1995), 271.

15. Photographic album containing 180 original *cartes de visites*, CM&MC.

16. *El Siglo* (Montevideo), 18 Sept. 1865.

17. On the origins of this conflict, see chap. 7.

18. The presence of other photographers at Paysandú during this time cannot be ruled out. José Murature (1804–80), commander of Argentine naval operations during the siege of Paysandú and the Paraguayan War, collected twelve photographic views; none, unfortunately, bear a photographer's name. See the Murature album, AHAA, Departamento de Iconografia.

19. Palleja, *Diario*, 1:286.

20. Cerqueira, *Reminiscências*, 42.

21. Quoted in Alberto Del Pino Menk, "Javier López, fotógrafo de Bate & Cía. W. en la guerra del Paraguay," *Boletín Histórico del Ejército* 68, no. 297 (1997): 66.

22. Quoted in José M. Fernández Saldaña, "La Guerra del Paraguay en fotografías de la época," *El Día* (Montevideo), 25 Aug. 1935.

23. *El Siglo* (Montevideo), 23 May 1866.

24. Aaron Scharf, *Arte y fotografía* (Madrid: Alianza Editorial, 1994), 159–63; Uruguay, Ley 9739, 17 Dec. 1937.

25. Cerqueira, *Reminiscências*, 63.

26. *El Siglo* (Montevideo), 31 July 1866.

27. *El Siglo* (Montevideo), 1 Aug. 1866; *The Standard* (Buenos Aires), 2 Sept. 1866.

28. These photographs are listed in Cuarterolo, *Soldados de la memoria*, 26 n. 11.

29. *El Siglo* (Montevideo), 13 Sept. 1866.

30. These photographs are listed in Cuarterolo, *Soldados de la memoria*, 26 n. 12.

31. *El Siglo* (Montevideo), 4 Nov. 1866.

32. *El Siglo* (Montevideo), 20 Nov. 1866.

33. José María Rosa, *La Guerra del Paraguay y las montoneras argentinas* (Buenos Aires: Hyspamerica, 1986), 216–17; Carlos Floria and Cesar García Belsunce, *Historia de los argentinos*, 2 vols. (Buenos Aires: Larrouse, 1992), 1:132.

34. *La Tribuna* (Buenos Aires), 14 Nov. 1866.

35. Cuarterolo, *Soldados de la memoria*, 25–26.

36. César's album is now housed in the Biblioteca Nacional, Rio de Janeiro, Seção Iconográfica, where two other albums on the war can also be found: *Lembrança do Paraguai* and *Excursão ao Paraguai*. These albums contain works by unidentified photographers who documented the Brazilian occupation of Asunción.

37. This photograph is reproduced in Salles, *Guerra do Paraguai*, plate 3.

38. Thompson, *Guerra del Paraguay*, 159.

39. *Album de la Guerra del Paraguay* (Buenos Aires), 1 July 1893. A copy of this photograph in the format of a *carte de visite* is in the Museo Histórico de la Provincia de Corrientes.

40. *La Tribuna* (Buenos Aires), 5 Jan. 1869. On Methfessel see Vicente Gesualdo, *Enciclopedia del arte en America* (Buenos Aires: Bibliográfica Omeba, 1969), n.p.

41. Alberto Armelán, *Bosquejos de la Guerra del Paraguay* (Buenos Aires: H. Tjarks, 1904).

42. José León Pagano, *Cándido López: El sentido de una vocación* (Buenos Aires: Ministerio de Cultura, 1949), 27.

43. Pagano, *Cándido Lopez*, 47.

44. José Ignacio Garmendia, *Recuerdos de la Guerra del Paraguay: Batalla del Sauce, Combate de Yataytí Corá, Curupaytí* (Buenos Aires: J. Preusser, 1883).

45. Gesualdo, *Enciclopedia*, n.p.

46. Maria Inez Turazzi, *Poses e trejeitos: A fotografia e as exposições na era do espetáculo (1839–1889)* (Rio de Janeiro: Funarte, 1995), 126.

47. Gesualdo, *Enciclopedia*, n.p. See also [João Zeferino] Rangel de S. Paio, *Combate naval de Riachuelo: História e arte, quadro de Victor Meirelles, notas para os visitantes da exposição* (Rio de Janeiro: Typographia Nacional, 1883).

48. Octavio Assunção, *The Art of Juan Manuel Blanes* (Buenos Aires: Fundación Bunge y Born, 1994), 25.

49. Enrique Zaracondegui, *Coronel de Marina José Murature* (Buenos Aires: Secretaría de Estado de Marina, 1961), 108.

50. Assunção, *Art of Juan Manuel Blanes*, 48. The painting is reproduced in *Paysandú en su bicentenario*, ed. Anibal Barrios Pinto (Montevideo: Editorial Minas, 1957), n.p. The photograph is in the Murature album, AHAA, Departamento de Iconografia.

51. Cuarterolo, *Soldados de la memoria*, 116–17.

52. Thompson, *Guerra del Paraguay*, 66.

53. The Gallery of Notable Warriors was a portrait section included in every issue of the *Album de la Guerra del Parguay*.

54. Gesualdo, *Enciclopedia*, n.p.

55. *The Illustrated London News*, which appeared in England in 1842, was the first periodical to include illustrations. In 1843 *L'Illustration* came out in France, and in 1855 the first issue of *Frank Leslie's Illustrated Weekly* appeared in the United States, followed by *Harper's Weekly* (1857) and *The New York Illustrated News* (1859).

56. *La Tribuna* (Buenos Aires), 28 Aug. 1865.

57. *El Correo del Domingo* (Buenos Aires), 29 Jan. 1865.

58. *El Correo del Domingo* (Buenos Aires), 12 Sept. 1866; Thompson, *Guerra del Paraguay*, 66. See also Cuarterolo, *Soldados de la memoria*, 142.

59. *El Correo del Domingo* (Buenos Aires), 2 July 1865.

60. *El Correo del Domingo* (Buenos Aires), 14 Oct. 1866.

61. *El Correo del Domingo* (Buenos Aires), 8 Mar. 1867.

62. *El Correo del Domingo* (Buenos Aires), 10 Aug. 1867.

63. Fernando Schulkin, *Sitiados: La epopeya de Paysandú* (Montevideo: Colección los Muros de la Patria, 2000), 89.

64. *El Siglo* (Montevideo), 23 May 1866.

65. On Brazilian illustrated newspapers during the war, see Mauro César Silveira, *A batalha de papel: A Guerra do Paraguai através da caricatura* (Porto Alegre: L&PM Editores, 1996).

66. José Antonio Vázquez and Osvaldo Salerno, *El Centinela: Periódico de la Guerra de la Triple Alianza* (Asunción: Centro de Artes Visuales, Museo del Barro, 1998).

## 10. The Paraguayan War

Portions of this paper were read before the LLILAS conference "Mercosul/Mercosur: The Market and Beyond," University of Texas at Austin, 27 Apr. 2001. The author wishes to express his gratitude for the comments of Hendrik Kraay, Jerry W. Cooney, and Juan Manuel Casal.

1. See Whigham and Potthast, "Paraguayan Rosetta Stone," 174–86. See also Whigham and Potthast, "Some Strong Reservations: A Critique of Vera Blinn Reber's 'The Demographics of Paraguay,'" 667–77.

2. *Webster's New Universal Unabridged Dictionary*, 2d ed. (New York: Simon and Schuster, 1983), 1196.

3. Whigham, *Paraguayan War*, 8–13, 17–20, 29–32.

4. The best overall treatment of Francia's Paraguay is Julio Cesar Chaves, *El Supremo Dictador: Biografia de José Gaspar de Francia*, 4th ed. (Madrid: Atlas, 1964).

5. Gerónimo Pérez, "La política," *Semanario*, 28 Feb. 1863 (as suggested by Michael Huner). See also "Nuestra nacionalidad," in *Semanario*, 9 May 1863; and Jerry W. Cooney, "Dubious Loyalty: The Paraguayan Struggle for the Paraná Frontier, 1767–1777," *The Americas* 55, no. 4 (Apr. 1999): 576–78.

6. Julio Cesar Chaves, *El presidente López: Vida y gobierno de don Carlos*, 2d ed. (Buenos Aires: Depalma, 1968).

7. This is not true of contemporary Paraguay, where the members of the Academia Nacional del Guaraní have proposed words to cover such "foreign" notions as "autobiography" (*oguekovemombe'u*), "democracy" (*porokua pavê reko*), and "telephone" (*ñe'émbyryha*). Very few of these terms have made their way into the popular consciousness, however, and most Paraguayans continue to call them by their Spanish equivalents. The same process has led over time to the development of a part-Spanish, part-Guaraní patois called *jopará*, which is so common in today's Paraguay as to be essentially a third language. The best Spanish-Guaraní dictionary remains that of Antonio Guasch and Diego Ortíz, *Diccionario castellano-guaraní, guaraní-castellano*, 6th ed. (Asunción: CEPAG, 1986). For general thoughts on the ambiguities of the language, see F. Ricardo Mello Vargas, *Enigmas de un idioma llamado Guaraní* (Asunción: Santa Rita, 1989).

8. Indeed, as a part of his push for modernity, López evidently tried to prohibit the use of Guaraní surnames because he felt that they summoned up images of an Indian, hence backward, past. His son found reasons to regret this stance after war broke out in the 1860s, and the use of Guaraní became a military necessity. The father's plan to eliminate Indian surnames clearly failed if we are to accept the evidence of the 1871 census in the largely Indian *pueblo* of Yaguarón. See "Censo general de la república del Paraguay según el decreto circular del Gobierno Provisorio de 29 de septiembre de 1870," Archivo del Ministerio de Defensa Nacional (Asunción).

9. To take one peripheral but rather telling example, when López designed a national coat of arms, he never considered deviating from standard European heraldic practice to include Paraguayan elements; the official Paraguayan lion, therefore, is the familiar long-maned animal of the Old World rather than the puma (which in the Paraguayan vernacular is nonetheless called *el león*). The atypical case of Paraguay in matters of national emblems is discussed in José Emilio Burucua and Fabián Alejandro Campagne, "Los países del Cono Sur," in *De los imperios a las naciones*, by Antonio Annino, Luiz Castro Leiva, François-Xavier Guerra (Zaragosa: IberCaja, Obra Cultural, 1994), 349–81.

10. The diplomatic history of Paraguay during this period is exceedingly complex. See Peter A. Schmitt, *Paraguay und Europa: Die diplomatischen Beziehungen unter Carlos Antonio López und Francisco Solano López, 1841–1870* (Berlin: Colloquium Verlag, 1963).

11. Pérez Acosta, *Carlos Antonio López*.

12. Warren, "Paraguay Central Railway," 3–22.

13. Pla, *British in Paraguay*.

14. The development of this defensive nationalism is an intriguing aspect of Paraguayan history. See John Hoyt Williams, "Race, Threat, and Geography: The Paraguayan Experience of Nationalism," *Canadian Review of Studies in Nationalism* 1, no. 2 (1974): 173–74.

15. Mary C. Karasch, *Slave Life in Rio de Janeiro, 1808–1850* (Princeton: Princeton University Press, 1987); João José Reis, *Slave Rebellion in Brazil: The Muslim Uprising of 1835 in Bahia,* trans. Arthur Brakel (Baltimore: Johns Hopkins University Press, 1993).

16. José Murilo de Carvalho, *A construção da ordem: A elite política imperial* (Rio de Janeiro: Campus, 1980).

17. On Brazilian politics at this time, see Barman, *Brazil.* On the emperor see Barman, *Citizen Emperor: Pedro II and the Making of Brazil, 1825–91* (Stanford CA: Stanford University Press, 1999); and Lilia Moritz Schwarcz, *As barbas do imperador: D. Pedro II, um monarca nos trópicos,* 2d ed. (São Paulo: Companhia das Letras, 1998), which analyzes the symbolism surrounding the monarchy.

18. Dave Treece, *Exiles, Allies, Rebels: Brazil's Indianist Movement, Indigenist Politics, and the Imperial Nation-State* (Westport CT: Greenwood, 2000); Gladys Sabina Ribeiro, *A liberdade em construção: Identidade nacional e conflitos antilusitanos no Primeiro Reinado* (Rio de Janeiro: Relume-Dumará, 2002).

19. Leitman, *Raízes sócio-econômicas da Guerra dos Farrapos.*

20. On the distinct character of the Rio Grande do Sul militia, the Guarda Nacional, or National Guard, see Uricoechea, *Patrimonial Foundations of the Brazilian Bureaucratic State,* chap. 6.

21. The principle of nationalism was ultimately linked in their minds to the practice of war. Although they were in no sense militarist, the Brazilians believed in expansionism. In this they resembled their European contemporaries, especially in the German states. Fichte and Hegel both thought war was the necessary dialect in the evolution of nation-states. As one deputy at the 1848 Frankfurt Assembly put it, "Mere existence does not entitle a people to political independence; only the force to assert itself as a state among others." Cited in Michael Howard, *The Lessons of History* (New Haven: Yale University Press, 1991), 39.

22. The best biography of Rosas remains Lynch, *Argentine Dictator.*

23. Tulio Halperín Donghi, *The Contemporary History of Latin America,* ed. and trans. John Charles Chasteen (Durham NC: Duke University Press, 1993), 110.

24. The phenomenon of *caudillismo* has received considerable attention from scholars. Most recently Noemi Goldman and Ricardo Salvatore have suggested major flaws in the accepted notion that the caudillo sat at the apex of a social pyramid arranged to facilitate patron-client relations; instead of this feudalistic system, they argue, the caudillo was a thoroughgoing capitalist who did what he did to advance the interest of the *estancieros* as a class. See *Caudillismos rioplatenses: Nuevas miradas a un viejo problema* (Buenos Aires: EUDEBA, 1998).

25. Cited in Nicholas Shumway, *The Invention of Argentina* (Berkeley: University of California Press, 1991), 111.

26. This "American" orientation perhaps explains why the Men of 1837 were so attracted to the romantic European nationalists like Mazzini, Kossuth, and François Guizot (who stressed the unique character of their own national experiences) and by the example of the United States, which had, it seemed, carved out its own

destiny regardless of European antecedents. See Domingo Faustino Sarmiento, *Viajes por Europa, Africa, y Estados Unidos*, 3 vols. (Buenos Aires: Belgrano, 1922). More generally see David Viñas, *De Sarmiento a Dios: Viajeros argentinos a USA* (Buenos Aires: Editorial Sudamerica, 1998).

27. Esteban Echeverría, *Dogma socialista* (Buenos Aires: Universidad Nacional de La Plata, 1947), 119.

28. Harris G. Warren, "The Paraguayan Image of the War of the Triple Alliance," *The Americas* 19, no. 1 (July 1962): 3–20.

29. Washburn, *History of Paraguay*, 2:81–82.

30. Abilio Cesar Borges to president of Bahia, Salvador, 18 Feb. 1865, APEBa/SACP, m. 3669.

31. Chiavenato, *Voluntários da Pátria*, 25–36; Beattie, *Tribute of Blood*, chap. 2.

32. Izecksohn, *Cerne da discórdia*.

33. *La Regeneración* (Asunción), 7 Oct. 1869; Warren, *Paraguay and the Triple Alliance*, 66–68.

34. Robert Conrad, *The Destruction of Brazilian Slavery, 1850–1888* (Berkeley: University of California Press, 1972); Warren Dean, *Rio Claro: A Brazilian Plantation System, 1820–1920* (Stanford CA: Stanford University Press, 1976); Emília Viotti da Costa, *Da senzala à colônia* (São Paulo: Difusão Européia do Livro, 1966).

35. Francisco de Azevedo Monteiro Caminhoá, *Documentos, juizo critico e orçamento relativos ao monumento patriotico do Brasil destinado ao Campo d'Acclamação no Rio de Janeiro* (Rio de Janeiro: Perseverança, 1874); João Baptista de Mattos, *Os monumentos nacionais: Estado da Bahia* (Rio de Janeiro: Imprensa do Exército, 1956), 314–16.

36. On Rio de Janeiro's monuments see *Monumentos da cidade* (Rio de Janeiro: S. A. Diario de Noticias, 1946).

37. José Murilo de Carvalho, *Os bestializados: O Rio de Janeiro e a República que não foi*, 3d ed. (São Paulo: Companhia das Letras, 1999); Carvalho, *A formação das almas: O imaginário da república no Brasil* (São Paulo: Companhia das Letras, 1990).

38. On the 1881 electoral reform see Graham, *Patronage and Politics*, 182–206. More generally see José Murilo de Carvalho, *Cidadania no Brasil: O longo caminho* (Rio de Janeiro: Civilização Brasileira, 2001), chap. 1.

39. Silva, *Prince of the People*, 71–89; Roderick J. Barman, *Princess Isabel of Brazil: Gender and Power in the Nineteenth Century* (Wilmington NC: Scholarly Resources, 2002), 178–85.

40. Michael R. Trochim, "The Brazilian Black Guard: Racial Conflict in Post-Abolition Brazil," *The Americas* 44, no. 3 (Jan. 1988): 285–300. On the violence in Salvador see British consul to envoy to Brazil, Salvador, 19 Nov. 1889, UK Public Record Office, Foreign Office 13, vol. 662, fols. 76r–77v; and Hendrik Kraay, "Introduction: Afro-Bahia, 1790s–1990s," in *Afro-Brazilian Culture and Politics: Bahia, 1790s–1990s* (Armonk NY: M. E. Sharpe, 1998), 21.

41. Marta Bonaudo and Élida Sonzogni, "Los grupos dominantes entre la legitimidad y el control," in *Nueva historia argentina*, tomo 4, *Liberalismo, estado, y orden*

*burgués*, ed. Marta Bonaudo (Buenos Aires: Editorial Sudamericana, 1999), chap. 1; Gabriel L. Negretto and José Antonio Aguilar-Rivera, "Rethinking the Legacy of the Liberal State in Latin America: The Cases of Argentina (1853–1916) and Mexico (1857–1910)," *Journal of Latin American Studies* 32, no. 2 (May 2000): 377–81, 385–90.

42. State efforts to inculcate civic virtues based on the examples of Belgrano and San Martín are part of the broad discourse on late-nineteenth-century education in Argentina. See Adriana Puiggrós, *Sujetos, disciplina y curriculum: En los orígenes del sistema educativo argentino* (Buenos Aires: Editorial Galerna, 1990); and Jorge María Ramallo, *Etapas históricas de la educación argentina* (Buenos Aires: Fundación Nuestra Historia, 1999).

43. Shumway, *Invention*; Tulio Halperín Donghi, "La historiografía: Treinta años en busca de un rumbo," in *La Argentina del Ochenta al Centenario*, ed. Gustavo Ferrari and Ezequiel Gallo (Buenos Aires: Editorial Sudamericana, 1980), 829–39; Aurora Ravina, "La historiografía," in *Nueva Historia de la Nación Argentina*, ed. Academia Nacional de la Historia, tomo 6, *La configuración de la república independiente, 1810–c. 1914 (continuación)* (Buenos Aires: Editorial Planeta, 2001), 429–51.

44. This choice of a "national" hero was decidedly odd, for Artigas himself never envisioned and never promoted a separate Uruguayan state, though he fought against the Brazilian occupation of the Banda Oriental. See John Street, *Artigas and the Emancipation of Uruguay* (Cambridge: Cambridge University Press, 1959). The ebb and flow of Artigas as a key figure in the national myth are detailed by Guillermo Vázquez Franco in two works, *La historia y los mitos* (Montevideo: Cal y Canto, 1994), and *Francisco Berra: La historia prohibida* (Montevideo: Mandinga Editor, 2001).

45. John Lloyd Stevens to Hamilton Fish, Montevideo, 5 June 1872, National Archives and Records Administration, Washington, M128, roll 3.

46. See anonymous report, Asunción, 19 Feb. 1870, in *The Weekly Standard* (Buenos Aires), 2 Mar. 1870.

47. Regarding the political reconstruction of the republic, see Decoud, *Sobre los escombros de la guerra*; and F. Arturo Bordón, *Historia política del Paraguay: Era constitucional, 1869–1886* (Asunción: Orbis, 1976).

48. The country only gradually recovered. See Warren and Warren, *Rebirth of the Paraguayan Republic*; Washington Ashwell, *Historia económica del Paraguay: Estructura y dinámica de la economía nacional, 1870–1925* (Asunción: Carlos Schaumann, 1989); Jan M. G. Kleinpenning, *Rural Paraguay, 1870–1932* (Amsterdam: CEDLA, 1992); Juan Carlos Herken Krauer, *El Paraguay rural entre 1869 y 1913: Contribución a la historia económica regional del Plata* (Asunción: CPES, 1984); Rafael Barrett, *El dolor paraguayo* (Montevideo: O. M. Bertoni, 1911); and Carlos R. Centurión, *Historia de la cultura paraguaya*, 2 vols. (Asunción: Biblioteca "Ortíz Guerrero," 1961), 1:315–495.

49. The division on this question was not strictly partisan, despite what many polemicists have argued. Not all Colorados saw López as a patriot. José Segundo Decoud, who acted as chief ideologue of the party for twenty years, had served in the anti-Lopizta Legión Paraguaya during the war. And the opposite was true for

certain Liberals. In a study frequently ridiculed by Paraguayans for its many errors and misconceptions, Paul Lewis gets this key feature of Paraguayan politics dead right. See *Political Parties and Generations in Paraguay's Liberal Era, 1869–1940* (Chapel Hill: University of North Carolina Press, 1993).

50. Francisco Tapia, *El tirano Francisco Solano López arrojado de las escuelas* (Asunción: Escuela Tipográfica Salesiana, 1898).

51. This "revisionist" school left an indelible mark on Paraguayan historiography and even today is still touted by the man in the street. For representative texts see Manuel Domínguez, *Causas del heroismo paraguayo* (Asunción: Talleres Nacionales H. Kraus, 1903); Juan E. O'Leary, *Nuestra epopeya* (Asunción: Imprenta y Libreria La Mundial, 1919); and Juan Natalicio González, *Solano López y otros ensayos* (Paris: Editorial de Indias, 1926).

# Contributors

**Juan Manuel Casal** is professor of history at the Universidad Mayor de la República Oriental del Uruguay. He received a graduate degree in history from the university in 1982 and a doctorate from the University of Iowa in 2001. He is author of six books, including *Historia institucional de la Facultad de Derecho de la Universidad Mayor del Uruguay* (2000), *Mariátegui: El socialismo indoamericano* (1992), *Historia política y social de Iberoamérica: Investigaciones y ensayos* (2 vols., 1992), and *El modo de producción colonial en el Río de la Plata* (1987). He has also published numerous articles and book chapters in Argentina, Brazil, and Uruguay.

**Jerry W. Cooney** received his doctorate in Latin American history from the University of New Mexico in 1971. Since then he has published extensively in journals on late-colonial and early national Paraguay. He is the author of *Economía y sociedad en la intendencia del Paraguay* (1990), *Paraguay: A Bibliography of Immigration and Emigration* (1996), and *Paraguay: A Bibliography of Bibliographies* (1997). In collaboration with Thomas Whigham he has edited several books. Currently he is collaborating with Frank O. Mora on a study of Paraguay–United States relations. He is professor emeritus of the University of Louisville and currently resides in a small town in southwestern Washington state.

The late **Miguel Angel Cuarterolo** was a professional journalist. He worked as photoeditor for United Press International, Reuters, and Agence France Presse and was a photoeditor for *Clarín* (Buenos Aires). In the 1980s and 1990s he devoted himself to the history of photography in Latin America. He published four books in that field: *Imágenes del Río de la Plata* (1983), *Los años del daguerrotipo* (1995), *El poder de la imagen* (1996), and *Soldados de la memoria: Hombres e imágenes de la Guerra del Paraguay* (2000).

**Ariel de la Fuente** is associate professor of history at Purdue University. He received his doctorate from SUNY–Stony Brook in 1995. He is the author of *Children of Facundo: Caudillo and Gaucho Insurgency during the Argentine State-Formation Process (La Rioja, 1853–1870)* (2000) and several articles and book chapters on *caudillismo* and is currently working on a book examining rural culture in nineteenth-century Argentina.

**Roger Kittleson** is assistant professor of history at Williams College and has taught at Northwestern University. He received his doctorate from the University of Wisconsin–Madison in 1997 and is currently completing a book-length study of political cultures in nineteenth-century southern Brazil. His other research interests include slavery, gender and abolition, and soccer.

**Hendrik Kraay** received his doctorate from the University of Texas at Austin in 1995 and has taught at the University of Calgary since 1997. He is the author of *Race, State, and Armed Forces in Independence-Era Brazil: Bahia, 1790s–1840s* (2001). He has edited *Afro-Brazilian Culture and Politics: Bahia, 1790s–1990s* (1998) and has published articles on recruitment for the Paraguayan War in *The Americas* and *Slavery and Abolition*. Kraay is past chair of the Brazilian Studies Committee of the Conference on Latin American History. His current research focuses on nineteenth-century Brazilian patriotic culture.

**Renato Lemos** is professor of history at the Universidade Federal do Rio de Janeiro. He has been a researcher at the Centro de Pesquisa e Documentação em História do Brasil Contemporâneo (CPDOC), where he worked on the second edition of the *Dicionário histórico-biográfico brasileiro pós-1930* (2001). He is the author of *Benjamin Constant: Vida e história* (1999) and has edited *Uma história do Brasil através das caricaturas* (2001).

**Barbara Potthast** is professor of history and director of the Institute of Iberian and Latin American History at the University of Cologne, from which she received her doctorate in 1986. She has previously taught at the University of Bielefeld. She has published widely on diverse aspects of Latin American history, including *Die Mosquitoküste im Spannungsfeld britischer und spanischer Politik, 1502–1821* (1988); *"Paradies Mohammeds" oder "Land der Frauen"? Zur Rolle der Frau und der Familie in der paraguayischen Gesellschaft im 19. Jahrhundert* (1994), translated as *"Paraíso de Mahoma" o "País de las Mujeres"? El rol de la mujer y la familia en la sociedad Paraguaya durante el siglo XIX* (1996). Most recently she has published *Von Müttern und Machos: Eine Geschichte der Frauen in Lateinamerika* (2003).

**Thomas L. Whigham** is professor of history at the University of Georgia. He received his doctorate from Stanford University in 1986. Author of *La yerba mate del Paraguay* (1991), *The Politics of River Trade: Tradition and Development in the Upper Plata, 1780–1870* (1991), *El Paraguay bajo el Dr. Francia: Ensayos sobre la sociedad patrimonial* (1996), and *The Paraguayan War: Volume 1, Causes and Early Conduct* (2002), he has also published numerous articles and book chapters and was named a corresponding member of the Paraguayan Academy of History in 1998.

# Index